TEXTILE ART in the CHURCH

TEXTILE ART

in the CHURCH

Vestments, Paraments, and Hangings
in Contemporary Worship, Art, and Architecture

Marion P. Ireland

ABINGDON PRESS   Nashville and New York

To my husband, Howard

Contents

Illustrations

Foreword

Marion Ireland, besides being a gifted ecclesiastical designer, has an extensive professional knowledge and experience of textiles. That she approaches her work with much more than mere craftsmanship is easily demonstrable. Not only is she a trained and competent organist as well as a designer; she has interested herself in such comparatively unusual art forms as color-music. More noteworthy still is Marion Ireland's resolute pursuit of intellectual truth. Most artists are content with such intellectual insights as they can glean in the exercise of their gifts, and feel no need for deeper reflection upon what they do. Not so in her case. Over a period of many years, after bringing up her children and in the course of running a family business, she found time not only to complete an A.B. degree but to go on to take the degree of M.A. twice over, in fine arts and in religion, writing, of course, a separate thesis for each.

No one having witnessed the diligence with which she conducted her researches could have had any doubt of her integrity, her energy, or her zeal. To her ecumenical vision she adds a sense of humor and a kindliness that together with her deep insight into the practical needs of churches render her as incapable of arbitrary faddiness as she is of pedantry. She is a safe guide for those who are involved in the use of textile arts in churches, such as clergymen and their congregations, building committees and altar guilds, church architects and artists, besides the people who actually embroider and weave. Marion Ireland is a practical person, professionally trained and widely experienced in the designing of vestments and paraments, according to sound

15

liturgical principles. Her aim in the present book is to stimulate an interest in the use of new creative designs for textiles for the expression of the life of the church in the contemporary world. She is, above all, a contemporary-minded woman who can say with the psalmist, "O Lord, I love the habitation of thy house, and the place where thy glory dwells."

With great pleasure, therefore, I accede to the request with which she has honored me: that I write an introduction to her book. Though I have no special knowledge of textiles, and had therefore no direct part at all in preparing the technical aspects of the book, my confidence in its author is such that I have no hesitation in commending her to her readers as one whose taste in such matters is dependable, being not only enlivened by her artistic talent, but informed by her academic training. Happy the parish that hears her precepts and ponders them in its assemblies.

GEDDES MacGREGOR D.D. (Oxon)

Preface

Art in the church—who needs it? One might as well ask: words—who needs them? A congregation that is truly striving to give full expression to the majesty and love of God, the creator of the universe, will exclude visual media no more than verbal ones. True, a vestment is still a vestment whether it employs symbolism or not, and the Sistine ceiling would keep out the rain without benefit of Michelangelo's magnificent frescoes. We could worship in a barn, but the same question arises as when one claims to be able to worship God on the golf course as well as in church. The question is, "Do you?"

There is, indeed, no question whether to use art or not. Human nature will use it. The only question is whether it will be good or bad. This is the crux of the matter. We must therefore examine the quality of the art on which we depend. Symbolism is the language of Christian love. He who loves Christ will learn it.

Beauty is not the exclusive possession of any single branch of the Christian church, and an effort has been made in this book to present evidence of the creative achievements in contemporary vestments and paraments among churches of many denominations, both in this country and abroad. The purpose of this book is to examine the role of art, particularly textile art, as a means by which the life of the church community may be enriched, and to note the extent to which this valuable asset may be put to good use. In some instances, much progress has been made in encouraging the development of artistic expression and appreciation. That is a real service to churches today.

In others, the textile art is woefully obsolete, bogged down by endless imitations of bygone days. Until there is a recognition of the value of informed artistic expression, a precious resource will be wasted.

The efforts and achievements of artists, architects, churchmen, and churchwomen are presented in this book in the hope of encouraging intelligent and discriminating use of art and beauty in the service of all Christian communions. I wish to acknowledge and thank the many artists, architects, clergymen, scholars, altar guilds, and other individuals who have contributed pictures and information. The names are too numerous to list here without the possibility of omitting some who deserve mention, but I have attempted to name each artist, architect, photographer, or writer where the contribution appears in the text or list of plates.

Photographs and permission for reproduction have been granted by the Victoria and Albert Museum, London; Kunsthistorisches Museum, Vienna; the Museum of Modern Art, New York City.

With profound gratitude I acknowledge the assistance of faculty members at the University of Southern California who served as advisers on my graduate study committees when the groundwork for this book was laid with the writing of two theses:[1] Dr. Edward S. Peck, Dr. Stephen C. Reynolds, Dr. Geddes MacGregor, Dean of the Graduate School of Religion until its dissolution in 1966, who has graciously written a foreword to this book. I have been fortunate indeed to have had the manuscript read by scholars from various Christian backgrounds, and to have received their helpful suggestions: Dr. Stephen C. Reynolds (Lutheran, Department of Religious Studies, University of Oregon, and formerly University of Southern California) Dr. Geddes MacGregor (Anglican, Distinguished Professor of Philosophy, University of Southern California); Dr. G. A. Lehmann (Baptist, Professor Emeritus, Colgate-Rochester Divinity School); Dr. C. E. Pocknee (Holy Trinity Vicarage, Twickenham, Middlesex); and A. W. Campbell (Episcopal layman, Edinburgh), a well-informed liturgical scholar who has devoted countless hours to research and correspondence in the preparation of both theses, and this book as well.

I am particularly indebted to the Swedish Institute for Cultural Relations and to the vestment studios which they arranged for me to visit and photograph: Licium, Libraria, and Märta Måås-Fjetterström in Stockholm. It is through the cooperation and generosity of these scholars, artists, and churchmen that many of the illustrations in this book have been made available.

MARION P. IRELAND
GLENDALE, CALIFORNIA

[1] *Contemporary Textile Art for the Church,* 1967, School of Architecture and Fine Arts, *The Historical Development of Liturgical Color Sequences with Reference to the Vestments and Calendar of the Christian Church,* 1966, Graduate School of Religion.

The Arts in Today's Context

O Lord, our Lord, how majestic is thy name in all the earth!
—PSALMS 8:9

The words of the psalmist are an utterance of genuine worship. Our generation has glimpsed wonders of creation never seen before. Spacemen have shown us our world in the midst of the firmament, and we marvel with the psalmist at God's handiwork. Science has made great strides into the unknown, and while some find in the unraveling of life's mysteries only the notion of man's self-sufficiency, others discover in these very wonders further evidence of God's love and power. The accelerated tempo and mobility of our technological age leave no traditional patterns unchallenged.

Moreover, the vastly increased scope of modern science does nothing to increase or deepen man's historical consciousness; it makes people inclined, on the contrary, to belittle all but the present segment of time. This is a foolish deprivation of a rich dimension of human experience. There is much to be learned from history and the genius of artists whose memory remains alive in their works. We cannot afford to turn our backs upon this rich heritage which provides a source of inspiration. We should learn to seek in it a means of nourishment for the creation of new works. The life of the church must encompass both past and present history if it is to help man to be mindful of his present spiritual needs. Therefore, any study of contemporary church art and its place in public worship must necessarily take into account the historical dimension.

Christian art, with contemporary theology and liturgy, faces a chal-

19

lenge today. Not since the sixteenth century have values and traditions been so questioned. For the Christian Church this is an age of experiment, a search for meanings and religious expression in a secular society. The liturgies, the art, and the music stand trial before the Christian community and must prove their usefulness in worship, no longer protected from criticism solely by the force of habit.

Two movements are at work within the contemporary church, the ecumenical movement and liturgical renewal, reshaping the accustomed patterns of worship at the same time that our very society is being shaken and reshaped. The two movements continually overlap as the search progresses toward a more adequate form of Christian action in the church and in the world. Church architecture, art, and music have a large role in both areas.

A secular society and a troubled world demand a long look at the accustomed traditions and an honest answer to the question of whether Christian churches are as effective as they can be. The ecumenical climate of the present day brings to light resources for the enrichment of worship that have been shunned for generations because of their association with the "other side," be it Protestant, Roman Catholic, Anglican, or Orthodox. Christianity on all sides is faced with the dilemma of ministering within a changing social structure, and the differences within the church are not as urgent as its mission.

The spirit of liturgical renewal that pervades an encouraging proportion of Christian communions today has prompted a search for every possible means of contributing to living worship, bridging the gap between a routine that has become dull and lifeless and an experience that makes something happen. There cannot be a "correct" music or art that will meet the needs of every congregation. The church must meet people on their own ground if it is to fulfill its mission. This has been done in the past, when, on the eve of the Reformation, religious leaders used whatever was at hand that could evoke a response.

Love songs and songs from the tavern were appropriated for religious use, with suitable alterations in the text, such as the Scottish "Gude and Godlie Ballades," and the German secular songs upon which so many of the Lutheran chorales were based. One of the most profoundly religious hymns we sing today, "O Sacred Head, Sore Wounded," was based upon a love song: *Mein G'muth ist mir verwirret, Das macht ein Mägdlein Zart* ("Confused are all my feelings, A tender maid's the cause"), from Hans Leo Hassler's *Lustgarten neuer teutscher Gesang* (1601). Although it was used as a hymn by Lutherans since at least 1613, it is now known generally as the Passion Chorale because of its several settings in the *St. Matthew Passion* by J. S. Bach (1729). It was a concern for reaching out to the spiritual needs of humanity that prompted the founders of the Salvation Army to use songs that people knew, to draw them to God. The words were altered from their often ribald verses to a spiritual message.

The modern jazz and folk masses reflect a phase of liturgical renewal, aimed at the religious involvement of a large and important segment of society: the youth, and particularly the youth that would be unlikely to be reached or affected by liturgical forms that are alien to them. As a matter

TEXTILE ART IN THE CHURCH

of fact, many who are not young attend a jazz mass out of curiosity and are caught up in the excitement of a fresh new setting, suddenly finding themselves listening intently to the words while reacting to the new sounds and rhythms. One observer who had attended a jazz mass for the first time remarked, "It makes you feel five years younger!"

The success of experimental forms, whether in music, liturgy, or art, depends on their individual merits. This is also true with respect to traditional forms. Neither alternative is foolproof. The eager borrowing that has been the result of ecumenical exposure is often ludicrous when the borrowing is not well conceived, such as a Protestant service with "bits" of the Mass. James F. White writes: "It would be indeed ironical if Roman Catholics took all the kneelers out of churches at about the same time that Protestants all put them in." [1] The very things that are adopted by some in a spirit of ecumenical enthusiasm are the things regarded as weaknesses that should be abandoned by their originators in a spirit of liturgical renewal. [2]

Today's church architecture shows the influence of modern design, but only occasionally is it allowed the scope of dramatic innovation that is accorded to other buildings. A restricting and artificial barrier separates sacred from secular architecture, placing the architect in a dilemma. A large segment of churchgoers demands a "church that looks like a church," whatever that might mean. Who is to define exactly what a church should look like? Should the early Christian basilicas, the Romanesque, the Byzantine, and other styles of church architecture be forgotten in order to exalt the Gothic or the New England steeple church, or whatever recollections we carry from childhood?

The first step in designing a church and its art in terms of today's needs is a thorough study of the nature of Christian worship, with special attention to the frame of reference of the particular congregation. Based upon a mutual understanding between the architect and those who have entrusted him with the planning of a building to meet these needs, a new church is designed. Good architecture is not guaranteed by this process, however, since the chief aim is sometimes motivated by a desire for novelty or the spectacular more than a space for the gathered Christian fellowship to worship and adore God.

"Churches are built to 'express' this and to 'symbolize' that. We have churches which look like hands folded in prayer; churches which symbolize aspiration or the anchor of the industrial pilgrim's life; churches which express the kingship of Christ; churches shaped like fishes, flames, and passion-flowers." [3] When a building committee buys a gimmick—for example, a novelty design for the church building patterned after a mother hen whose wings cover her chicks, in the form of Sunday school rooms—we are inclined to feel that they deserve the ridicule outsiders give them. But one cannot help lamenting the hardship for the rest of the congregation that is striving toward genuine worship.

The contemporary liturgical movement has encouraged increased interest in

---

[1] *The Worldliness of Worship* (New York: Oxford University Press, 1967), p. 45.

[2] Massey H. Shepherd, Jr., ed., "The History of Liturgical Renewal," *The Liturgical Renewal of the Church* (New York: Oxford University Press, 1960), p. 46; Peter F. Anson, *Fashions in Church Furnishings, 1840-1940* (2nd ed., London: Studio Vista, 1965), p. 365.

[3] Peter Hammond, ed., *Towards a Church Architecture* (London: The Architectural Press, 1962), p. 24.

the Christian year as a useful basis for design of paraments, vestments, and banners. The various colors associated with special festivals and seasons offer an occasion for the representation of a sequence of events and liturgical subjects. The rich colors and designs of paraments in the chancel lead the eyes of the congregation to the scene of the liturgy as it progresses from lectern to pulpit, and finally to the altar, the focal point of the church.

This book deals with a particular kind of art (textiles), for a particular purpose (liturgical), and a particular time (now). This must be approached within the context of the church for which it is designed. The textile artist may find a great opportunity for experiment and creativity, both in method and in contemporary symbolism or composition. There is no excuse for mediocrity or ignorance of the liturgical function and significance of the object to be made. As in the case of music, church art is most effective when the artist directs his work toward the comprehension of the congregation, appropriating whatever methods and materials that are seemly. In acquiring a work of textile art for the church, whether it is a tapestry, banner, parament, or vestment, one should go beyond saying "I like it" or "I don't like it" and appraise it from the standpoint of good art and theological relevance.

The Function and Form of Textile Art in the Church

Holiness is to religion what beauty is to art.
—R. G. COLLINGWOOD

Textile arts are a continuation of long-established tradition in Roman Catholic, Lutheran, Anglican, and Orthodox churches. Paraments, dossals or tapestries, banners, and ministers' stoles are now being seen in an increasing number of Protestant churches as well. The current interest in experimentation has prompted a search for resources with which to quicken the religious consciousness and reach a deeper level of understanding and response on the part of the worshiping community. Well-designed cloth hangings and vestments are an effective means toward the enrichment of worship both because of their visual appeal and because they are continually changed in color and symbolism to represent the progression of the calendar of the Church year.

The key word in this case is "well-designed." The artist is expected to understand the function of the work, and this entails a conception as to the kind of art that is required and the kind of worship that is to take place. When we speak of worship that takes place in a church, we should be referring to corporate worship rather than a purely personal activity. The community of believers unites in an activity between God and man, and requires participation—putting something into worship. One would not have cause to complain about getting nothing out of the service if he were aware of his obligation to put something into it. One of the chief causes for failure to achieve genuine worship in churches is the separation between performers and spectators, and one of the chief objectives of the current liturgical movement is to remedy this. The total involvement of each member of the congregation must be engaged if corporate worship is to be real. Protestant worship in particular became primarily verbal, with emphasis on the Scriptures and the spoken word, from the time of the Reformation. The limited observance of sacraments afforded little visual attraction, and the indifference or outright animosity toward beauty offered even less. While remnants of this aesthetic poverty are still with us, there are encouraging signs that it is on the wane.

Changing trends that have a direct bearing upon vestments and hangings include a revised interpretation of the sacrament of Holy Communion. There is a tendency now to emphasize the table concept instead of the older idea of altar. Altar suggests mainly a place of sacrifice, whereas table stresses the communal and banquet nature of the Eucharist. Roman Catholic churches should now have a "freestanding" altar for celebration of Mass, and the medieval style of altar and frontals seems to be going out of fashion. The position of the celebrant facing the congregation has resulted in the chasuble being at least as decorative in front as in back, and there is a trend toward the full, flowing shape of the ancient *paenula* from which the chasuble was derived.

Although the practice of facing the congregation for the Eucharist is attributed to the early church, there is evidence that this was not generally the case. The early churches and basilicas were usually oriented so that the priest and the people faced the East, or Jerusalem, to pray.[1] In the Eastern Orthodox rites, which have preserved the traditions of the primitive church more faithfully than in the West, all churches are oriented so that the bishop takes the eastward position, with his back to the congregation. While the position of the celebrant facing the people may not be a return to the practices of the first centuries, it does bring about a closer union between priest and people.

A current view in liturgical circles seeks to modify the older distinction of "sacred" and "secular," and to see all life as celebrated in the liturgy, at any time and in any place. God acts in the world, and we are God's people at work in his world, not just at an hour and place set apart for worship on a Sunday morning. James F. White writes: "In a sense the term 'secular' is useless, since all depends upon God. 'Secular' is only employed when one limits a small sector of life to the so-called 'sacred' and another adjective must be found for the rest."[2]

It is false to speak of "sacred art" or "sacred music" since neither can be sacred in and of itself. We can, however, distinguish between "religious art" and "liturgical art." Art which produces a religious feeling, or transports one outside of one's self into a supernatural realm—such as a stirring painting or piece of music with religious subject matter—may be described as "religious art" or "religious music." It would be just as accurately described, whether it was seen or heard in an art gallery, concert hall, or church. "Liturgical art," on the other hand, serves a definite function within the framework of liturgical

[1] Cyril E. Pocknee, *The Christian Altar in History and Today* (London: A. R. Mowbray and Co., 1963), ch. 5, pp. 88-99.
[2] *The Worldliness of Worship,* p. 92.

worship. It need not be great art; indeed, it may even be of the simplest and most primitive sort. It must, however, serve a purpose beyond itself in supporting and directing the activity of worship. Paraments and vestments are included principally in this class, although they may function in both a liturgical and religious sense. Both liturgical and religious art are appropriate in a church.

The Function of Vestments and Decorative Cloths

Beautiful and colorful garments and coverings are visual stimuli, directed toward encouraging a contemplative and reverent attitude for worship. People respond emotionally and intellectually to that which is seen as well as that which is heard. The ornamentation and colors of the priestly garments and veils of the temple are described in detail in the Old Testament, and the churches of the Middle Ages are known to have employed richly decorated fabrics, along with a wealth of symbolical and representational art of all sorts.

We are conditioned today to respond to visual imagery through various media. Television, magazines, newspapers, billboards, and movies all exert a subtle influence on our thinking. Therefore, we can and do respond one way or another to what we see in church, and beauty is not the least important part of our visual encounter. A change of paraments from one season or festival to another attracts attention on entering the church and suggests contemplation on a particular theme, in preparation for the worship service.

Liturgical worship includes contemplation, praise, revelation, and offering. Liturgical art participates in all these actions. A splendid work of artistry in embroidery or weaving of paraments and vestments may be a joyful thing— a celebration, an act of praise, an offering on behalf of the artist and the congregation. It may also be a testimony to God, an affirmation of faith, and an alleluia. Art need not necessarily be beautiful, however, in order to serve a liturgical function. It may, instead, be a sorrowful reminder of the terrible price paid for our redemption. Not all aspects of Christian faith are lovely. Birth in a stable and death on a cross are bitter, and to express them prettily is to rob them of their nobility and power. Some of the most moving works of Christian art have been based upon suffering and death.

The trite phrase "aids to devotion" is inadequate when it is applied to truly worthy church needlework. The term implies a limited and purely personal area of worship. It also represents a weak and sentimental type of art that has been rejected by both Puritan and Catholic as unworthy. The term "message" art is also open to some question. Roger Hazelton suggests that the word "disclosure" would be a more apt term for what liturgical art is intended to do:

There is undoubtedly a kind of paradox involved in speaking of art as disclosure. On the one hand, it is plainly true that art seeks to establish a world of its own and to invite us into that world. Arthur Miller, commenting upon his recent play *After the Fall*, asserted that the play was not *about* something, but hopefully *was* something. An artist is a maker who wants what he has made to stand by itself. But on the other hand, art that deserves to be called great possesses a strange capacity to lead us beyond its presented surface toward quickened awareness . . . wider and deeper than art's own.[3]

[3] *A Theological Approach to Art* (Nashville: Abingdon Press, 1967), p. 31.

A great deal is said of the didactic or teaching function of the symbolism employed in church art. It would be more accurate to assume that the observer already recognizes the symbol if he finds meaning in it; therefore, it has reminded him rather than taught him. One of the principal benefits of the use of symbolism, however, is this very function: a calling to mind of what is already known, but more fully, at a new and deeper level of understanding.

Form, with Reference to Time and Place

The value and effectiveness of any work of church textile art must be judged by its relationship to the situation in terms of time, place, architectural style, and liturgical propriety.

Time

When referring to contemporary art, it is important to bear in mind that every age has had its contemporary art. Westminster Abbey, for example, has celebrated its nine-hundredth anniversary—nine hundred years during which various artists contributed to its architectural setting, development, and furnishings. Each was contemporary with his time and each contributed what was then contemporary with a specific period. This is true in many famous churches and cathedrals all over Europe today.

Every age has known conflicts between "traditionalists" and "innovators" and ours is no exception, the traditionalists accepting only the styles inherited from the past and the innovators claiming the freedom to find a new artistic language adapted to the church art of our day. The very term "contemporary art" is anathema to the traditionalist, to whom the only "correct" manner is that which has been hallowed by oft-repeated use. In the embroidering of vestments, needlework guilds are often guilty of perpetuating styles of a bygone era, led by teachers who are skilled in the "correct" methods of executing the traditional designs, but who are heedless of the possibilities in creative experimentation. At a large gathering of altar guild ladies, I overheard the remark made that there are really only about three authentic stitches for church embroidery. How dull this would be if it were true! Fortunately, there are now several fine teachers who have freed themselves from these restricted paths, and are introducing their pupils to the adventure of an immediate experience in church needlework. The sheer weight of years does not make a form of art more sacred.

The furnishings and decorations of churches are governed by fashion—either that of the day or an attempted recreation of some earlier time which appears in retrospect to have been more valid, according to Peter F. Anson. He goes on to say that the wheel of fashion has gone full circle in the past hundred years. "The pioneers revive the fashions of the past, with slight adaptations." [4] This statement treats the matter only stylistically, however, and does not take into account the immense theological change that has affected the vestments and decorative cloths today. The current emphasis on the church in the world,

[4] *Fashions in Church Furnishings, 1840-1940*, p. 356.

1 Poncho for Mass, St. Joseph's Church, Pisinimo, Arizona

involved in all phases of life, requires its own artistic language, and it is this language that today's textile artists are seeking to express in Christian art.

Place

Liturgical fitness depends considerably on the accommodation of the work of art to its intended situation. It makes a great deal of difference whether a particular work is intended for a cloister, a cathedral, a parish church, or the mission field.

A provocative question was raised in a letter to the editor of *Liturgical Arts*.[5] A picture was submitted showing a priest at St. Joseph's Church in Pisinimo, Arizona, a Papago Indian reservation near the Mexican border (Illustration 1). The priest is pictured officiating at Mass wearing a poncho woven by his Indian craftsmen. The caption about the picture asks: "In this particular case is anything wrong? If so, why?" The correspondent writes: "Is it not better to use such a poncho (a very close relative to a chasuble) with the attractive designs of the Indian craftsman, rather than the more usual leftovers of italianate, abbreviated chasubles which are sent to poor parishes as a misplaced gesture of generosity by more affluent, but little discerning, parishes in other parts of the country?" Certainly medieval European ecclesiastical dress would have little meaning to a Papago Indian.

A more conventional provision for the use of indigenous textile art on

[5] Letter from Fritz Kaeser (Vol. XXXIV, Aug., 1966).

2 Chasuble, Tekawitha Vestments,
made by Indian craftsmen

3 Chasuble, Tekawitha Vestments,
made by Indian craftsmen

3

2

Courtesy of *Handweaver and Craftsman*

Courtesy of *Handweaver and Craftsman*

traditional vestments was illustrated in *Handweaver and Craftsman* in an article "Vestments by Indian Craftsmen, a Cooperative Enterprise of the Lummis, Navajos, and Sioux." [6] The vestments are designed by a member of the Dominican Sisters of the Perpetual Rosary in New Jersey, woven by the Lummi Indians at Marietta, Washington, embroidered by the Navajos in Arizona, and made at the Sioux reservation at Marty, South Dakota. A royal purple chasuble (Illustration 2) is embroidered with a corn motif in yellow and green, over a white moon, the symbol of the Tekawitha Vestments, the company that markets the vestments in New York. Another chasuble (Illustration 3) in rich maroon with an orphrey of black and gray embroidery on white, shows a geometric pattern of Indian design.

Art and Architecture

The relationship between a church embroidery and its setting involves not only the design itself but also its scale or proportions, color scheme, and even its texture. The era to which the building belongs must be taken into account, and the relevance of the design to the church today. This by no means implies that a church of another era with regard to architectural style, such as Norman, Gothic, Jacobean, and others, should not use a design that is contemporary with our own times. There must be a harmonious relationship, however, between the church and its furnishings.

[6] (Winter, 1967), pp. 6-8.

Courtesy of C. H. Ferguson

An outstanding example of synthesis of different eras is to be seen in England at Chichester Cathedral, built in the eleventh and twelfth centuries in Norman style, rebuilt after a fire in 1187 in Transitional style. Whenever anything new was required during the cathedral's seven hundred years of history, it was done in the contemporary manner. Old styles which had gone out of date and lost their inspiration were never copied. The reredos behind the high altar is a particularly successful blend of old and new: a bold and vigorous tapestry, designed by the modern artist John Piper, to be hung in sections on a sixteenth-century screen. Unsuccessful attempts had been made during the last hundred and fifty years to provide a worthy setting for the high altar, and John Piper, who is distinguished both for his talent as a creative artist and his extensive knowledge of old churches, was consulted for a solution. His brilliant tapestry, woven by Pinton Frères at Felletin, near Aubusson, is the result. He chose tapestry because of its affinities with old stonework and woodwork, and viewed the screen with its crest of medieval canopies as an ideal setting for seven strips of tapestry which could "read" as a whole across the six narrow buttresses between the strips. The three central panels represent the Trinity, with an equilateral triangle among flames, the Father symbolized with a white light, the Son with a Tau cross, and the Holy Spirit with a flamelike wing. The elements (earth, air, fire, and water) are shown at the top of the two panels at each end, and the four Evangelists beneath (Illustration 4).

The three-hundred-year-old chapel at Emmanuel College, Cambridge, designed by Christopher Wren, is the setting for the frontal designed by Beryl

THE FUNCTION AND FORM OF TEXTILE ART IN THE CHURCH 29

5 Altar frontal (center section), Emmanuel College, Cambridge, by Beryl Dean

6 Altar frontal (section), Chelmsford Cathedral, by Beryl Dean and Patricia Scrase

Courtesy of the artist

Courtesy of Beryl Dean

Dean (Illustration 5). The design and its techniques are definitely modern, and yet the frontal blends well with the furnishings of other eras.

A dramatic altar frontal for Chelmsford Cathedral, by Beryl Dean and Patricia Scrase (one end of which is shown in Illustration 6), demonstrates a contemporary treatment of the legendary phoenix rising from the flames, using modern techniques of hand and machine embroidery, including appliqué of many bits of fabric.

St. Margaret's Church, King's Lynn, is a twelfth-century Norman church, which was rebuilt in the thirteenth century to perpendicular Gothic style. A huge nineteenth-century gilded and carved reredos, added in 1899, dominates the altar. The festal frontal is designed with variations of the Greek cross arranged as a balanced but not symmetrical pattern, presented as a collage of metallic textures. A variety of effects is attained on a single shape, repeated

7 Altar frontal, St. Margaret's Church, King's Lynn,
  by Beryl Dean

From *Embroidery*, Diamond Jubilee Issue, 1966; courtesy of Beryl Dean

within a close-knit composition (Illustration 7). The dimensional effect belies the flat surface upon which the embroidery is laid, carrying a relationship to the sculptured reredos and Gothic columns and arches.[7]

Occasionally, the blend of old and new is reversed, and a new, original architecture is equipped with a trite cliché of the past. On an architectural tour of interesting new churches, this blunder was seen in a fine little church with free-form shape and thick adobelike walls in keeping with the pioneer heritage of the locale. The pulpit, lectern, base of the communion table, and communion rail resembled the rough bark of trees. The color scheme of neutral and wood tones was accented with vivid orange kneeling cushions and covering for the clergy's chairs. Shortly before the tour, some misguided person apparently consulted a catalog and ordered a limp white ribbed cloth with a conventional cross and gold fringe for the pulpit. The architect's concern for roughness of texture of the walls and wood had not been taken into account in selecting the textiles or designs for the parament. How effective a rough, handwoven fabric in natural unbleached color could have been as a foundation for a design worthy of such a church.

Not only church architecture but also church furniture is subject to changes in style. While some Roman Catholic altars are beginning to resemble tables, many Protestant communion tables look like altars. This is a matter of theology and liturgics, not just design. The trend in the current liturgical movement

[7] Beryl Dean, "Embroidery for the Church," *Embroidery* (Diamond Jubilee issue, 1966).

is away from the concept of altar and sacrifice and toward the centrality of the Lord's table and the sacred meal. A zeal for traditionally correct furnishings on the part of architects, manufacturers of church furniture, and the purchasers themselves has led many Protestants to install an altar and use it as a table. The altar with an enclosed shape originally contained relics and represents a tomb. In recent centuries it was placed against the wall, although this is no longer the favored position. As a table, it is open beneath, with a base or legs for support, and is brought forward so that the minister or priest faces the congregation. The communion rail now extends around all four sides of the table in many churches, in an attempt to express the spirit of the liturgy (*leitourgia*), the work of the people. An altar frontal is inappropriate for a table, and a more suitable cloth must be devised for its vesture.

Variations in altar or communion table designs occur both in the base, which may be open as table legs, solid as a tomb or pedestal, and in the shape of the top (the *mensa*), which may be any of a number of shapes: rectangular, tapered toward the ends, curved, oval, or some other form, depending on the choice of the architect, designer, or buyer. The illustrations throughout this book show an assortment of furniture styles and shapes of paraments, both conventional and novel. Pulpits are also designed in different ways: some with a modern version of a sounding board overhead, some suggesting the prow of a ship, and at least one that I have seen resembling a Jack-in-the-pulpit (which has caused some amusement, and perhaps some embarrassment as a result). Obviously, conventional shapes of paraments cannot be used on these shapes of furniture. A style and proportion must be determined that bears a relationship to the altar or pulpit, as well as to the chancel and entire church interior.

A number of different shapes of altar cloths are used today. The full frontal extending over the entire length and height of the altar, and the frontlet running the full length across the upper edge, are more closely related to the altar-tomb concept than the altar-table. A central rectangular-shaped cloth or a pair of hangings placed toward the ends of the altar are more customary today. An enormously long altar in St. Thomas Church, Stockholm-Vällingby, has an unusual frontal draped in seven sections, with a scalloped superfrontal in contrasting color (Illustration 8). The altar, described by G. E. Kidder Smith as "rather fussily dressed," [8] is purposely large to represent a table for the entire congregation.

The central rectangular shape of altar antependium is seen more and more often, both in this country and abroad, and affords an opportunity for strong and easily visible design. An uncommon use of parallel cloths is seen in some of the churches designed by architects Sövik, Mathre, and Madson. A particularly effective example is the Trinity Lutheran Church, Lisbon, North Dakota (Illustration 9), where a strong Trinitarian symbolism is carried out. Three cloths are grouped together, allowing the triple-inverted arches of the base of the altar to be seen. The grouping emphasizes the Trinity and the placement at one end of the altar balances the asymmetrical arrangement of the chancel. The shapes and proportions of the cloths are parts of the whole architectural composition. In the case of the Shepherd of the Hills Lutheran Church, Edina,

[8] *The New Churches of Europe* (London: The Architectural Press, 1963), pp. 244-47.

8

From G. E. Kidder-Smith, *The New Churches of Europe*

8 St. Thomas Church, Stockholm-Vällingby;
Peter Celsing architect

9 Trinity Lutheran Church,
Lisbon, North Dakota

9

Courtesy of Sövik, Mathre, and Madson; Robert Warn

10 American Lutheran Church,
Oslo, Norway

11 Our Saviour's Lutheran Church,
Austin, Minnesota

Minnesota, the architects explained that one reason for designing a three-panel altar table parament was to avoid a large cloth area that would conflict in scale with the tapestry behind the altar (Illustration 150*). It also makes a strong Trinity symbol. A two-panel parament was designed by the same firm for the American Lutheran Church in Oslo, Norway (Illustration 10), relating to the separated pedestal base of the altar. A cloth of generous proportions was designed for the long altar table for Our Savior's Lutheran Church of Austin, Minnesota, also by Sövik, Mathre, and Madson (Illustration 11), allowing the ends and legs of the altar to show. The embroidered design and the candlesticks, as well as the altar table, are placed at the extreme right of the chancel, as parts within a complex organization.

The plan for the altar cloths at the San Marino Congregational Church (United Church of Christ), San Marino, California, was prompted by the design of the altar, where an overlay of light wood is placed on a darker wood for

*P. 256.

34

12a

12 Altar antependia, San Marino
Congregational Church,
United Church of Christ,
San Marino, California,
paraments by Marion P. Ireland:
(a) green Trinity design;
(b) red Pentecost design

12b

Marion P. Ireland

the face of the altar. This effect is repeated on the green antependium (Illustration 12a), with a variegated material in shades of green and harmonizing bands acting as a background for the main area of the cloth. A similar treatment is used on the red parament (Illustration 12b) with accents of appliquéd brocades. The deep blues were used on the red paraments to relate to the pale

13

13 Pulpit marker, San Marino Congregational Church: official insignia of the United Church of Christ, by Marion P. Ireland

Marion P. Ireland

gray-blue carpet, walls, and ceiling. The pulpit of the same church has an indented panel down the center front, into which a pulpit hanging is fitted, ornamented with bands of various textures and hues of fabrics to match the altar cloth, and embroidered with the official insignia of the United Church of Christ (Illustration 13).

At St. Mark's Lutheran Church, Chula Vista, California, the position of the pulpit in relation to the altar, the solid pedestal base upon which the long altar rests, and the vertical lines of paneling on the walls behind the altar all suggested the use of a pair of altar antependia (Illustration 14). They are placed close to the base of the altar, so that they will be seen with the pulpit cloth as a group, thereby strengthening the effect of the green, which, in this case, must compete with a great deal of red carpeting. Since only one set of paraments is used at a time, the same plan need not be used on all sets. There-

14 Paraments, for altar and pulpit, St. Mark's Lutheran Church, Chula Vista, California; Des Lauriers and Sigurdson architects, by Marion P. Ireland

15 St. Mark's Lutheran Church, Chula Vista, California:
Pentecost paraments, first prize award from the Guild for Religious Architecture, 1968. Designed and embroidered by Marion P. Ireland

16 Paraments, First United Methodist Church, Escondido, California, by Marion P. Ireland

arion P. Ireland

15

16

arion P. Ireland

Marion P. Ireland

fore, a large rectangular altar cloth was made for the red set for St. Mark's Church, creating a strong mass of color, with the red pulpit hanging showing directly above it, an effect that is appropriate for the spirit of excitement related to the Pentecost color (Illustration 15).

A successful balance is achieved in an asymmetrical arrangement of the whole interior of the First United Methodist Church of Escondido, California, designed by architect Hal C. Whittemore (Illustration 16). There is no central passageway, central window, or central cross behind the altar. Rather, a central *composition* groups the wall of stained glass, cross, and altar in subtle balance with one another. Large masses of angular shapes and textures of stone, stained glass, elaborately carved wood, exposed ranks of organ pipes, and organ chamber make the chancel wall three-dimensional rather than a flat surface. Strictly vertical lines are avoided in the treatment of shapes, and the

17 Pulpit antependia, First United Methodist Church,
Escondido, California, by Marion P. Ireland

18 Paraments, Herrick Memorial Chapel,
Occidental College, Los Angeles, California,
by Marion P. Ireland

18

17

Glenn B. Wa

handsomely carved pulpit is tapered narrower at the bottom than at the top, sloping forward at the top. The designing of the paraments is based upon this architectural arrangement. To carry out the nonparallel lines already established by the architecture and furniture, the hangings for the pulpit are shaped on the lines of a minister's stole—narrow at the top and wider at the bottom (Illustration 17). A large rectangular cloth is placed between the center and right end of the altar table, balancing with the cross suspended above the left end. A figured damask and banding are used to blend with the surface textures of the woodcarving and cut stone nearby.

The gracefully contoured cruciform shape of the Herrick Memorial Chapel of Occidental College, Los Angeles (Illustration 18), by architects Ladd and Kelsey, suggested a theme for the paraments. The circular motif of the pulpit and lectern, the dais at the crossing, and the stained-glass oculus overhead, is repeated in harmonizing shades of red-violet and blue-violet as a background for the Advent and Lenten symbols on the purple paraments and the symbols of the Lord's Supper on the pulpit fall (Illustration 19). The white paraments carry the same distinctive cross, with a suggestion of the stained glass in embroidery accenting the ends of the cross, highlighted by crowns and monograms in gold kidskin.

19 Pulpit and lectern antependia,
   Herrick Memorial Chapel,
   Occidental College, Los Angeles,
   by Marion P. Ireland:
   (a) lectern fall, Advent
   and Lenten symbols;
   (b) pulpit fall, symbols
   of the Lord's Supper

19a

19b

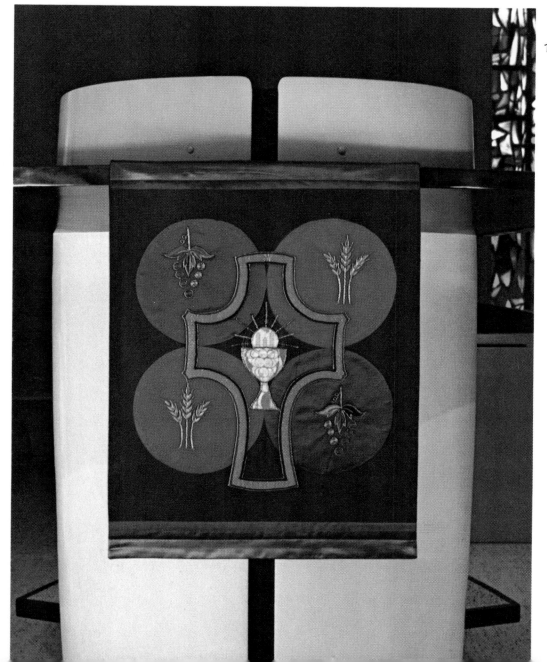

Art Waldinger

20 Herrick Memorial Chapel, Occidental College, Los Angeles:
paraments by Marion P. Ireland:
(a) interior;
(b) pulpit antependium for Pentecost;
(c) lectern antependium

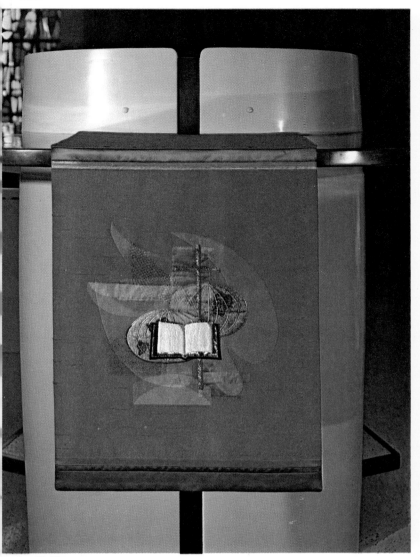

Art Waldinger

Art Waldinger

The designing of the red paraments for this chapel was influenced by the vivid colors of the red pew upholstery and the fragmented patterns from the stained-glass windows against the off-white walls upon which the sunlight streaming through the glass casts reflections (Illustration 20a). The spirit of Pentecost determined the composition of the red paraments. A collage technique was used to create an atmospheric quality and an effect of flames, by means of overlapping of semi-transparent and opaque fabrics and stitchery. A flame-colored dove of variegated material forms the background for each of the two hangings, and upon this appliquéd foundation the symbolism was worked. The pulpit design (Illustration 20b) portrays the Church at work within the world; the lectern design (Illustration 20c) portrays the ship as a symbol of the Church, the net with fish for the disciples as "fishers of men" and the anchor as a symbol of hope: "Which hope we have as an anchor of the soul" (Hebrews 6:19). The symbols are as old as the Church, but they are expressed in a new way which suggests the *feel* of the Pentecost experience, and a message of its pertinence in our day.

The principal aim in each of the above examples has been to use the Christian symbols in such a way that they are not reserved for the initiated, but can be understood at least to some extent by anyone who enters the church and sees them, awakening an emotional, intellectual, and aesthetic response.

Liturgical Propriety

It is assumed that an artist commissioned to do liturgical art will be concerned with its propriety. Often the result is good art, but unsuccessful in its liturgical function. Bold experiments have been made in selecting non-Christian artists on the basis of their talent, and the results have been by no means failures. P. R. Régamey argues the case quite convincingly in a chapter called "The Non-Christian Artist in the Service of the Church," pointing out that some of our best artists are outside the church, while some of the worst examples of art for the church are produced by the most devout believers.[9]

Roger Hazelton writes that while artists usually mean what they say, they do not always say exactly what they mean.[10] When the artist is working in the capacity of the servant of the church, it is of the greatest importance for him to know what the *Christian* means. On the other hand, a thing or an event may have quite a different meaning to an outsider than to one who stands within the faith. Yet it is possible that the outsider may hit upon something from his objective vantage that is so obvious that the Christian fails to note its significance.

The Church of Notre-Dame-de-Toute-Grâce at Assy is a notable example where "unbelievers" were brought in and each was invited to do just what he seemed best fitted to do. It was here that the Marxist Lurçat did his finest masterpiece, the large Apocalypse tapestry over the altar (Illustration 21). The conflict between the artist's atheism and the necessity for a Christian iconography over the altar was resolved by choosing the subject of St. John's visions in the Apocalypse. This theme appealed particularly to Lurçat because of the magnificent tapestry, the Apocalypse of Angers, completed in 1382 for the Duke of Anjou, a work which made a deep impression on Lurçat and influenced his mature style.

The Lurçat tapestry is designed in zones which depict a symbolic struggle between good and evil. The main zone shows a heavenly woman with child, clothed with the sun (Revelation 12:1), and a great dragon (Revelation 12:3), representing good and evil respectively, both looking forward rather than engaged in struggle. The horizontal zone beneath the main panel shows the Archangel Michael triumphing over the dragon. The vision is treated imaginatively by Lurçat, allowing vast scope for his decorative style and studies of bestiary.[11] The artist's personal attitudes toward religion could not allow him to portray deity as a Christian would, but he could in all honesty interpret the war between good and evil. To the Christian, however, the apocalyptic monsters are somewhat disturbing and oddly pagan in an area that is traditionally reserved for Christ in Majesty.

Henri Matisse was not a religious man, but his last major work was the decoration of the interior of the Chapel of the Rosary, for the Dominican nuns at Vence. The most controversial part of his design has to do with the unconventional arrangement of the Stations of the Cross (Illustration 22):

[9] P. R. Régamey, O.P., *Religious Art in the Twentieth Century* (New York: Herder and Herder, 1963), p. 177.

[10] *A Theological Approach to Art*, p. 28.

[11] Lurçat's symbolism stems from study of medieval bestiaries adapted to the scriptural theme of his tapestry. See Jean Lurçat, *Le Bestiaire de la tapisserie du moyen âge* (Geneva: Cailler, 1947).

Courtesy of the Guild for Religious Architecture

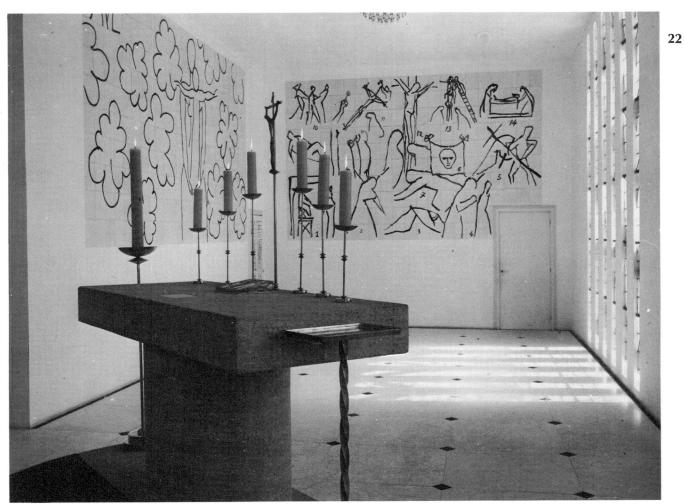

Hélène Adant, Paris

21 Church of Notre-Dame-de-Toute Grâce at Assy, France:
tapestry "Apocalypse" by Jean Lurçat

22 Stations of the Cross, by Henri Matisse,
Chapel of the Rosary, Vence, France

This mature work by a major artist lacks, nevertheless, in functional competency. Matisse either failed to remember, or could not be bothered with, the *why* of his decoration. For example, when making the stations of the cross, one should take a few steps between stations in imitation of Our Lord's last journey. Hence the fourteen pictures spaced around the nave in orderly display. To make the stations in the Vence chapel, distracted faithful must meander in front of the single wall on which the stations are crowded in disordered tiers, with the hazard of colliding against each other in mid-devotion.[12]

There was a purpose behind this apparently haphazard arrangement, however. Matisse rejected the traditional idea of a procession of stations and portrayed a drama instead, with Christ the central and culminating figure, on the cross. The figures of Mary and John and the stations below form a pedestal for Christ's feet. Two oblique lines, the cross of station eleven and the ladder of station thirteen, frame the figure of the Crucified Christ, whose outspread arms soar heavenward in a gesture of hope and victory.

In designing the vestments, Matisse was apparently not too concerned about the necessity for relating the symbolism and liturgical color to the particular season when it is to be worn. Although he designated the color for each chasuble, there is no apparent relationship between the liturgical significance of the design and the seasonal color. The butterfly, a symbol of the Resurrection, appears on a purple chasuble which belongs to the Advent and Lenten seasons, and flames—more appropriate for the red of Pentecost—are used on the green chasuble. His emphasis is first upon art and the effect he wanted to achieve, and liturgical propriety is second. The magnificence of the little chapel, however, far overshadows whatever faults one might find in its details.

Abstract Design

Nonrepresentational or abstract design is more readily accepted in stained glass and mosaic than on the vestments and paraments which serve a liturgical function. Symbolism that can be recognized and understood is more direct and effective in its didactic capacity than nonrepresentational design. In the function of encouraging reverent contemplation, however, there is much to recommend in parament designs that do not try to "say" something. A subject that is readily identified may be as readily dismissed or may cause one's attention to drift along on some superficial train of thought. Art that is apprehended on an intuitive level engages the observer, enabling him to draw upon his inner resources to see beyond the surface.

The question is not whether we should have subject matter or not, and whether the aim is to tell us something or to make us feel something. There are hymns to express the full range of the liturgy—adoration, supplication, repentance, instruction, and the rest. Why not visual art?

Viewed together, the pulpit and its antependium seen in Illustration 97,* show both representational and abstract art. The antependium was designed as an abstraction because of the subject matter carved on the pulpit. There is no need to place symbol upon symbol, each competing with the other. The important consideration here is the unity of design of both textile

---

[12] Jean Charlot, "Catholic Art in America: Debits and Credits," *Liturgical Arts,* XXVII (Nov., 1958), p. 22.
*Pp. 186-87.

and wood carving together. At the same time, both are complete in themselves.

Subject matter is only incidental to the abstract, sculptural design of gold kidskin on the altar cloth shown in Illustration 92,* made from the negative shapes where crosses, circles, and other pieces had been cut out and the remaining pieces used as building material. Although there is a suggestion of symbolism, it is not necessary to the character of the abstract design, which leaves the observer free for his own contemplation.

A comparison is often made between the nonrepresentational character of some forms of art and music. Organ music that was written for church use can usually be recognized as such, just by hearing it played, and religious emotions can be deeply stirred by music without asking what it means. When the organ music is based upon a chorale tune, the words associated with the tune provide subject matter for anyone who recalls the words. It is not essential, however, to know the words in order to be religiously affected by the music. This can be true of the designing of paraments and vestments as well.

A serious criticism of abstract art for liturgical use is that the meaning is so obscure that it is reserved for the elite. This is contrary to the communal concept of Christian worship. The liturgy literally means the work of the people, and it is for and by all of the people who gather together with one accord to worship the Lord. A major principle of liturgical renewal is the total participation of the whole worshiping assembly. Anything that is limited to a select few threatens a return to the passive spectator attitude and barren worship against which the Church is now struggling. Nonrepresentational art admittedly lacks the ability to convey didactic content, but fortunately the Church is not dependent on the message of the paraments and vestments for its teaching function, and can allow them to perform their aesthetic functions quite apart from whether symbolism is employed or not.

The altar table is a symbol, and so are the paraments. It is quite possible to make a complete set of vestments and paraments in all colors without putting a single symbol on any of them, if circumstances make it desirable to do so. What needs to be recovered is the inherent symbolism of *cloth itself.*

In the ancient world, cloth was used and apprehended as "drapery," in the sense that large, whole, free-falling pieces were used both for clothing and for curtains, tablecloths, and so forth. The aesthetic properties of these articles were determined by the free draping, falling, enveloping character of the cloth. The "massive" effect of large curtains, or of large, enveloping garments, excluded a tailored appearance. The simple, geometrical form of the chasuble, tunicle, etc.—"seamless" garments made of a single web—was integral to their symbolic function. As covers (clothing and tablecloths) they *simplify* and *unify* the underlying form, which is *concealed* by being covered and then again *revealed* by the drape and fold of the cloth over it. This calls for generous use of relatively large and uncut pieces. As curtains, the cloth concealed what lay behind it until drawn open, and then revealed and enframed it—again requiring generous use. This is the symbolic *value* of the cloth, inherent in its nature: simplification and unification of forms, the concealment/revelation

*P. 176.

of underlying forms. Symbolic *interpretation* was specific to circumstance: the words "clothe" and "veil," for example, appear under many different circumstances in the Bible, as is easily verified in a Bible concordance, and medieval allegorical interpretation develops from this.[13]

This ancient aesthetic of cloth was preserved well down to modern times in folk art, especially in Eastern Europe,[14] but the modern, tailored aesthetic has led to the idea of paraments, stoles, etc., as mere backgrounds for symbols, which could be stiff stuff and un-clothlike. Stiff stuff has been used in the Roman Catholic Church from the late Middle Ages to the modern revival of the original forms. Where garments equivalent to church vestments have remained in daily use, they have also remained very full and uncut; the best examples are the *burnūs* in Morocco (a cope) and the *djellaba* (tunicle).

An awareness of the symbolic nature and value of cloth and the historical development of its use as ecclesiastical clothing, covering, and drapery will guide us in our search for the most worthy handling of this time-honored resource.

[13] For example of ancient use of cloth, see F. van der Meer and Christine Mohrmann, *Atlas of the Early Christian World* (London: Thomas Nelson and Sons, 1958), figs. 232, 235, 457-460; and comments by Basil Minchen, *Outward and Visible (London: Darton,* Longman and Todd, 1961), pp. 66-68. See also Ernst Kitzinger, *Early Mediaeval Art* (Bloomington: Indiana University Press, 1966), plates 18, 20, 24, 28; and David Talbot Rice, *The Beginnings of Christian Art* (Nashville: Abingdon Press, 1957), plate 26a; C. E. Pocknee, *The Christian Altar.*
[14] Tancred Banateanu, *et al., Folk Costumes, Woven Textiles, and Embroideries of Rumania* (Bucharest: State Publishing House for Literature and the Arts, 1958), fig. 360 and plates XXII and XXXVI.

Vestments and Hangings: Origin and Development

Worship the Lord in holy array.
—1 CHRONICLES 16:29

Ornamental textiles have been used both as garments for the officiants and as coverings for use in places of worship throughout Judeo-Christian history. The use of distinctive vestments exhibits the dramatic function of the clergy and their identification with the liturgical scene. They are no longer "Mr. Jones," "Dr. Smith," and "Father Green," but the servants of the sanctuary. This is true of the historic and traditional vestments of the Roman Catholic, Anglican, Eastern Orthodox, and Lutheran communions, and the black preaching robe in the Reformed tradition as well.

Vestments, Past and Present

The designing of vestments for the church requires both religious propriety and artistic merit. For the former, it is necessary to clarify our use of the term "vestments" and to include a brief description of the various articles and their purposes. In some quarters, the use of the word "vestments" is limited to those worn during the Eucharist, whereas others employ both a general use for all special attire for religious services and a specific term "eucharistic vestments" for sacramental use. *The Oxford Dictionary of the Christian Church* defines vestments as "the distinctive dress worn by the clergy when performing the liturgical and other services of the Church," and defines eucharistic

47

23a Representative vestments—Eastern: (a) sticharion, worn by deacon or acolyte; (b) orarion, worn by deacon or acolyte; (c) sticharion, worn by bishop or priest; less elaborate than that of the deacon or acolyte, since other vestments are worn over it; (d) epitrachilion, worn by bishop or priest; (e) zone, or girdle, worn by bishop or priest; passed through the slits in the sticharion and tied around the waist; (f) gauntlets, worn by bishop, priest, or deacon; tied over the sleeves of the sticharion; (g) felonion, worn by the priest over his other vestments, illustrated spread out flat; (h) phelonion, front view; (i) phelonion, back view; (j) sakkos, worn by the bishop; (k) epigonation, suspended from the hip of a priest; (l) omophorion, worn by the bishop, before the Great Entrance in the liturgy, and called "megalo-omophorion," comparable to the Western pallium; (m) omophorion, worn by the bishop, after the Great Entrance, and called "micro-omophorion" or broad stole

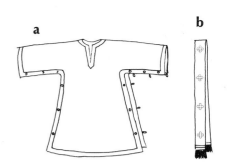

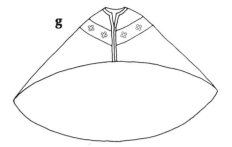

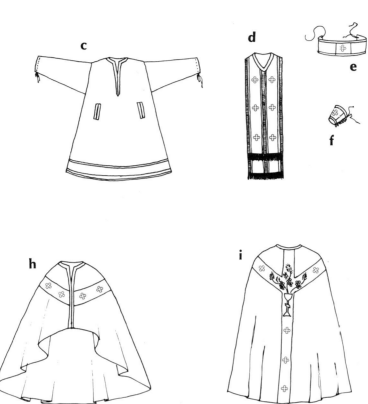

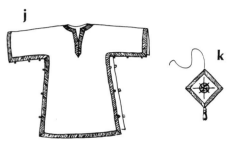

VESTMENTS: WESTERN AND EASTERN COUNTERPARTS

Western	Greek	Syriac	Armenian	Coptic	Ethiopian
Alb	stichárion	kuthina; sudra	shapik	stichar(ion)	gamīs
Cincture	zónê	zundāra; hasa	goti	zunar(ion)	zenār
Amice	anabó-loeon; anago-loeon	sanwarta; masnaftho	varkas	kidaris	hebanie; ghelbab
Cuffs	epimani-kia	zande; kepi, kummīn	bazpan	kamas(ion)	akmām; edjgē
Deacon's stole	orarion	urara	urar	orar(ion)	(?mothat)
Priest's stole	epitrachê-lion	hemnikho; bitrashīl; urara rabba	porurar	orar(ion)	mothat
Chasuble	phelónion	feno; pagīlā; paina, ma'pra; ridā	shurchar	felon(ion) kuklion; amforion	gābā

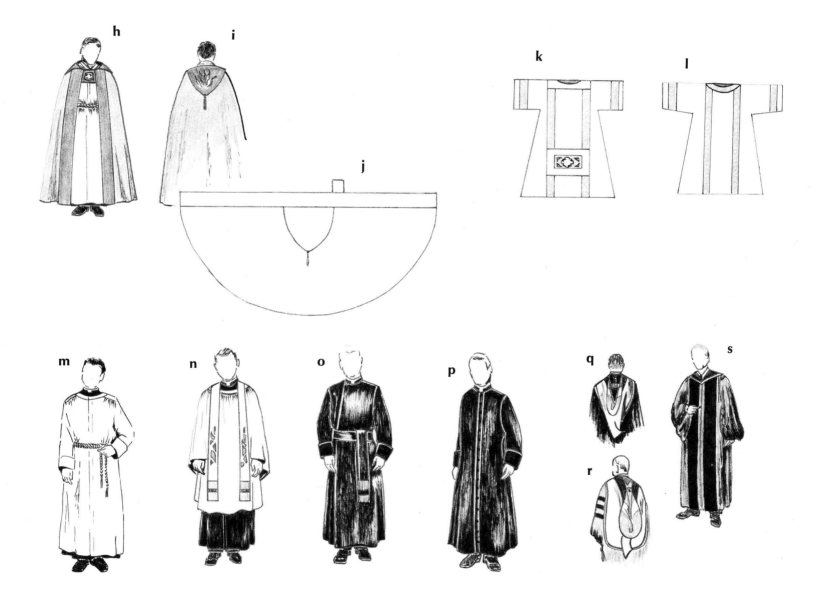

23b Representative vestments—Western: (a) chasuble, full cut, worn with amice, alb, and stole; (b) chasuble, modern modification of Gothic shape; (c) chasuble, conical; (d) conical chasuble, before seaming together in front; (e) amice, with apparel; (f) stole; (g) maniple; (h) cope, worn with amice, alb, and rope cincture; (i) cope, with hood, back view; (j) cope, spread out flat; (k) dalmatic, one of many variations in shape and ornamentation; (l) tunicle; (m) alb; worn with rope cincture or girdle, over a cassock; (n) surplice, illustrated over a cassock, with a stole; (o) Anglican cassock, with cloth cincture; (p) Roman cassock; (q) Bachelor's hood. The color of the velvet indicates the field in which the degree is taken, and the lining indicates the college or university, or seminary. A Master's hood is the same shape but larger; (r) Doctor's hood and Doctor's bars or chevrons on the sleeve of the robe; (s) black preaching robe with academic hood

24 Ordination of bishops in Uppsala Cathedral, Sweden.
Bishops kneeling are vested in copes; officiants in copes
and mitres; attending clergy in chasubles

vestments under a separate heading.[1] The term "vestments" will be used in its general sense throughout this book to include both eucharistic vestments and others, which include the cassock, surplice, and stole generally worn by Lutheran clergy in this country, and the black preaching robe that is worn for regular worship services in the Reformed tradition. The stole is coming into greater use in Protestant churches as a result of the spirit of liturgical renewal and an increased emphasis on the Christian year, designated by the liturgical colors on the paraments as well. In the Episcopal Church, the stole is reserved for sacramental use, signifying *priest,* and is worn for the Eucharist. For nonsacramental services, the tippet is worn instead. In some Lutheran churches, particularly abroad (Illustration 24), the eucharist vestments are worn, as they are by Roman Catholic and many of the Episcopal clergy in the United States. Orthodox vestments follow a separate tradition.

The terms "parament," "antependium," "hanging," or "fall" may be applied to the cloths for the altar or holy table, the pulpit, and the lectern. These are also vestments in the sense that they clothe, or cover, the furniture used for religious services.

It is universally agreed today that the vestments set apart for sacred use originated not from the priestly robes of the Old Testament, but from secular Roman dress. Even before the end of Christian antiquity, a special vesture was worn by the officiant—at first merely more costly and precious than the holi-

[1] (London: Oxford University Press, 1957). See also "vestments" in standard dictionaries such as Oxford or Webster.

TEXTILE ART IN THE CHURCH

day clothing of the populace. Then, when fashion decreed a newer, shorter costume, the liturgical vesture became a stylized version of several types (dalmatic, tunic, etc.) of the old Roman imperial dress.

Alb

The alb, or *tunica,* is of classical Greek and Roman origin, but received its name at the time of Charles the Great, the word in Latin referring to its color, white. It was the ordinary form of dress in the pictures in the catacombs. Changes in shape were introduced—long garments with sleeves introduced from the East, a longer and fuller garment reaching to the ground, but kept in position with a girdle around the waist, at the time of Charlemagne. Colored bands attached as ornaments were derived from the *clavi* of antiquity, which had ceased to be used when the alb came to be worn under a dalmatic. The fashion of attaching ornaments or "apparels" grew in the eleventh and twelfth centuries, and consists of decorative bands in color on the hem, front and back, and on each wrist.

A similar garment worn in the Eastern Church is also derived from the ancient tunic, and is called a *sticharion.* It is worn by all who are vested, from the reader to the patriarch (Illustrations 25-27, 29). It is not an alb; rather, it shares the same origin as the alb—the tunic. In the Armenian Church, the tunic is a *shabik* and is without ornamental bands at shoulder, cuff, or hem.

Surplice

The surplice is not used in the Eastern rites but is entirely Latin and Western. It is fuller and generally shorter than the alb, from which it was developed, with full sleeves, whereas the sleeves of the alb are narrow. The alb is confined at the waist with a cincture, but the surplice hangs free. The alb is a eucharistic vestment, while the surplice is intended for most other occasions.

Stole

It is generally agreed by liturgical scholars that the stole was derived neither from the Latin *stola* nor the Jewish prayer shawl. The term *stola* appeared in early Christian literature, referring to the long, flowing garment worn by Roman matrons, and was the white garment put on by the candidates on Easter Even for their baptism/confirmation.

The stole was first known as *orarium* (or *orarion*) a term derived from the Latin *oro,* meaning "to pray." The stole and pallium were ensigns worn by Roman officials, comparable to a policeman's badge (i.e., secular), the term *orarion* meaning the pallium when applied to the bishop's vesture, and the stole when applied to that of the priest or deacon. The change in name from *orarion* to *stola* took place in the ninth century, a Franco-Germanic innovation, and it was not until after the twelfth century that the new name "stole" became generally used. By the sixteenth century the stole had become a badge of the bishops, priests, and deacons—the three higher orders of clergy—each of whom wore it over the shoulder in a distinctive way.[2]

[2] See Daniel Rock, *The Church of Our Fathers as Seen in St. Osmund's Rite for the Cathedral of Salisbury* (London: John Murray, 1905), I, 343-43; C. E. Pocknee, *Liturgical Vesture: Its Origin and Development* (London: A. R. Mowbray and Co., 1960), pp. 21-23.

25 Greek Orthodox Divine Liturgy,
Epiphany Day Service,
Long Beach, California

Steven N. Brussa

The *orarium* was originally nine or ten feet long and a uniform two to three inches wide, but by the twelfth century the ends were terminated in a rectangular compartment giving the appearance of a Tau cross. The tapering stole was a later innovation. The end terminated in a fringe and in earlier times was sometimes finished with little bells. Pope Innocent III gave a religious significance to the stole, which was originally a secular garment, by calling it the "easy yoke of Christ."

At the close of the Middle Ages, the stole suffered the overall degeneration of other liturgical vestments, being altered to a shorter, wider shape, with an excessive splaying at the ends. Pugin wrote in the 1840's: "The large, unmeaning, shovel-shaped ends, generally used in France and thence brought into England, have not been introduced much above a century ago; they have never been used in Rome, and are not only extravagantly large, but most ugly in form."[3] The trend today is toward a narrower stole than was current in the early part of the twentieth century.

In the Eastern Orthodox tradition the stole has various forms. The *orarion* is a long band, worn by the deacon and subdeacon, sometimes over the left shoulder and sometimes crossed upon the breast and back (Illustration 25), according to the occasion and office of the wearer. The priest's stole, the

[3] A. Welby Pugin, *Glossary of Ecclesiastical Ornament and Costume, Compiled from Ancient Authorities and Examples,* 3rd ed. rev. by Bernard Smith (London: Bernard Quaritch, 1868), p. 218.

TEXTILE ART IN THE CHURCH

26 Greek Orthodox Archbishop Iakovos,
of the Greek Orthodox Arch-diocese of
North and South America,
wearing sticharion, sakkos,
epigonation, and broad stole

27 Greek Orthodox vestments,
Epiphany Day Procession,
priests wearing sticharion,
phelonion, epitrachilion,
and zone (not shown)

Steven N. Brussa   Steven N. Brussa

epitrachilion, is wider than the orarion, worn around the neck and joined its
full length in front. It is stiffened with an interlining, and is held in place by a
zone, or girdle, around the waist. In the Eastern Orthodox Rite, the omophorion is a counterpart of the Western pallium, but unlike the Western
pallium it is not restricted to metropolitans who receive it from the Pope. It
is worn as a pall, hanging down in front and behind in a manner symbolizing
the Saviour Christ who, as the Good Shepherd, carried the lost sheep upon
his shoulder. The omophorion is worn before the reading of the Epistle, and
is then replaced by the short, broad stole (Illustration 26).

Maniple

The maniple, or fanon, is a small version of a stole, worn on the left wrist,
originally a napkin which was carried about for cleansing the sacred vessels.
It is now merely an ornament. It was made optional in the Roman Catholic
Church in May, 1967, and is obsolescent. It has not been used in Lutheran
churches which retained vestments, but is still often found in Episcopal (Anglican) churches.

Chasuble

Originating as the outer covering of classical Roman dress, the chasuble
was known by various names, including paenula, planeta, and casula (meaning
"little house" or "tent"). The paenula was worn by the Etruscans as early

as the fourth century B.C., and by Tacitus' time, it replaced the toga for Senatorial dress. The shape was gradually modified by lengthening and being closed in front, with an opening for the head. It was then called a *casula*, from which the liturgical chasuble evolved. Although some scholars maintain that it was originally a flat circle of material with an opening for the head, overwhelming evidence indicates that the primitive chasuble was conical or bell-shaped. The conical chasuble is produced by sewing together the radii of a semi-circle of cloth, the seam being concealed beneath a decorative strip (orphrey).

Chasubles worn by deacons and sub-deacons and lower clergy were shorter and of inferior material and elegance than those of the celebrant. Later, the deacon's and sub-deacon's chasubles came to be the characteristic garment of the celebrating priest. The evolution of the shape of the garment is illustrated briefly in the series of diagrams (Illustration 28)[4] representative of various centuries and locale. These examples are by no means intended to represent the predominant shape at a particular time and place, since examples, illustrations, and records of chasubles throughout the centuries and from place to place show that there has always been a variety in the shapes and ornamentation. Certain trends and characteristics may be observed, however.

The full, flowing lines of the ample garments in the early centuries were altered to allow freedom of motion. Evidence from the sixth century shows the chasuble cut back or draped on the shoulder on the right side (b), or both sides (d). Following the eleventh century, a reaction to this mutilation resulted in a fuller shape. The ample conical-shaped vestments continued to the thirteenth century. The elevation of the Host, a ceremonial innovation of the thirteenth century, led to further mutilation of the shape of the chasuble. The celebrant at the Mass was required to hold the Host above his head with both hands so that it could be seen by the entire worshiping congregation. To do this, it was necessary to fold back the material of the chasuble over the shoulders, and so it became expedient to cut away the sides to allow freedom for the arms.[5]

In the Byzantine Rite the chasuble *(phelonion)* is not cut away at the sides, but in front, to allow freedom of movement (Illustration 27). Sometimes buttons are sewn onto the chest of the garment and the front lower edge. In the "lesser" Eastern churches the chasuble remains very full but is not sewn together (only pinned or buttoned), so that it looks rather like the Western cope. The Eastern *phelonion* is not only worn at the Eucharist, but at all other sacramental rites such as baptism, marriage, and funerals, as well as the offices of matins and vespers.

In the West, along with the clipping away of fabric, there was an increase in the heaviness of ornamentation. Now, in place of a full garment hanging in graceful folds, there was a flat panel, often shaped into a fiddleback, stiff with embroidery and jewels. Distinctive shapes were favored in various countries, yet the love of splendor crossed national borders.

[4] These diagrams were selected from a collection published by Louis Grossé Ltd. of London in a pamphlet "History of the Chasuble by Monuments"
[5] Cyril E. Pocknee, *Liturgical Vesture,* p. 30.

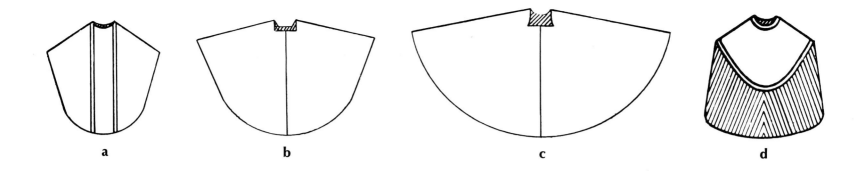
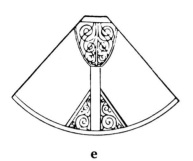
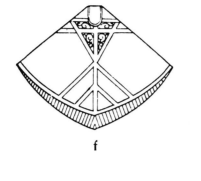
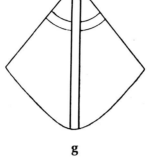
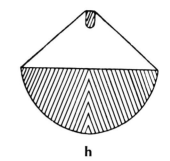
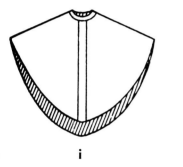

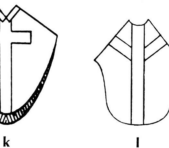

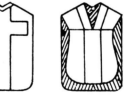
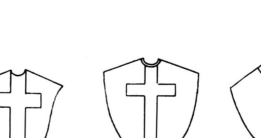

28 The development of the chasuble from its prototype, the paenula, a secular Roman garment, through the centuries of Christian use as a priestly vestment: (a) paenula; (b) 6th century, narrowed on one side—Ravenna; (c) 7th century—Rome; (d) 11th century—Rome; (e) 11th century—Hildesheim; (f) 12th century—Sens; (g) 13th century—Maubeuge; (h) 13th century—Rheims; (i) 14th century—Aix la Chapelle; (j) 14th century—Cologne; (k) 15th century—Rome; (l) 15th century—Danzig; (m) 16th century—Rome; (n) 16th century—Florence; (o) 16th century—Brussels; (p) 17th century—Rome; (q, r) Roman shape, cross at the back; (s) Spanish; (t) Polish; (u) Austrian; (v) Gothic; (w) Large Gothic

Much of the beauty of the chasuble as a vestment derives from the draping of the material, which in turn depends on the cut of the garment. The Gothic shape with seams at the shoulders and the full, circular style allow the folds to hang vertically, while the stiffer, abbreviated shapes have less attractive horizontal folds when the arms are raised. A movement in the nineteenth century to return to the original form of the chasuble resulted, instead, in a revival of the Gothic style. Today attention is given more and more to the beauty and dignity of the draped fabric and less to the application of symbols, since the chasuble and stole are symbols in themselves. Many of the finest vestments today are devoid of the orphreys and symbols considered necessary in the era from which we are emerging. The ideal situation is when the ornamentation and chasuble are designed as a single entity, with consideration as to the various effects obtained through the liturgical motions when it is worn.

Dalmatic and Tunicle

The dalmatic is worn over the alb by the bishop and deacon; the tunicle, by the subdeacon, acolytes, and minor clerics. Both are counterparts of the celebrant's chasuble at the Eucharist, the dalmatic being more elaborate than the tunicle. A similarly shaped vestment in the Eastern Church is the *sakkos*, of Byzantine imperial origin (Illustration 29), worn by the bishop, symbolical of Christ's coat without a seam. A tunicle-like garment of very full cut, the *djellaba*, is still in common use in Morocco.

The traditional form of dalmatic which remained in use for many centuries is to be seen in early mosaics at Ravenna, Milan, and elsewhere, and in frescoes of the second and early third centuries in the catacombs outside Rome (Illustration 30). In these, the distinguishing trim consists of two vertical stripes or *clavi* with matching pieces on the edges of the sleeves and across the bottom, front, and back, as ornament. Considerable contrast is seen in shape, dimensions, and ornamentation in comparing dalmatics of the Holy Roman Empire (Upper Germany, about A.D. 1320, Illustration 31), a dalmatic of the Order of the Golden Fleece (Netherlands, about mid-fifteenth century, Illustration 32), and modern dalmatics shown in Illustrations 33 and 34.

The dalmatic is presently about knee length, with broad sleeves; the tunicle similar, but often somewhat scantier and less ornamented, in keeping with its designation for the lower orders. It was customary by the thirteenth century to have sets of vestments of the same color and material, consisting of chasuble, dalmatic, tunicle, stole, and maniple, as is illustrated in the modern set shown in Illustration 33.

Cope

Like the chasuble, the cope was originally a large weather cloak with a hood for covering the head. This vestment was in ceremonial use as early as the sixth century, when it appeared in a mosaic at St. Apollinare Nuovo, Ravenna, and at St. Apollinare in Classe. The primitive form of both chasuble and cope, the *paenula*, was varied in construction, sometimes open at the front and sometimes closed, with or without a hood. In the West the chasuble became confined to the celebrant at the altar (Illustration 35), while the open

29 Greek Orthodox bishop wearing sticharion, sakkos, epigonation, and broad stole; acolyte wearing sticharion, orarion, and zone

30 Fresco in the Catacombs of St. Callistus, Rome. Praying figure is wearing dalmatic, ornamented with clavi

31 "Eagle Dalmatic," insignia of the Holy Roman Empire, Upper Germany

32 Dalmatic, Mass vestments of the Order of the Golden Fleece, Netherlands

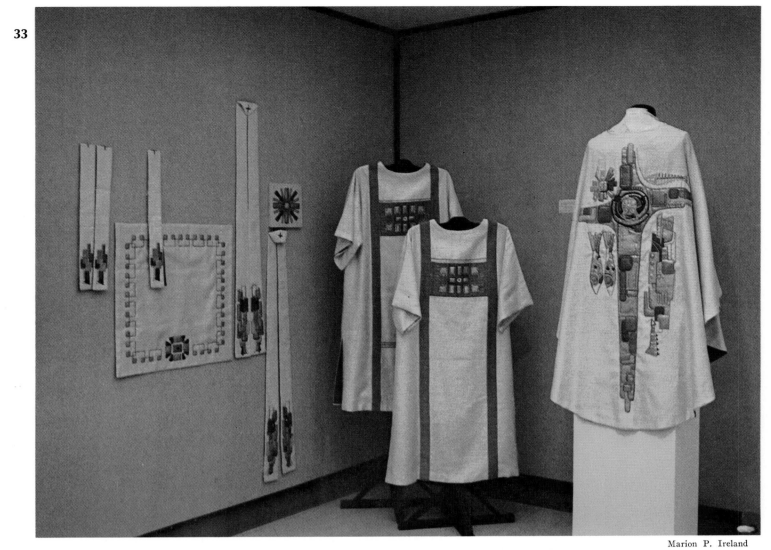

Marion P. Ireland

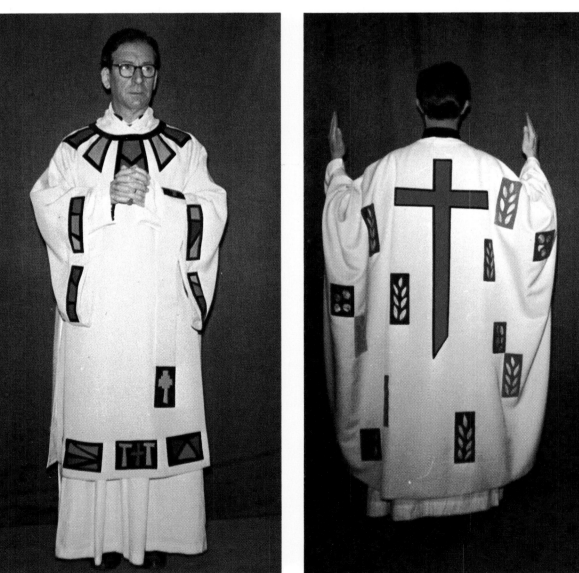

Courtesy of Louis Grossé

Courtesy of Louis Grossé

33 Eucharistic vestments made for the Church of the Resurrection,
New York City, by Beryl Dean and Elisabeth Hopper

34 Dalmatic and maniple for St. Paul's Cathedral, Peoria, Illinois,
by Louis Grossé

35 Chasuble for St. Paul's Cathedral, Peoria, Illinois,
by Louis Grossé

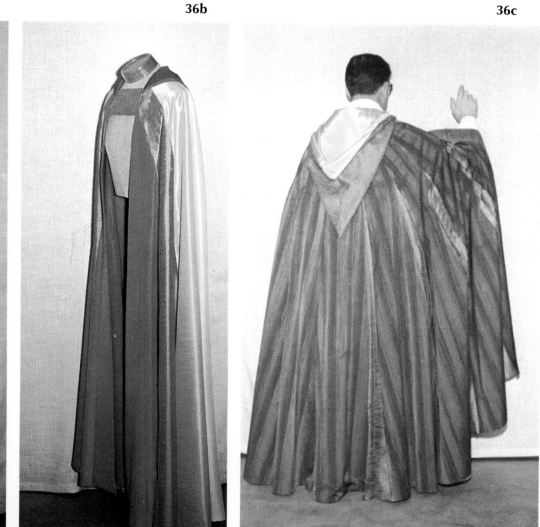

36a   36b   36c

Marion P. Ireland

36 Modern copes: (a) back view;
(b) front view; (c) cope with hood,
by Louis Grossé

form, or cope (Illustration 36), came to be worn by others than the officiant, and at other times than the celebration of the Eucharist. The bishop's mantle, or *mandias,* is worn in the Eastern Church, and a very full cope, or *burnūs,* complete with hood, is also used in Morocco.

The hood of the cope was originally functional as a head covering, but by the fifteenth century it had become a mere token, a shield-shaped flap for the display of ornamentation. Even the pretense of a hood was lost when the piece was mounted below the orphrey rather than at the top of the garment. The desire to return to the early form of the traditional vestments has led to a revival of the hood hanging in folds down the back of the cope (Illustration 36c). Sometimes it is eliminated altogether.

Black Preaching Robe

The black robe, used principally in the Reformed tradition but also in non-liturgical services occasionally in Lutheran churches, is derived from the academical dress of the universities. The rise of the universities, dating back to the twelfth century, occurred in a church-dominated society where most masters and scholars were in religious orders. A sober form of dress was worn as a uniform of sorts, as befitting a secular clerk, and the loose cape and hood were worn as protection against the weather, the same as any citizen would wear. A gradual development [6] led to the black robe and academic hood,

[6] See W.N. Hargreaves-Mawdsley, *A History of Academical Dress in Europe until the end of the Eighteenth Century* (Oxford: The Clarendon Press, 1963), for a well-documented study.

VESTMENTS AND HANGINGS: ORIGIN AND DEVELOPMENT   59

representing the degree and faculty, that is now worn by ministers. The use of the historic liturgical vestments did not cease abruptly among all leaders of the Reformation.[7] Although Zwingli and others declared vestments impermissible, Luther used both the traditional vestments and his doctor's gown, sometimes wearing his doctor's gown in the pulpit, and the chasuble for the Communion Office, a custom that is followed today in Sweden. The scholarly robe has been adopted in Protestantism as compatible with the emphasis on the Word over the sacraments. The hood is frequently worn because of its relationship to the university robe, and to add color to relieve the somber black. It is also introduced to regain the use of color that was lost with the rejection of the eucharistic vestments. Criticism is leveled at the use of stoles in the colors of the Church year on the black robe, since it is a mixture of liturgical and academic vesture. This seems no more objectionable, however, than wearing an academic hood over a surplice, a tradition acceptable to most Anglicans.

A thorough and complete presentation of all items of ecclesiastical attire has not been intended in this book, which is concerned primarily with design and color of garments and decorative cloths and their suitability for use in the Church. Several fine books have been written about the history and use of vestments, and these are listed in the bibliography for the benefit of the reader who wishes more complete and documented information on the subject.

Choir Robes

Although choir robes are not strictly a part of a discussion of art in the church, something should be said about styles and colors, since they have a prominent place in the worship service today. A distinction has been made between the traditional vestments of the clergy and the academic preaching robe and hood adopted by Protestant ministers. Both traditions are observed in the vestments worn by choirs in various branches of the church: a liturgical style consisting of cassock and surplice (or cotta), and an academic robe patterned after a bachelor's robe, relating to the minister's preaching robe. Attempts to find a historical precedent for proper choir attire are not entirely successful, as there was no direct counterpart of the modern choir of men and women from the congregation. The nearest similarity would be the choristers associated with the Anglican cathedrals. One cannot argue a traditionally correct vestment based on choirs of monks, canons, or clerks in minor orders. So there is also no "correct" color. Ceremonial vestments for the choir are, therefore, subject only to good taste and modesty. The "black" school has no more on its side than any other.

The purpose of choir robes is to provide a decent covering for everyone and a uniform appearance, so that individuals do not stand out in the group. Since a large number of people serve a visual as well as an aural function, their appearance must be provided for without giving them undue prominence. It is frequently argued that black "goes with everything," where-

---

[7] See Arthur Carl Piepkorn, *The Survival of the Historic Vestments in the Lutheran Church After 1555* (2nd ed., Graduate Study Number I, St. Louis: Concordia Seminary, 1958).

as in some cases it goes with nothing. In fact, sometimes a large mass of black robes is far more distracting than a neutral or subtle shade of color that blends with its surroundings. A general rule is that the choir should be in keeping with the type of liturgical worship in which it is participating.

Unfortunately, freedom of choice often leads to ill-advised results, when it is left to individual taste or a decorator's selection without regard for the choir's liturgical function. A church building is planned with great care, and yet the choice of colors for choir robes, carpets, and furnishings is frequently left to a series of committees acting independently of one another.

From the aesthetic standpoint, an effort is made to cause the visual impression of the entire worship service to be beautiful and inspiring, reflecting the joy of Christian fellowship. Churches would do well to bring color back into use to express this joy, on vestments, paraments, dossals, and other arts. The admonition is to let "all things be done decently and in order" (I Corinthians 14:40).

Chancel and Altar Hangings

The terms "Lord's table" and "altar" appeared side by side in the writings of the first centuries. The "table of the Lord" is referred to in I Corinthians 10:21, and Hebrews 13:10 refers to an "altar from which those who serve the tent have no right to eat." The Christian altar originated as the table at which the Last Supper was shared, and it was at just such tables that the sacred meal was perpetuated in private houses during the first three centuries. The cloth coverings used traditionally and those that are used today reflect the aura of sacrifice and communion associated with "altar" and "holy table" and, most frequently, an overlapping of both.

It is a false generalization to assume that the more Catholic a church is, the more emphasis is placed on liturgical furnishings, and the more Protestant it is, the more these furnishings are rejected. The contrary is often the case. There has been a continued effort since the 1930's, through a liturgical movement which began much earlier in France, Belgium, Holland, Germany, and Austria, and far more as a result of Vatican II, to lead the Roman Catholic Church toward a return to forms of worship of the primitive church of the catacombs.[8] Moreover, certain Roman Catholic traditions—for example, the Cistercian—have always favored austere simplicity.

At the same time, there has been an increased interest in the use of liturgical vestments and hangings associated with the observance of the Christian calendar on the part of churches in the Reformed tradition. In *Fashions in Church Furnishings, 1840-1940* (the second edition of which contains an epilogue bringing the material up to 1965), Peter F. Anson describes a state of confusion arising from efforts toward liturgical reform. His account is enlightening, though possibly exaggerated.

[8] An extensive list of studies of the liturgical movement is included in the bibliography, covering both Roman Catholic and Protestant Churches. See Ernest B. Koenker, *The Liturgical Renaissance in the Roman Catholic Church*, first published in 1954 by the University of Chicago Press (St. Louis: Concordia Publishing House, 1966), p. vi: "An Austrian Jesuit working in Rome in connection with Vatican II declared in November 1964, 'We have seen more changes in the past three weeks than in the previous 1600 years.'"

37 Frescoes from the Catacombs of St. Callistus, second or early third century:
(a) Eucharistic banquet;
(b) Jesus and his disciples

37a

While Catholic churches on the continent of Europe were growing more and more like Calvinist places of worship, nonconformists were hurrying in a Papalist direction. In some Scottish Presbyterian kirks the communion tables were shoved back against the east wall, and vested with richly embroidered frontals. . . . The more courageous Presbyterian ministers even dared to put wooden or brass crosses on their communion tables, just when many Catholic priests were trying to find valid reasons for removing them. . . . Some Presbyterian ministers may have wished they could introduce eucharistic vestments, but a fair number compromised by pulpit-falls and book-markers of the liturgical colours, usually those of the Roman rite, of the seasons of the Christian year. In the United States the practice of furnishing Baptist, Congregational, Methodist, Presbyterian and even Unitarian places of worship with altars and reredoses, usually copied from medieval Gothic examples, continued. In the Catholic church, where the modern Liturgical Movement had been introduced, the aim was a reversal to the Puritan tradition of the eighteenth or nineteenth century "meeting house." [9]

Always of central importance, the altar was expanded from the small, cube-shaped free-standing altar of the early centuries to a tremendous length during the Gothic period, when the great size was further supplemented by a towering reredos directly behind the altar. Frescoes in the catacombs show wooden tables of various shapes: square, round, semicircular, occasionally with three legs but more often four. From the fourth century, stone became the more usual material but wood continued to be used, at least until the eleventh century (Illustration 37).

From the earliest times it has been almost universally considered that the

[9] Pp. 365-66.

altar should be covered, as a mark of respect toward it as the holy table. In the early centuries the small cube-shaped altars were covered with a large cloth, shaped as a "throw-over" covering all four sides and hanging in folds at the corners. Canon law in the Church of England orders the altar to be "covered in time of Divine Service, with a carpet of silk or other decent stuff." [10] A number of these "carpets" of the seventeenth and eighteenth centuries are still in existence. The throw-over style which enveloped the entire free-standing altar was the type of covering used before the Oxford Movement, and marked a return to the older form in use before the fourteenth century.[11] Illustration 86* shows a modern free-standing altar with the so-called "Laudian" or "throw-over" covering.

Frontals and Frontlets

The elongation of the altar and its placement against the east wall were a result of the Gothic spirit and the elaboration of the Mass. The large number of priests participating required more space around the altar, and when the altar was pushed against the wall, separated from the people by a large space in the choir, the Mass became a spectacle to watch and the people became spectators. With the dramatization and lengthening of the altar, the front was ornamented the full length and height with a frontal, either of material or

[10] Canon 82 of the Canons Ecclesiastical of 1604.
[11] Cyril E. Pocknee, *The Christian Altar*, p. 48.
*P. 166.

38 Obsolescent church furnishings: (a) prominent pulpit and lectern; (b) pulpit-dominated chancel

Marion P. Ireland

Marion P. Ireland

precious metal. The frontal was portable and could be changed according to the seasons. A frontal stretched on a frame lacked the beauty of the old style of cloth which hung loosely, because the appearance of drapery was lost. The special qualities of cloth should be exploited rather than transformed into a boardlike appearance. A frontlet (mistakenly called a superfrontal, since the term superfrontal originally referred to a cloth hung above the altar) hangs from the front edge of the altar to hide the suspension of the frontal. The frontal is traditionally made according to the colors of the Church year, and there may be either a set of matching frontlets or one permanently used in one color or combination of colors.

Frequently, for economic reasons or because of the design of the altar front, only a frontlet has been used. In this event, it should be of the color of the day or season. A frontlet without the frontal has been used a great deal during the last century in churches where the altar is placed against the wall, but in new or remodeled churches where the altar is brought forward with access from all sides, this practice is becoming increasingly uncommon. The shape of the altar antependium today is determined as often by aesthetic considerations as by canon law.

While a Gothic revival was going on in Anglican churches at the end of the nineteenth century and the beginning of the twentieth, churches in the Reformed tradition were following a different path, with emphasis on the spoken word predominating over the sacraments at the altar. Although not representative of the best in churches of the Reformation, Illustration 38 shows

Marion P. Ireland

what was (and still is) going on in rural America. The altar (Illustration 38a), laden as it is with eight candles, two vases, missal stand, offering plate, and neon cross, can scarcely have room to function as an altar. It is more a repository for memorial gifts from members of the congregation. Furthermore, the altar takes second place to a disproportionately bulky pulpit and lectern. The towering pulpit in illustration 38b reduces the holy table to a mere chest, indicating where the heart of the worship service lies.

The tradition of using linen communion cloths for the entire congregation in the pews, called "houselling cloths," in the Church of Scotland (Presbyterian), is shown in Illustration 39, in the Parish Church of St. Columba, Burntisland.[12] The church was built in 1592 and ready for use in 1594. The present building is the original one. It has a central plan within a square; enclosed pews are on all four sides, both at the ground level and the balconies, with the pulpit high enough for the minister to face the people at the balcony level.

Pulpit Cloths

The origin of the pulpit is traced to the ambo, a large stand or desk in the primitive church where the liturgical lessons were read. The sermon was preached from the bishop's chair (the cathedra), the ambo, or the altar steps. Examples from sixth-century basilicas show large marble pulpits with steps

[12] A plaque in this historic church states the date on which, in this place, King James ordered the translation of the Bible which was to become known as the King James Version.

40 Marble pulpit by Giovanni Pisano,
at the Cathedral in Pisa, Italy

mounting up to them, predecessors to the modern pulpit. These pulpits were
first used for the singing of the Psalms and alleluias; later, the bishop mounted
the ambo, in order, as Chrysostom says, "the better to be heard." [13] A separate pulpit came into general use in the twelfth or thirteenth century when
sermons were preached apart from the liturgy. One of the famous monuments
of Gothic sculpture is the marble pulpit (1302-10) by Giovanni Pisano, in Pisa
Cathedral (Illustration 40). Although pulpits are known to have been in use
for preaching since the twelfth century in England, the earliest examples now
existing are a few from the fourteenth century.

At first a single structure, the pulpit developed in size and ornamentation,
particularly in the sixteenth century. A canopy or sounding board appeared
in the fifteenth and sixteenth centuries, and in the seventeenth and eighteenth
centuries many pulpits were placed very high. Three-decker pulpits of the

[13] van der Meer and Mohrmann, *Atlas of the Early Christian World*, p. 137.

TEXTILE ART IN THE CHURCH

41 Pulpit, church at Dunfermline Abbey, Scotland

Marion P. Ireland

seventeenth to nineteenth centuries were found in England and elsewhere. The shifting of emphasis from the sacraments to the preaching of the Word in churches influenced or formed by the Reformation brought the pulpit into a place of prominence, so that in many instances it towered over the communion table. The pulpit (Illustration 41) at Dunfermline Abbey in Scotland is placed on a high pedestal over the tomb of the Scottish king, Robert the Bruce. This splendid Norman building was built in two stages in the twelfth century, the east end and transepts being replaced in the early nineteenth century. The chancel furnishing is in Gothic revival style.

An interesting account of the origin of colored cloths on the pulpit appears in *The Warham Guild Handbook:*

In former times when the preacher had the degree of doctor it was customary to lay a cloth over the pulpit before him. At the trial of Ridley a cloth was laid before him because he was a doctor; but when Latimer was brought in the cloth was removed because he had no such degree. This was the origin of the modern pulpit cloth or banner.[14]

In some churches today a pulpit antependium is the only cloth that is used; in other cases it is part of a set for the altar, pulpit, and lectern. A variety of shapes and proportions is used, depending upon the pulpit itself and its position with regard to the rest of the chancel, and a generous assortment of examples is illustrated throughout this book.

[14] (2nd ed. rev., London: A. R. Mowbray and Co., 1963), p. 131.

Lenten Array

The use of the Lenten Array is probably the most distinctive "Sarum" feature to remain in vogue today, and a fair number of the greater churches in England today observe this custom. Frequently the term is used to imply color, such as Lenten white or unbleached linen; however, it refers to the shrouding of crosses and images during Lent. Until the eleventh century the crucifix over the altar portrayed Christ in Majesty, the *Christus Rex*. From the twelfth century on, piety centered on the suffering of Christ upon the cross, and particularly in the Lenten season. Therefore, the Christus Rex was draped in mourning during that period. Eventually it became customary that all crosses and images were veiled during Lent, whether the crucifix was a portrayal of the kingly or the suffering Lord. The veiling of images and crosses was not necessarily always in white, but occasionally in some other color, such as blue or black.

The Lenten Veil

The custom of using a great veil between the chancel and the nave was widespread in the medieval churches from the beginning of Lent until Easter Even. Mention of such a veil appears in Matthew 27:51, referring to the veil of the temple which was rent at the Crucifixion. Chrysostom wrote: "When thou beholdest the curtains drawn aside, then think that heaven is parted and the angels are descending." [15] Although this reference applies to fourth-century Syria, the altar is not concealed by a veil or curtain in the Byzantine liturgy today, except when the preparation of the chalices might present a distraction from the liturgy that is in progress. Use of the Lenten veil was a usual procedure in medieval English churches, and in France until the Revolution. J. Wickham Legg wrote of the Lenten veils he saw in Spain and Sicily in 1884, which were drawn up for a moment to allow the people to see the chalice and Host at the Elevation.[16] The veil, in Spain, was short enough that one could see under it, and was often thin enough to allow the light of the candles on the altar to be seen through it. In one instance, however, it appeared to be of the consistency of a Persian carpet.[17] The medieval Elevation of the Sacrament made it necessary to shorten the veil so that it could be seen by the worshipers. The custom of drawing a veil across the sanctuary during Lent was also practiced in Germany, known as the *Fastenvelum*, and is still being used in some places today.[18]

Banners

The current exploration of new media for visual expression has focused attention upon a historical tradition of processional banners, which are as ancient as the triumphal banner of Constantine and the standard of a king rallying his forces in battle, and as contemporary as the signs carried by demonstrators in our own times. The ancient hymn *Vexilla Regis*, "The royal banners forward go, the cross shines forth in mystic glow . . . proclaims the

[15] St. John Chrysostom, "In Epistolam ad Ephesios Commentarius," in *Patrologiae Graeca*, ed. J. P. Migue, LXII, 29 (Paris: Garnier Fratres, 1862).
[16] J. Wickham Legg, "The Lenten Veil in Spain and Sicily To-day," *Essays Liturgical and Historical* (London: S.P.C.K., 1917), p. 166.
[17] *Ibid.*, pp. 166-67.
[18] Pocknee, *The Christian Altar*, p. 62.

TEXTILE ART IN THE CHURCH

Courtesy of the University of Chicago

King of glory now," presumably composed in the year 569, has been used since the tenth century as a vesper office hymn from Passion Sunday to Wednesday in Holy Week. The *vexillium* was the old Roman cavalry standard which, after Constantine, was surmounted by a cross instead of the Roman eagle.[19]

Religious flags and heraldic flags are by nature processional, and therefore mobile. Their use may or may not be desirable in certain congregations, but they are textiles, and as such they are of interest to church textile artists. Banners carried in procession and displayed during a religious celebration perform a liturgical function more than when mounted to the walls, where they tend to become mere stationary decoration. However, being suspended in space over the aisles of the nave (as in Illustration 42), they move in the air,

[19] This processional hymn is supposed to have been composed by Vanantius Honorius Fortunatus for the occasion when the relics of the True Cross, sent by the emperor Justin II to Queen Rhadegonda, were received in the monastery at Poitiers.

suggesting the mobility of a cloth flag and a sense of the "here and now."

A variety of banners for special occasions is preferable to a few which are always used together in every procession. Banners have backs as well as fronts, and an effort should be made to make both sides interesting. An unusual collection of forty-four contemporary liturgical banners was designed by Norman Laliberté for the Vatican Pavilion of the New York World's Fair in 1964-65. These works were acquired by art patron Earl Ludgin and given to the University of Chicago as the Mary McDonald Ludgin Memorial Collection of Liturgical Banners, and are displayed in series of sixteen in the Rockefeller Chapel of the university. Each year a different series from the permanent collection is shown (Illustration 42). The spontaneity of design and the rich coloring add a vitality and excitement to the sense of permanence and stability of the historic and stately architecture of stone.

This brief sketch of the origin and use of vestments and ornamental cloths is not intended to be a comprehensive history, nor does it represent the rubrics of a particular communion. The purpose is to clarify the various uses to which textile art is put, within a wide cross section of churches. Christian art is not a denominational prerogative; its enjoyment is available to all who choose to accept it. The extent to which traditional vestments and paraments are used varies from one communion to another, and within each communion. A contemporary expression of religious devotion through art belongs to all.

Liturgical Colors

The dwelling itself you must make out of ten curtains, making them of fine twisted linen, violet, purple, and scarlet material, with cherubs, the work of artists.

—EXODUS 26:1 (Smith-Goodspeed)

Anyone who recalls the excitement of seeing color photography, motion pictures, and television in full "living" color for the first time can appreciate the added dimensions of life that are gained. We are immediately spoiled for going back to the shadow world of black and white pictures to which we had been accustomed. We do not live in a black and white world. Indeed, we live amid a panoply of color. Yet when it comes to the Lord's house, how many are unadorned with what is sedately called "neutral" tones of off-white or cream-colored walls, clear glass windows, brown wood, and a carpet that doesn't show the soil. *What* does this *say?*

Color is a language, and we use it naturally, as we use all other forms of language. Expression and response through the language and symbolism of color are among the most primitive and basic and, at the same time, sophisticated and subtle instincts. We see red and feel blue; we know black despair, and are green with envy. It is a natural phenomenon for colors to be used in religion, the innermost concern of our being, and for them to be developed into a grammar through which the pageantry of the events of the Christian year move in orderly procession.

There is a long tradition of using vestments and cloths, the colors of which

71

vary according to the seasons and festivals of the Christian calendar. This tradition of color sequences has been retained in Roman Catholic, Lutheran, and Anglican churches. Today, more markedly in the United States than in Europe, there is also a widespread use of such sequences by Methodists, Presbyterians, Congregationalists (United Church of Christ), and some other denominations. The increase in this practice is attested by the appearance of recommended sequences in one after another of the yearbooks of denominations where the tradition had earlier been ignored. The present liturgical revival could be traced in a comparative study of successive editions of the books of worship, denominational plan books, and pamphlets of each communion. The appearance of a liturgical color sequence in such a source does not necessarily mean that the recommended practice is followed in the majority of churches within a denomination, nor does the absence of such a sequence in some official writing indicate that colors are of no consequence to that denomination. Liberals and conservatives may be found in almost every group, but there has been a definite trend toward the adoption of stoles for the clergy and paraments in the seasonal colors within the past decade.

The use of color sequences is linked with the greater concern for the Christian year as a basis for the lectionary readings and lessons, which have been discovered to be of value in proclaiming the *whole* word of God. Without a plan that includes an orderly progression of readings, there is a likelihood that, just as in the case of repeating the same few hymns over and over, only certain favorite passages of the Scriptures will be read and expounded.

The renewed appreciation for the merits of a comprehensive order of the Christian calendar has prompted an increasing number of clergymen and congregations to adopt or reassert its use. With commercial interests usurping the most wondrous of holy days—Christmas and Easter—for merchandising drives, and folk festivals returning them to the rank of winter solstice and rites of spring, it is high time for the Church to rise up and proclaim her own prior rights to celebrate her festivals. The use of vestments and vesture in accordance with a color sequence provides an easily understood means of stressing the theme of each day and season.

Symbolism of Colors

The common practice of referring to "correct" colors for liturgical use, to specify the proper hue for "church" red, "bishop's" purple, "liturgical" green, or "Mary" blue, shows little comprehension of the complexity of traditions which contributed to the limited color sequences of today.

Origins

Symbolic use of color is to be found in some form in most periods of mainstream Christianity. The medieval church brought the symbolical, mystical, and historical development of color use to its highest peak. Elaborate networks of symbolism and theology were developed, and there was an ardor for grounding ceremonial in antiquity. Theories on the source of liturgical colors were influenced by theories as to the source of the liturgical vestments themselves, which were believed to have derived from the Levitical vestments of the Jewish Dispensation.[1] Modern scholars reject this theory, arguing that, while our use involves the full scale of primary and secondary colors, the Mosaic cult had only white, scarlet, and two kinds of purple. Also, ours changes according to the times and occurrences, where the Mosaic colors were the same for every day, except for the great day of reconciliation, on which only white vestments were worn. Therefore, it was not in remembrance of the Mosaic vestments but to express the tendency, the character, and the mood of the church festivals that color was assigned to paraments.[2]

References to colors in both Old and New Testament indicate that there were symbolic overtones. The soldiers put a scarlet cloak on Jesus (Matthew 27:28), the color worn by Greek and Roman soldiers. The Lord was arrayed in white garments at his Transfiguration (Mark 9:3). The black horse of the Apocalypse (Revelation 6:5) signified death, and the white horse (Revelation 6:2) carried its rider to victory. White was the robe for newly baptized Christians in the primitive church, and the color of the sacred vestments worn by the Essenes in the Qumran community.

The everyday dress of the Romans, from which the liturgical vestments were derived, had its own hierarchy of colors appropriate to the rank and station of the wearer. The toga was white on days of rejoicing and dark (*pullus, fuscus*) in times of mourning. The toga of the emperors was purple, and later gold. These four colors are the forerunners of the liturgical colors, white, black, red, and gold, which appear in early Christian documents and mosaics.[3]

The purple worn by emperors was an intense purple, called *holoverae*, and was forbidden to be sold to individuals, although emperors from the time of Constantine on occasion allowed it to be used for decoration of churches. Vitruvius (a first-century Roman writer) distinguished four kinds of purple resulting from the climatic effects upon a certain kind of marine shellfish from which the dyes were extracted. In northern waters the shellfish produced a dye that was almost black (*atrum*); a little farther south, blue (*lividum*); still farther south, a violet color (*violaceo colore*); and under the equator, red (*rubum*). The shade *blatta* was an inferior purple, inclining to blood-red.[4]

Medieval Colors

Although the medieval mind displayed a sensuous interest in colors and a zeal in explaining their symbolism, there was no general agreement as to what different colors signified—above all, blue. As a substitute for violet, blue vestments were sometimes worn during Advent and Lent, and, in a few dioceses of Europe, on feasts of confessors and saints. A papal ban by Pius V in 1570 on the liturgical use of blue did not prevent it from becoming more and more closely associated with the Virgin Mary.[5] The liturgical use of blue for the Holy Virgin cannot be traced much further than the sixteenth century, and then only in Spain where it is associated with the festival of the Immaculate Conception. Anciently in England, her color was either white or red. The

[1] J. Wickham Legg, "Notes on the History of the Liturgical Colours," *Transactions of the St. Paul's Ecclesiological Society,* I (London: 1882), 95.

[2] Joseph Braun, S.J., *Die liturgischen Paramente in Gegenwart und Vergangenheit* (Freiburg im Breisgau: Herder and Co., 1924), p. 45.

[3] Legg, "Notes," p. 96.

[4] Pugin, *Glossary of Ecclesiastical Ornament and Costume,* pp. 198-99.

[5] Peter F. Anson, "Blue Vestments," *Liturgical Arts,* XXXVIII (May, 1961), p. 65.

latter was used as she was called the "mystic rose." [6] In paintings, until about 1300, it was the exception for the Virgin's cloak to be blue. By 1400 it was still more exceptional to see her without the blue mantle:

> Mary can always be recognized by her azure cloak. Yet, if they study the older stained glass with any care, they will find that green, red, and golden yellow are by far the Virgin's favourite colours. For this there must be a very natural reason: the Queen of Heaven must be royally arrayed; red and green side by side with gold, were the two most aristocratic colours for dress in the Middle Ages. [7]

A sacred iconography governed the colors for the garments of the saints and holy personages in keeping with their spiritual character, and each could be identified by the color and symbolism. Medieval colors were a liturgical kaleidoscope in their diversity. Old records show such hues as crimson, red-purple, rose, pink, horse-flesh, for red. Green might be termed yellow, saffron, or tawny. Black included violet, blue-purple, blue, azure, gray, etc. [8]

Symbolism of colors is not confined to religious meanings, and there are many widely varying accounts of mystical interpretations in history. According to one heraldic view, green was regarded as the color of madmen, and black signified prudence. According to the Chinese, five symbolic colors refer to the five elements: red for fire, black for water. green for wood, white for metal, and yellow for earth. Contradictory customs, sacred and secular, disrupt attempts to attach symbolical meanings to various hues in a universal sense. In some cultures, particularly in the Orient, white is for mourning and black is for joy, exactly contrary to most Western tradition.

In the Western tradition, symbolical meanings have become attached to each color and have grown familiar through long use. Although the distribution of usage has varied among churches, the meaning of each color has a general theme with variations, since colors have inherent characteristics as well as the theological implications associated with them.

White is the purest of all colors, being pure light, and represents perfection, light, joy, and glory. It is therefore generally used to celebrate the Saviour's birth and resurrection as well as additional occasions that vary from one communion to another, and from one time and place to another. Red suggests fire and blood; in Christianity it represents the fervor of Pentecost, the Holy Spirit, divine fire, love, and the blood of Christ and the martyrs. Green, color of nature and growth, promises life and hope through Christ. Purple, a dark, somber color, suggests royal mourning and repentance in the seasons of preparation for the Lord's birth and crucifixion, Advent and Lent. Black is total darkness, the absence of light or color; therefore, it symbolizes death, although in some traditions white is used for the death of infants, because of their innocence.

As has already been said, however, and cannot be too strongly emphasized, this brief outline is not a hard-and-fast guide. It is an easy error to assume that

[6] Percy Dearmer, The Parson's Handbook, rev. by Cyril E. Pocknee (13th ed.; London: Oxford University Press, 1965), p. 62, n. 4.
[7] G. G. Coulton, Medieval Faith and Symbolism (Torchbook ed.; New York: Harper & Row, 1958), p. 264.
[8] E. G. Cuthbert F. Atchley, "Liturgical Colours," Essays on Ceremonial, ed. Vernon Staley (London: Alex. Moring, 1904), pp. 101-4.

the so-called Western tradition is a rule wherever liturgical colors are used. In all except the Roman Catholic Church, the use of any color system is at most a recommendation and subject to variation.

Color Sequences

A liturgical color sequence is a firmly established use of specific colors assigned to the various seasons and days of the Church year. We must remember that the use of colored vestments came first, and a systematic arrangement of colors particularly suited to certain occasions followed. No special rules dictated the choice of colors in the primitive church, or for long afterward. The various records that have survived which describe colored vestments can only tell us that these colors were used then. They do not prove that these were the traditional colors for specific holy days. Moreover, even after sequences became fully developed according to the entire Church year, they were not universally accepted. Each locality had its own customs.

Earliest Known Liturgical Uses of Colors

Before the development of appointed colors for the various festivals and fasts of the Church, the guiding principle in the selection of suitable vestments was based upon their beauty and quality; the most handsome and valuable, with the most elaborate embroideries, were used for the most solemn and important festivals, and the others used for lesser occasions. This is still the rule in the Eastern churches.

References to vestments of several different colors in early times suggest that some sort of rule was evolved which allotted different colors to different seasons and feasts. None is known, however, except by annual records here and there. It is natural to expect a great increase in splendor in the fourth century, when Christianity emerged from persecution and began to be a universal religion. Contemporary records show that this is so. One example of the Emperor Constantine's patronage is a record of a cloth-of-gold vestment sent by him to the Bishop of Jerusalem for use at baptisms.

Black, purple, blue, yellow, and perhaps green chasubles were worn at Centulum in the ninth century, according to an inventory made in 831 of a monastery there.[9] Red is seldom mentioned until the eleventh or twelfth century, yet even though there are so few notices of red in antiquity it is possibly one of the oldest liturgical colors, descended from the imperial purple.[10]

The gift of the Gregorian sacramentary from Pope Hadrian to the Emperor Charlemagne in 788, caused liturgical innovation to pass from Rome to the Carolingian empire. The old Gallican liturgy was proscribed (though not abolished since bits appeared in Alcuin's supplement) when the emperor made the Roman books obligatory throughout his domains. The Roman Rite, which came to prevail in most of Catholic Europe, has almost entirely supplanted the Gallican Rites. All color sequences, except the Ambrosian and the old Sarum, belong to the Roman rite—or to a derivative of it. While there

[9] Legg, "Notes," pp. 98-99, referring to Luc d'Achery, *Spicelegium*, Paris, 1723.
[10] *Ibid.*, p. 98.

was great variety and richness of colors in the Carolingian churches, there do not seem to have been any attempts to formulate a regular sequence. The variety was rather a result of the symbolism of the period.[11]

The Jerusalem Sequence

The earliest known sequence covering the festivals of the entire year was compiled during the Latin domination of Jerusalem which lasted from 1100 to 1187, served by the Augustinian or Black Canons. The Black Canons took their liturgy with them in the Holy Land, and so of course the colors they used differ but little from the liturgical colors in use in the Middle Ages in Western Christendom.[12]

The Jerusalem colors are summarized as follows:[13]

Advent	black
Christmas	red, white, and gold
St. Stephen	red
Epiphany	blue, gold
Purification	black
Lent	black
Easter	white
Ascension	blue
Pentecost	red
SS. Peter and Paul	red
Feast of the Holy Cross	red

A most striking point is the strange fact that black is assigned to feasts of the Blessed Virgin. In practically all liturgical books, white is the color for the Blessed Virgin, although there are cases where red is used to represent her as the mystic rose. There is also the exception in Spanish dioceses where blue is allowed. Since black and violet were considered interchangeable, black during Advent at Jerusalem is not too different from violet as it is used today.

The Innocentian Sequence

The Innocentian sequence of colors, which was later incorporated into the Roman Missal by Pope Gregory V as the Color Canon for the Roman Catholic Church, was at first merely an account of the practice that existed in the church at Rome itself, before Innocent III became pope in 1198. His record was not written with the intent to impose a rule on other churches, but pertained to its own locality, as each locality had its own usages. There are four chief colors: white, red, black, and green. The principal change from this early sequence to the present Roman use is from black to purple during Advent and Lent. Today we assume that there is a particular, limited range in what is considered to be red, black, or any of the other colors. However, the variety of shades included under these four headings was far more inclusive in the time of

---

[11] Archdale King, *Liturgy of the Roman Church* (Milwaukee: Bruce Publishing Co., 1957), p. 115.

[12] J. Wickham Legg, "An Early Sequence of Liturgical Colours," *Essays Liturgical and Historical: Studies in Church History* (London: S.P.C.K., 1917), p. 159.

[13] Compiled from King, *Liturgy of the Roman Church*, p. 116.

TEXTILE ART IN THE CHURCH

Innocent III than it is today: for example, crimson (*coccineus*) interpreted as red, violet as black, saffron as green.

Sarum Use

The history of developed sequences of color usage in England begins in the thirteenth century, the most prominent and earliest being Sarum (c. 1210), set forth in St. Osmund's rite for the Cathedral at Salisbury.[14] The Sarum use represents the general trend of liturgical practice in the later Middle Ages in Northern Europe. Its origins lie in the Romano-Germanic Pontifical compiled at Mainz about 950. It was brought to England during the time of Edward the Confessor (d. 1066).[15] A considerable amount of legend has been built up around the "Sarum" uses, which are imperfectly known. What is today called Sarum use is of necessity only based upon what the ancient records actually showed, and filled in from other data where the Salisbury records were silent. To add to the confusion, there is no one document, issued once and for all, but a rule that was perpetuated and corrupted with numerous additions and variations, generation after generation. Colors for the greater part of the Christian year and many important festivals in the early Sarum rites are unknown:

> It would be as reasonable to conclude that only red and white were used at Sarum in the twelfth century, because this rubric speaks only of red and white, as to conclude that only the festivals spoken of in this same rubric were observed. It is known that other colours were in use at this time from their appearance in the inventory of 1222 (*purpureus, indicus*) although this of course gives us no sort of clue to the sequence in which they were used.[16]

The ancient practice of using the best and most elaborate vestments and altar cloths for the most festive occasions, regardless of color, appears in the Sarum records as in other inventories throughout Christendom; hence, the reference to "the best" in the table on the following page.

The Golden Age of Color Sequences

It was not until the seventeenth and eighteenth centuries that color sequences reached their period of greatest elaboration. A comparative table of liturigcal colors compiled by J. Wickham Legg[17] lists sequences of prominent dioceses in groups, according to the peak period of their development: Anglican sequences from the thirteenth to fifteenth centuries (a special use of the term "Anglican" since it precedes the breach between the Church of England and Rome); Gallican uses at Paris, Lyons, etc., from the seventeenth and eighteenth centuries (also a special use of the term "Gallican" by nineteenth-century liturgists for what is now called "neo-Gallican"); Spanish use during the sixteenth century; German use in the seventeenth century, and Italian (Milan) at the end of the eighteenth century.

While there are many instances of general agreement, there are few oc-

---

[14] Daniel Rock, *The Church of Our Fathers as Seen in St. Osmund's Rite for the Cathedral of Salisbury.*

[15] See M. Andrieu, *Les Ordines Romani du haut moyen âge,* I (Louvain, 1938), 507-10; also *Le Pontifical Romano-Germanique,* 2 Vols. (Rome, 1963), pp. 73-74.

[16] Legg, "Notes," p. 119.

[17] "Notes," p. 112.

TABLE I

A TABLE OF LITURGICAL COLORS ACCORDING TO SARUM USE
COMPARING EARLY RECORDS AND
CURRENT RECONSTRUCTION[18]

| | Salisbury - Sarum | | | St. John the Divine New York |
	13th-14th centuries	14th-15th centuries	present use	
Advent	?	Unknown ?White	Red (Sundays) Blue (weekdays)	Blue
Christmas	?	Unknown ?White	White Red	The Best or White
St. Stephen	Red	Red	Red	Red
St. John the Evangelist	White	White	White	White
Holy Innocents	Red	Unknown ?Red	Red	Red
Circumcision	?	Unknown ?White	White	White
Epiphany and Octave	?	Unknown ?White	Red	The Best or Red (Octave)
Epiphany Octave to Candlemas	?	Unknown ?White	Red	Red
Candlemas to Septuagesima	?Red	Red	Red	Blue
Ash Wednesday	Red	Red	Lenten Red vestments	Blue
Lent ?	Unknown	Unknown ?Ash	Lenten Lenten vestments	Unbleached linen
Passiontide	Red	Red	Red	Red (oxblood)
Palm Sunday	Red	Red	Red	Red (oxblood)
Maundy Thursday	Red	Red	Red	Red (oxblood)
Good Friday	[Red]	Red	Red	Red (oxblood)
Easter and Octave	White	White	White	Best or White
From Low Sunday	White	White	White	White
Pentecost (Whitsuntide)	White	Unknown ?Red	White	White (in a few places, Red)
Trinity Sunday	?Red	Unknown ?Red	Red	White
Trinity to Advent			Red	Red

[18] The columns listed in the table above have been compiled from the following sources: 13th-14th cent., William St. John Hope, "Comparative Table of English Colour-Sequences," *On the English Liturgical Colours*, p. 272; 14th-15th cent., Legg, Comparative Table of the Liturgical Colours, "Notes," p. 112; Salisbury present use, questionnaire received from Dean of Salisbury Cathedral, the Very Rev. K. W. Haworth (1966); Cathedral of St. John the Divine, New York, from "A Table of Liturgical Colours According to the Ancient Use of the Church of England (Sarum)", received from the Rev. Canon Edward N. West, Canon Sacrist of the Cathedral of St. John the Divine.

casions when there is not some exception, in the broad span of both time and place listed above. *Feria* is a term denoting a weekday on which no feast is celebrated. The ferial use between Trinity and Advent varies generally between red and green. However, exceptions include violet, blue, and saffron. Milan used red until the third Sunday of October and then green until Advent. An interesting reoccurrence of the division between red and green in this long span of the liturgical year is the system now in use in The United Methodist Church in the United States: red is used for Sundays after Pentecost until the last Sunday of August (Kingdomtide), when the color is changed to green. Presbyterian churches today also divide the long time span between red and green: red until the first Sunday of October, when the color changes to the use of green for the season of God the Father, until Advent.[19] Correspondence with members who had served on commissions in these two Protestant bodies when the changes were adopted indicates that there was no relationship between these independently formulated systems and the Ambrosian use at Milan.

Little is known of medieval color sequences in Scandinavian countries, although there are records of a great variety of colored vestments. Prior to the nineteenth century, when the colors were reduced to red and black, all the liturgical colors were used in Sweden. Gray was used on Ash Wednesday, but surviving examples are rare. Violet was a rare color in Scandinavian churches in the Middle Ages; blue and red, on the contrary, were customary colors.[20] When the colors were reduced to red and black in nineteenth-century Sweden, it is curious to note that red was the festal color, whereas in the Middle Ages, it was often the ferial color.

Color Usage in Eastern Churches

Since color use in the various bodies of Eastern Christendom has been on the basis of recommendation or suggested use rather than legislated by canons of law, there has been little publication of either historical or present color use associated with the different rites. Therefore, the work of Philipp Hofmeister is particularly helpful in noting those uses that are distinctively Eastern, and those that have been influenced by, or agree with, Western use.[21] A necessarily brief summary will be made here, but the reader will find the work useful as a basis for further research through the documentation of sources as well as the original research of the author.

Today, Hofmeister reminds us, a liturgical color system is wholly unknown to the Orient, and only among the Russians does a definite practice appear to have been established. In general, soft and bright colors are favored. In the Byzantine Rite a commentary ascribed to St. Sophronius, Patriarch of Jerusalem (d. probably 638), mentions both white and red *phelonions* and knows a meaning for each, although wearing a red *phelonion* only in fast and

---

[19] *The Book of Common Worship, Provisional Services and Lectionary for the Christian Year* (Philadelphia: The Westminster Press, 1966), published jointly for the Cumberland Presbyterian Church, the Presbyterian Church in the United States, and the United Presbyterian Church in the United States of America.

[20] Bengt Stolt, *Kyrklig skrud enligt svensk tradition* (Stockholm: Diakonistyrelselses Bokförlag, 1964), p. 30.

[21] Philipp Hofmeister, O.S.B., Nereshrim, "Gibt es in den Ostkirchen einen liturgischen Farbenkanon?" *Ostkirchliche Studien*, XIV (1965), 149-61.

in services of mourning appears still unknown in this work. Later mention of this practice appears by the second half of the twelfth century, however.

The Ruthenian Provincial Synod of Lemburg of the year 1891 sought to establish rules through the ordinance *"sequentem norman proponere sacerdotibus opportunum judicat"*:[22] (a) white is to be used on feasts of the Virgin and saints who were not martyrs, excluding feasts of the Sorrows of Mary, the beheading of John the Baptist, and the Holy Cross, on which violet paraments are used; (b) red is used on feasts of martyrs, except on Sundays, when white is used, the Resurrection taking precedence; (c) violet is worn on vigils of Christmas and Epiphany if they fall on a feast day, and Lent and Holy Week until the reading of the Gospel on Holy Saturday, before which the violet is removed and white put on; (d) black for services for the dead, except all days of Easter week, when white is used; (e) *mixtus* (green) is worn for days with ferial office except on Wednesday and Friday, when, in view of the office of the cross and the fast, violet is worn.

The Ukrainians regarded this regulation as a latinization and held to the old tradition of the Eastern Church, using bright and red colors. On high feasts white is used; on feast days, for feasts of martyrs, and for burials, red is used. About the same uses are observed by the Orthodox Greeks and Ukrainians of the Byzantine Rite. In Russia red dominates on high feasts; white is prescribed from Easter until Ascension, and also for burials; during Lent, the vestments are usually a dark color, mostly blue or violet, but also at the Liturgy dark red is worn, reminiscent of the blood of Christ. Hofmeister quotes Braun[23] in saying that black is usual at burials and on Good Friday, but does not cite his source for saying that white is used for burial.

Melchite Uniates adopted the Western color sequence, but in recent years have returned to the old Eastern custom, with almost no regulation. A notable exception is a rubrical prescription of white for Good Friday.[24]

The Armenians at the time of the Crusades had relations with the Greeks and with Rome. A Plenary Council in 1307 ruled in favor of the Roman custom. Neither the Uniates nor the dissidents have a color canon. A letter from the Rector of the Armenian College in Rome to Hofmeister states that red is preferred, also on Easter, and Masses of the dead are always white. Among both the Eastern and Western branches of the Syrians, most groups have no color canon. The Syro-Malankanese Rite has no color rule and excludes black. In the Alexandrian Rite, the Canons of Hippolytus (third century) and of St. Basil (thirteenth century) mention only white vestments, but other colors came into use. The Coptic Uniate Synod of Cairo of 1898 recommended white or red on Sundays and feasts, violet in Lent, and black at funerals.

In his conclusions, Hofmeister calls attention to the striking opposition to black, expressly forbidden by Ruthenians, Armenians, Maronites, and Malankanese. This exists among the Latins, too, he says, and at the Plenary Council of Argentina of 1953, it was necessary to specify dropping the use of black as an error. The only instance of the Roman sequence in an Eastern rite

[22] *Acta & decreta Synodi Provincialis Ruthenorum Galiciae habitae Leopoli an. 1891* (Rome, 1896).

[23] *Die liturgische Gewandung im Occident und Orient* (Freiburg im Breisgau, 1907), pp. 730 ff.

[24] Hofmeister, n. 6: R. Janin, *Églises orientales et rites orientaux* (Paris, 1955), p. 37.

TEXTILE ART IN THE CHURCH

is Malabar; it was connected with a real latinization in which the authentic forms of vestments, etc., were replaced, and, as he points out, it was probably illegal to begin with (Latin bishops cannot legislate for other rites), and was abandoned as soon as the latinization was rejected. Otherwise only Uniate churches have recognized the Roman sequence, and then only by way of a little-observed recommendation. Hofmeister cites the case of the Ruthenians, who regarded even recommendations as to color sequences as a latinization, and resisted. He argues that such recommendations are not a latinization, but rather, a fulfillment, or improvement, from a simple to a more developed form. When a better form is available, he asks, why not take it? This argument is doubtful, however, since it could be used to "prove" that Rome ought to exchange *its* sequence for one of the much more elaborate eighteenth-century French ones. His conclusions concerning Western influences on Eastern color usage, in general, give very little recognition to non-Roman Western sequences.

Liturgical Decline

The Reformation dealt the first great blow to the use of vestments in the colors of the Christian festivals, along with the abolition of the liturgical year by the radical reformers. Luther stood equally against those who demanded their discontinuance. The color sequences were preserved for vestments where the liturgical use was retained, principally in the Lutheran churches of Europe (mainly German and Scandinavian), and to a very limited extent, until the nineteenth-century revival, in the Church of England.

Various movements contributed to the gradual decline in the use of vestments in color sequences of the Church year. Among these were Pietism and Rationalism. The Hundred Years' War hastened the decline in Germany. By the eighteenth and nineteenth centuries, red and black had replaced the old sequences in some countries, and the black robe of the clergy replaced the traditional eucharistic vestments. Bengt Stolt reports that in Sweden, vestments of black were not only acquired, but the presently owned ones were often dyed black, or material was purchased and dyed black before making the vestments.[25]

The effects of this poverty of color use still linger today, even though the full use of liturgical colors is practiced universally among Roman Catholics and, without a sequence, also among the Orthodox and other Eastern Christians. It is widely found also among Anglicans, Lutherans, and Protestants of many denominations. If only one set of paraments or vestments is available, altar guild manuals often direct that the universal color shall be red—the color (with black, which is an absence of color) to which the liturgical use was reduced at its lowest ebb, in the eighteenth and nineteenth centuries.

Liturgical Renewal

The reawakening, which has become general though not universal during the twentieth century, began at different times in different parts of the Christian world, and involves most major communions, in one form or another. The problems and goals of both Protestant and Roman Catholic liturgical

[25] Stolt, *Kyrklig skrud enligt svensk tradition,* p. 207.

movements are too complex to be covered here, but the literature of the movement is enormous.[26]

In the Roman Catholic Church, the movement began in France in 1840 with Dom Prosper Guéranger and the restoration of pure Benedictine practice and the Gregorian chant, at Solesmes. The first Liturgical Week for laymen at Maria Laach in Holy Week of 1914 marks the beginning of an important era in Germany. In Belgium a Liturgical Week was held in 1911, and the First International Congress was held in 1930 at Antwerp. Similar movements took place in Holland, Austria, and Switzerland. The movement has had papal encouragement since 1903, became widespread in the 1930's, and, after the Second Vatican Council of 1962-65, reached the peak of official recognition in 1967 with the introduction of a completely vernacular liturgy in most parts of the world. Undoubtedly, the most far-reaching changes have resulted from Vatican II, the proceedings of which were watched and weighed by Christians of all affiliations throughout the world.[27] The liturgical movement was brought to the United States by the Benedictines in 1925, to St. John's Abbey in Collegeville, Minnesota, where a liturgical magazine *Orate Fratres* (now *Worship*) was published, which made the aims and methods of the movement widely known.

In the Church of England, the Oxford or Tractarian Movement of the 1830's and the related Cambridge Camden Society, which was later the Ecclesiological Society, led to new stress on worship and its setting. At the turn of the century, a new impetus was given on the basis of local tradition by the Alcuin Club and its chief spokesman, Percy Dearmer. In the Church of Scotland (Presbyterian), from the 1860's, Anglican example led to the refashioning of services on quasi-liturgical lines, exemplified finally in the 1940 *Book of Common Order*, though most Scottish Presbyterian congregations are still indifferent to traditionalist ordering. In the United States the Episcopal Church has always used the *Book of Common Prayer* and liturgical renewal has followed much the same lines as in the Church of England.[28] Most Protestant churches in the United States have official service books, which are followed with varying degrees of exactness, but, generally speaking, there has been more attention to externals than to the liturgy or to the Eucharist, its true center.

Liturgical Colors Today in the United States

Liturgical color sequences were adopted in this country a little over a century ago by High Church Episcopalians, under the influence of the Oxford Movement and its American followers. From them the custom spread to middle-of-the-road Episcopalians. It was also adopted, probably independently, by the Lutherans and has now spread to the traditionally nonliturgical churches, which are concerned to dignify and enhance their worship procedures. The present color systems outlined in the various calendars and denominational publications are of very recent origin in some cases, and of long standing in others. While the Western or Roman sequence is most generally followed,

---

[26] See bibliography.
[27] See *The Documents of Vatican II*, ed. Walter M. Abbott, S.J. (New York: Guild Press, American Press, Association Press, 1966).
[28] The Protestant Episcopal Church in the U.S.A., with many other churches throughout the world, including the Church of England, form part of the Anglican Communion, recognizing each other as possessing one common, ancient, Anglican heritage.

there are notable exceptions and variations. Sarum colors are preferred in some Protestant Episcopal churches, and there is a difference in custom in the use of violet (or purple, and in some instances blue) as a pre-Lenten color starting with Septuagesima, a practice that is followed in Roman Catholic and some Anglican and Lutheran churches. The chief objection that is made to this practice is that it takes away from the Lenten season.

Color sequences are secondary to the liturgical calendar of seasons and special days, on which the lectionary is also based—a calendar that differs from one communion to another. Sundays following Pentecost (Whitsunday) are treated in various ways, depending on whether the following Sunday (Trinity Sunday) is regarded as a single day or the beginning of an entire season. Some liturgies number Sundays after Pentecost; others list Sundays after Trinity. While green is used most often today for Sundays between Trinity and Advent, medieval sequences in England and France showed red to be used at least as much as green. A season called Kingdomtide in The United Methodist Church, beginning on the last Sunday in August, marks a change in color from red for Sundays after Pentecost to green for Kingdomtide, lasting until the first Sunday of Advent.

A revised order of worship and lectionary for the Christian year, prepared by a joint committee on worship for three branches of Presbyterianism apportions the year into three sections: God the Son, starting with Advent (violet for Advent and Lent, white for Christmas, Epiphany, and Easter); God the Holy Spirit, starting with Pentecost (red); God the Father, Creator, beginning with Worldwide Communion on the first Sunday in October (green).[29] Here again, as in the Methodist use, the period between Pentecost and Advent is divided between red and green. These plans allow a greater use of red than when it is assigned only to Pentecost Sunday and special days for martyrs, Reformation, Thanksgiving, and dedications or ordinations, where observed. Another unusual feature of the Presbyterian use is the continuation of white from Christmas until the beginning of Lent, instead of an interval between Epiphany and Lent when a ferial or ordinary color is customarily used.

Colors have qualities in themselves to act upon those who have the sensibilities to respond. There will always be some who are immune, but it is possible that they may also be immune to anything with any degree of subtlety, including music and other arts that serve the Church. When the use of liturgical colors on paraments and vestments is a matter of choice and we do not employ them, we are making a choice. On the other hand, if we do choose to use them, we are obliged to have some basis of knowledge on which to proceed. It is convenient to consult a chart that tells us exactly what to do—what is right and what is wrong. The problem here is, who is going to tell us and on what basis? We have tradition, but tradition gives us variety instead of uniformity. Most communions stay clear of laying down a rigid set of rules to govern the matter since the intuitive response to symbols—color symbolism, in this case—like love, must be voluntary if it is to have any meaning. It must be adapted to the capacity of each congregation to cherish and be spiritually nourished by it.

In order to avoid setting down a rule that is nothing more than a sweeping

[29] *The Book of Common Worship: Provisional Services.*

generality, and at the same time offer encouragement to any who seek the rudiments of a color sequence, I shall list the principal festivals and seasons that occur in a large segment of Roman Catholic, Anglican, Lutheran, and other Protestant churches in this country. Since it is inaccurate to assign a single color that applies universally to each, the first color mentioned will indicate the most general present use.[30] To show the greater richness and variety in medieval history as compared to the very limited range today, a few additional colors that appear in old records from England, Sweden, and countries in Western Europe are listed, although not in any order of popular use.

TABLE II

LITURGICAL COLORS PRESENTLY IN USE IN ROMAN CATHOLIC, ANGLICAN, AND PROTESTANT CHURCHES IN THE UNITED STATES WITH SUPPLEMENTARY MEDIEVAL COLOR USES

Feast or season	Liturgical colors presently used	Medieval variations in addition to present colors
Advent	Violet, Blue	Black, Red, White
Christmas	White, Best	Red, Gold, Brown
Epiphany	White, Red	Best, Yellow, Green
Septuagesima to Lent	Green, Violet, Blue	Red, Indigo, Black
Lent	Violet, Ash-color, Unbleached	Red, Blue, White
Good Friday	Black, Violet, Red, None	Ash-color
Easter	White, Best	Red, Green, Black, Violet
Pentecost	Red, White	Best, Saffron, Black, Purple, Brown
Trinity Sunday	White	Best, Red, Green, Violet, Gold
Trinity to Advent	Green, Red	Violet, Saffron, Blue, Old or Shabby

[30] Present use refers to suggested or recommended uses in denominational books of worship, bishops' directives in some dioceses, canon law in the Roman Catholic Church. It does not include isolated or unusual uses, nor does it pretend to be complete. It is intended merely as a guide, and further study into the position and publications of specific denominations is recommended in order to arrive at a well-informed procedure.

TEXTILE ART IN THE CHURCH

Symbolism: The Language of Christian Art

There is no more welcome gift to men than a new symbol.
—EMERSON

Symbolism is the vocabulary with which the artist expresses a concept or an idea, today as well as in the past. The language of symbolism has been a rich and natural source of expression, not only in Christianity but in all religions—from the most primitive to the most sophisticated. Each age and culture has found symbols for its religious life and has adapted symbols from antiquity and from neighbors to meet its own needs. As the pattern of society shifts from the pastoral, agrarian life in biblical times, through eras of the Middle Ages, the Renaissance, the Industrial Revolution, and our present urban culture in the space age, the language must be adapted and reformed to meet the people's needs, whether the language be words, music, or art. Certain symbols of our faith, however, spring from the fountainhead of Christianity and remain alive through the ages.

Many of the Christian symbols accumulated through the centuries have lost their power to function and have become outmoded. As a result, either the use of symbolism in church art tends to become neglected altogether, or new symbols are sought to take the place of traditional ones. Often the problem is not with the symbol, but with a lack of understanding of the function of a symbol, a failure to relate it to the present time, and an inability to comprehend that which lies beneath the surface. The latter is a serious handicap in understanding the Scriptures as well, where so much is taught in parables and with signs and symbols.

85

Hymns are apt to become as obsolete as symbols in art, yet no thinking Christian would advocate dispensing with congregational singing on that account. A close examination of the texts of many favorite hymns reveals many examples of words that have little bearing on the present age, and there is a great need in this area also to seek contemporary expression. Texts such as "bringing in the sheaves" are used as symbolic language in hymns, but had more relevance in the rural life of previous generations than in the urban framework of science and industry today. There is a close parallel between liturgical music and liturgical art. In both cases the symbolism is set within a form of beauty that engages the emotions in some form of response. The words of the psalms and hymns are more readily learned when associated with a familiar melody, and the Holy Word is called to mind by visual symbols in art. Furthermore, the emotional appeal of stirring music or art may greatly increase the power of the symbol.

There is a real need to give thoughtful attention to the kind of symbols we elect to use in church art if they are to have meaning in today's context. Too often, books of symbols are regarded as lists from which to select appropriate designs for wood carving, stained glass, or to attach to colored cloths, for the decoration of churches. An intelligent use of this visual language demands that we understand the historical process of adapting certain basic symbols to meet the spiritual needs of every age. When we have determined what we expect of a symbol, it will be easier to recognize what makes some symbols die, while others endure, and new ones come into being. Man needs symbols to see beyond the surface to a wider and deeper dimension of comprehension, a shorthand embodiment of ideas and ideals. We look to God's word as found in the Scriptures as our source of instruction for the Christian life. Here are the truths and lessons that are ageless. It is in endeavoring to apply these teachings to the difficult moral and social problems of today that we may discover the symbols we are seeking.

Symbols and Representations

Both symbols and likenesses or representations have been employed in Christian art from the times of the early centuries until now. Likenesses of saints and other holy personages have identifying characteristics, such as the garment of animal skin worn by John the Baptist; the winged man, lion, ox, and eagle symbolizing Matthew, Mark, Luke, and John; the tri-radiant nimbus set apart for the triune God: Father, Son, and Holy Spirit; and countless other identifying symbols. A *symbol* leads to the conception of an idea or object; a *likeness* is of a particular person or object. In the frescoes and mosaics of the early Christian catacombs, stories from the Old Testament are illustrated pictorially (likenesses or representations). These are usually interpreted as *types,* or forerunners of New Testament persons and events. Thus the ark surviving the flood was a forerunner or type of the ship which is the church of God, and the sacrifice of Isaac prefigures the crucified Christ. Symbols such as the fish are also to be found in ancient burial places and places of worship of the early Christians. The great cathedrals of Europe give abundant evidence

TEXTILE ART IN THE CHURCH

of the continuous use of symbols, types, and representations through the centuries.

In the early church, the creed was a symbol delivered by the teacher to the candidates for baptism (*traditio symboli*), who in turn recited the creed (*redditio symboli*) to the presiding bishop at the time of their baptism. The word "symbol" is derived from the Greek *symbolon*, wherein a coin or contract was broken into two pieces by two contracting parties, each preserving one part, as a sign or token of their agreement. The sign of the cross is a symbolical gesture for baptism and confirmation which dates back to the time of Tertullian (c. 160-c. 220), when it was employed also as a means of sanctifying every activity of daily life, for encouragement in times of trial, and for mutual recognition in times of persecution.

In Christianity, primary symbols are used in the sacraments: the water of baptism, the bread and wine of the Eucharist, the oil of confirmation. These are not only symbols, but means of grace; they are dramatic rather than pictorial.

Ancient Sources

The sources from which our present body of symbolism derives include Judaism and its neighboring religions, and the Greco-Roman world in which the young church emerged.[1] Both Christianity and Judaism were influenced by the Hellenism of their day, and even though both Jews and Christians hated paganism, evidence found in the remains of catacombs and synagogues shows their own and pagan symbols combined in the same paintings and mosaics. A synagogue at Dura on the Euphrates, rebuilt in A.D. 245 and finally destroyed in 256, was discovered in 1932, and has proved to be a sort of Rosetta Stone for interpreting Judaic symbolism of its time and the influences of Hellenism upon it. Here and in the tombs, the menorah and the shofar are combined with winged victories, dolphins, birds eating grapes, and other pagan symbols.[2] Goodenough reminds us that in the early days of the church, religions were not mutually exclusive, and symbols were borrowed for their "value" rather than their "explanations." Jews now borrow the Christmas tree, not for the doctrine of incarnation but for joy, the evergreen tree being an old life symbol predating the Christian era; likewise, Christians sometimes use a seven-branched menorah on the altar, signifying the Christians as the Chosen People.[3] Another ancient synagogue of Palestine which has provided evidence of the interrelatedness and adaptations of Judeo-Christian art and symbols is at Beth Alpha, where the mosaic floor provided the basis for Bernard Goldman's study, *The Sacred Portal*.

Primitive Symbols

Many symbols of antiquity which have recurred in one religion after another are found also in primitive Christianity. The fact that they adapt so readily to diverse religions attests to their universal character and provides a clue as to

[1] See bibliography.
[2] Goodenough, *Jewish Symbols in the Greco-Roman Period*, XII (New York: Pantheon Books, 1953-1965), 71.
[3] *Ibid.*, p. 94.

their lasting value as symbols. Their significance varies according to the religious doctrines to which they are attached, and often they are imbued with many interpretations within a single faith. Among such symbols are elements of nature, such as water, fire, vines, flowers and leaves, trees, blood; heavenly bodies including sun, moon, and stars; living creatures—birds, fish, animals, man; a sacramental meal, with fish, bread, and wine; crowns, lamps, geometric figures, and numerous other devices, including the cross.

Bread, Wine, and Fish

The most universal and important religious symbols are those connected with rituals and sacraments, having to do with the sanctification of life: baptism and regeneration, communion and mystical union, and immortality.[4] The cup and broken bread blessed by Christ and shared with his disciples at the Last Supper became the central act of Christian worship, known variously as the Lord's Supper, Holy Communion, the Eucharist, and the Mass. Both the fruit of the vine and the humble loaf of bread have appeared as sacramental food elsewhere in Christian, Jewish, and pagan accounts. In the Old Testament, Melchizedek brought out bread and wine, and blessed Abraham (Genesis 14:18). The Dead Sea Manual of Discipline directs the communal meal, attended by at least ten men, one of whom must be the "priest" who blesses with bread and wine before the group may eat.[5] Rabbinic tradition has the cup filled to overflowing and the formula, "Blessed art thou, O Lord our God, King of the universe, who created the fruit of the vine." [6] The Sabbath and four chief festivals of the Jews in the rabbinic tradition are consecrated with the wine and bread that have been blessed. In Judaism, bread sometimes represents the offering of the first fruits wherein the patriarchs offered themselves as the first fruits to save the Jewish people, and the Jews became the first fruits for the nations. As a symbol of salvation, Christ became the first fruits of those who sleep.[7] In the Old Testament, manna was the bread of heaven which kept the Children of Israel alive during their wilderness wandering, and Elisha fed multitudes during a famine with loaves and grain. In the New Testament, Jesus fed the multitude with loaves and fishes. Later, talking with his disciples, he compared himself with the manna sent by God, saying, "I am the bread of life; he who comes to me shall not hunger, and he who believes in me shall never thirst" (John 6:35).

Loaves of bread in baskets and baskets of offerings appeared in paganism long before Christianity, as well as the custom of a funeral meal (refrigerium) at the burial place of a loved one. In the catacombs outside Rome, such as St. Domitilla and St. Callistus, frescoes show such a meal, alluding to the celestial banquet and to the Eucharist. In the catacombs of St. Callistus (second and early third century), seven figures are shown seated around a table with loaves of bread and seven baskets and fish (Illustration 43a). The seven derives from the seven disciples on the shores of the Sea of Tiberias after the Resurrec-

[4] See Evelyn Underhill, *Worship* (Torchbook ed.; New York: Harper & Row, [1936] 1957), for discussion of the nature and development of sacrament and worship.
[5] Goodenough, *Jewish Symbols* XII, 124. Goodenough devotes two entire volumes, V and VI, to "Fish, Bread, and Wine" in addition to introductory and concluding remarks in volumes I and XII.
[6] *Ibid.*, p. 124.
[7] *Ibid.*, p. 104.

43a Frescoes, Catacombs of St. Callistus,
celestial meal with the seven disciples

43b Frescoes, Catacombs of St. Callistus,
second or early third century,
loaves and fish

tion, partaking of the loaves and fish offered them by the risen Christ (John 21:1–13). This theme disappeared in the fourth century.[8] A fresco in the catacombs of St. Callistus shows Jesus seated with his disciples, a Last Supper scene (Illustration 37b*). Loaves and fish were often portrayed in association with the eucharistic banquet (Illustration 43b) in the first centuries.

The most familiar interpretation of the fish as a sacred symbol to Christians is the acrostic of the Greek word for fish, translated, "Jesus Christ, God's Son, Saviour," a sign of recognition and secret language between Christians during times of persecution. The fish has been identified with baptism by the early Christian writers, such as Tertullian who wrote: "But we, little fish, are born in water." [9] The contrast between the Dead Sea, where there are no living things, and the River Jordan or the Sea of Galilee, whose water is abundant

[8] van der Meer and Mohrmann, *Atlas of the Early Christian World*, p. 55.
[9] *Bapt.*, I, 3.
*P. 63.

with fish, was apparent to the early followers of Christ. Therefore, it was natural for fish to represent life and for living water to be associated with baptism. The River Jordan, before it falls into the Dead Sea, was a sign of living water to John the Baptist. In Jewish art, water filled with fish signifies resurrection.[10]

Water

The symbolism of water, in addition to its baptismal context, is interpreted in a biblical sense denoting God as the fountainhead or source of life, and in a Christian sense denoting the Holy Spirit.[11] A distinction is made between running water or spring water and standing water. The *Didache*[12] directs the use of living water for baptism and the alternative, still water, when running water is not available—a necessary consideration in a semiarid climate. Living water symbolizes God, the source of life, in Jeremiah 2:13: "They have forsaken me, the fountain of living waters." Water for purification is recorded in Ezekiel 36:25: "I will sprinkle clean water upon you, and you shall be clean from all your uncleannesses, and from all your idols I will cleanse you." Baptism in the Holy Spirit is foretold by John the Baptist in Matthew 3:11: "I baptize you with water for repentance, but he who is coming after me . . . will baptize you with the Holy Spirit and with fire." Living water is mentioned repeatedly in the New Testament. Jesus said to the woman of Samaria at the well: "If you knew the gift of God . . . he would have given you living water" (John 4:10), and "Every one who drinks of this water will thirst again, but whoever drinks of the water that I shall give him will never thirst; the water that I shall give him will become in him a spring of water welling up to eternal life" (John 4:13-14).

Crown

Eternal life is symbolized for both Jews and Christians by a crown. The Jewish feast of Tabernacles is celebrated with a procession round the altar, wearing crowns consisting of wreaths of various kinds of leaves or foliage. The Apocalypse of St. John (Revelation 2:10) promises: "Be faithful unto death, and I will give you the crown of life," and in James 1:12 we read: "Blessed is the man who endures trial, for . . . he will receive the crown of life which God has promised to those who love him." Peter 5:4 refers to an "unfading crown of glory." Daniélou cites a number of references that would indicate that the crowns referred to in both Jewish and early Christian writings were of foliage, relating to the leafy arbors (*skenai*) of the feast of Tabernacles, the nosegay (*lulab*) of willow, myrtle, and palm, and the citron (*ethrog*) symbolizing the fruit of the tree of life.[13] While there is no doubt that the crown of thorns, made of branches woven or entwined together, fits into this category, other references point to a golden crown set with jewels: the plate of pure gold engraved with the signet, "Holy to the Lord" (Exodus 28:36-37) for Aaron; the kingly crown "the weight of it was a talent of gold, and in it was

[10] Goodenough, *Jewish Symbols* V, 36-61.
[11] Daniélou, *Primitive Christian Symbols*, pp. 42-57.
[12] One of the earliest "Church Orders," containing instructions on baptism, fasting, prayer, the Eucharist, etc., probably dating from the beginning of the second century.
[13] Daniélou, *Primitive Christian Symbols*, pp. 1-24.

a precious stone; and it was placed on David's head" (II Samuel 12:30); the "jewels of a crown" (Zechariah 9:16); and the "crown of fine gold" (Psalms 21:3). The victor's prize, which was customary in the Greco-Roman world, was a garland of leaves, and is referred to in I Corinthians 9:25 as a "perishable wreath" (RSV) or a "corruptible crown" (KJV).

Tree of Life

The tree of life is an ancient symbol, and has appeared frequently in Near Eastern art. Its fruit was believed to bring immortality. Two trees, the tree of life and the tree of knowledge, were specifically mentioned in the Garden of Eden (Genesis 2:9); anyone who ate the fruit of the tree of life would live forever (Genesis 3:22), but it was from the tree of knowledge, the forbidden fruit, that Adam and Eve ate and were banished from Paradise. Hippolytus wrote: "In this Paradise were found the tree of knowledge and the tree of life. In the same way today, there are two trees planted in Paradise, the Law and the Word." [14] The faithful are referred to as God's planting, in both Old and New Testaments, a concept carried further by the early church fathers. Isaiah 60:21 refers to "the shoot of my planting" and 61:3 to "the planting of the Lord."

Closely related to the tree of life is the vine, also a part of the "planting" theme. [15] In the parable of the vineyard, we find that "the vineyard of the Lord of Hosts is the house of Israel" (Isaiah 5:7). Many of the parables of Jesus pertained to the vine: laborers in the vineyard, new wine in old wine-skins, and others. The most familiar passage concerning the vine is found in John 15:1-7. Jesus says, "I am the true vine, and my Father is the vinedresser," signifying that he is the true Israel; and "I am the vine, you are the branches," symbolizing the union of Christ with his disciples. Jesus blessed the cup containing the fruit of the vine, as was the custom of the Jews at the Passover, and gave it to his disciples, saying, "I shall not drink again of this fruit of the vine until that day when I drink it new with you in my Father's kingdom" (Matthew 26:29).

The Good Shepherd and the Lamb

Among the many references to the shepherd in the Old Testament, undoubtedly the most familiar is the twenty-third psalm, beginning: "The Lord is my shepherd, I shall not want." Isaiah (40:11) describes the Lord God as a shepherd: "He will feed his flock like a shepherd, he will gather the lambs in his arms, he will carry them in his bosom, and gently lead those that are with young." References to Jesus as the Good Shepherd are principally based on the parable in John 10:1-16. Jesus says: "I am the good shepherd; I know my own and my own know me. . . . I lay down my life for the sheep." The example of the ninety and nine sheep and the one who went astray (Matthew 18:12-13) prompted portrayal of a young shepherd carrying a sheep on his shoulders, representing Jesus as the Good Shepherd, a theme that was used until the beginning of the fourth century (Illustration 44).

[14] *Com. Dan.,* I, 17; *Griechische christliche Schriftsteller,* p. 29, lines 16-19.
[15] Daniélou, Ch. II, "The Vine and the Tree of Life," supplies numerous references and interpretations to be found among the literature of the early Christian Fathers (*Primitive Christian Symbols,* pp. 25-41).

TEXTILE ART IN THE CHURCH

44 The Good Shepherd,
Catacombs of St. Callistus, fourth century

The lamb was originally sacrificed for the Jewish Passover; therefore, Jesus became the fulfillment: "Christ our paschal lamb has been sacrificed" (I Corinthians 5:7). John the Baptist identified Jesus as the one who ranks before him, saying: "Behold the Lamb of God, who takes away the sin of the world" (John 1:29). This is the text of the *Agnus Dei* in the liturgy of the Mass, and a favorite theme for artists. The *Adoration of the Mystic Lamb*, the Ghent Altarpiece painted by Jan and Hubert Van Eyck in the fifteenth century, is based upon Revelation 5:12, and is a monumental masterpiece. The lamb has been symbolized also with the book with seven seals (Revelation 5–8) or upon Mount Zion (Revelation 14).

The Four Evangelists

The four winged creatures symbolizing the four evangelists are described in Ezekiel's vision (1:5-10) and in the Apocalypse of St. John (Revelation 4:7). The association of the evangelists with the winged man, lion, ox, and eagle that appeared in two different accounts of visions, in both Old and New Testaments, was due in some measure to the symbolic significance of numbers. Groups of twelve were associated with the twelve tribes of Israel, the twelve apostles, or the twelve minor prophets; four indicated the evangelists or the four major prophets; seven, the gifts of the Holy Spirit; three the Trinity, or faith, hope, and charity; two, Christ's humanity and divinity, and so on. There is no indication in either Ezekiel or Revelation that the four winged creatures referred to the evangelists, and early writers differed in their identifications of the four. Irenaeus associated them with attributes of Christ, and also as prophetic symbols of the evangelists: Matthew, the winged man; Mark, the eagle; Luke, the calf; and John, the lion. Athanasius attributed the calf to Mark and the lion to Luke. Augustine and the Venerable Bede both attributed the lion to Matthew, the man to Mark, the calf to Luke, and the eagle to John.[16] The interpretation that has carried through the Middle Ages to the present identifies the winged man as Matthew, because the lineage of Jesus is found in this Gospel. The lion pertains to Mark [17] because his Gospel begins with the account of John the Baptist, the voice crying in the wilderness. The ox belongs to Luke because of the account of Christ's sacrificial death, and the association with the ox as a sacrificial animal. The eagle suggests the soaring of the Gospel of John heavenward in contemplation of Christ's divinity. Hence, the lectern from which the Gospels are read is often shaped like an eagle. These brief explanations are only a small part of a highly developed symbolism for a theme that has been portrayed in textiles, stone, paintings, and manuscripts through the centuries. Two outstanding tapestries of contemporary design which include the symbols of the four evangelists are the "Christ in Majesty" by Graham Sutherland at Coventry Cathedral (Illustration 65*) and the John Piper tapestry at Chichester Cathedral (Illustration 4†).

The Cross

The cross, the most distinctive symbol of the Christian faith, was used in many civilizations before the Christian period. It had many shapes and forms, usually equal-stemmed, and often appeared on coins. The earliest Christian use was the sign of the cross, traced on the forehead of the catechumen at the time of baptism and confirmation. The cross was not depicted realistically as the instrument of Christ's suffering until about the fifth century, but its form was recognized in various objects such as the mast and yard of a ship, the plow, ax, anchor, etc. (Illustration 45a). The equal-armed cross was most commonly used in both the East and West in the early centuries, but the term "Greek" cross for this shape was not used until the Middle Ages. The Latin cross, with a long stem, was in common use from the sixth century.

In the first centuries, the cross was a triumphal symbol and a sign of the elect. A likeness of the cross on Calvary would have been like the hangman's noose or the electric chair today: the fate of the criminal. St. Paul said: "We preach Christ crucified, a stumblingblock to Jews and folly to Gentiles" (I Corinthians 1:23). The earliest known crucifixion picture was a graffito scratched on the wall of the pages' room on the Palatine, at the end of the second century, blasphemously portraying a figure on the cross, with the head

[16] F. R. Webber, *Church Symbolism. An Explanation of the More Important Symbols of the Old and New Testament, the Primitive, the Medieval and the Modern Church* (Cleveland: J. H. Jansen, 1938), p. 186.
[17] Vistors to Venice are reminded by the great Cathedral and Square of St. Mark, and by the winged lions over the city gate and all through the city, that St. Mark is the city's patron saint.
*P. 139. †P. 29.

45a Anchor,
Catacombs of St. Callistus

45b Graffito, third century A.D.
Rome, Terme Museum

of an ass, and a youth standing by, and the inscription: "Alexaminos adores his god" (Illustration 45b). After Rome was conquered by the Goths, the triumphant monogram with the sacred chi (X) rho (P), the first two letters of XPICTOC, or Christ, in a circle or laurel wreath, was displaced by the crucifix, or cross of suffering.[18] Daniélou concludes his chapter on the cross in primitive Christianity thus:

> The sign of the cross is seen to have its origin, not in an allusion to Christ's passion, but as a signification of his divine glory. Even when it comes to be referred to the cross on which he died, that cross is regarded as the expression of the divine power which operates through his death; and the four arms of the cross are looked on as the symbol of the cosmic significance of that redeeming act.[19]

The cross is adaptable to use on textiles but is often too lavishly used. It is, nevertheless, the symbol of the very foundation of the Christian faith, and I am not suggesting the discontinuance of it as a symbol. On the contrary, a more worthy use should be made of the cross as a symbol than the scattering of mediocre shapes of crosses on every piece of furniture in the chancel, including crosses on the altar front, embroidered on the frontlet, placed upon the altar, and mounted on the wall above the altar. Its use is more effective when more sparing. Its poignancy is diminished rather than intensified by idle repetitiousness.

[18] The cross + represents the instrument of Christ's suffering; the X is the first letter of his name. See "Croix" by Dom Henri Leclerq, *Dictionnaire d'archéologie chrétienne et de liturgie* (Paris, 1907-37).
[19] Daniélou, *Primitive Christian Symbols*, p. 145.

46 Pulpit antependium,
by Marion P. Ireland;
Los Altos United Methodist Church,
Long Beach, California;
Culver Heaton architect

Marion P. Ireland

Symbolism for Today

A symbolism for our own times depends upon the foundations of our faith; that is, the same basic ideas that formed the symbols of the past. At the same time, the conditions of modern life and the scientific advances that have widened our horizons bring us, or force us to invent, an added vocabulary of symbols for modern church art. Religious symbols from the earliest times reflect two major concerns. One is man's mindfulness of his environment: the world and the firmament, the sun, moon, and stars, the unseen forces that govern the elements, the living things upon the earth. The other chief concern is man's role within his environment: his origin and destiny and his relationship with his Creator. A comparison of the primitive symbols mentioned on the foregoing pages and the symbols sought for in the present age reveals the same core of human existence and religious response dealt with in the framework of each succeeding age.

Symbolism must be built upon both the old and the new: the needs of the times are dealt with in the manner in which the artist interprets and renders his subject. For example, the cosmos and the order of the universe may be suggested by a modern symbol such as the atom (Illustration 46) with electrons in their orbits around the nucleus of protons and neutrons, or the orbits of the solar system, reminding us of the universal laws of God beyond the comprehension of man. The ineffable majesty of creation is suggested in the force relationship exhibited in the atom, the same orderly forces as in the solar system around the sun, or on a larger scale in the whole cosmos. On the other hand, creation may be portrayed in contemporary design, based on the Genesis account as illustrated in Illustration 47a. The firmament is suggested in a composition based upon the theme of "Worldwide Communion" (Illustration 48a). The elements of nature (earth, air, fire, and water) are included in the symbolism of the Chichester tapestry by John Piper (Illustration 4*). Scriptural passages were favorite subjects in the art of the catacombs and are a source for church art today; cf. the loaves and fish in the second century fresco in the Roman catacombs (Illustration 43b†) and the feeding of the multitude at the Sermon on the Mount, portrayed in Illustration 47b. The Parable of the Sower (Illustration 47c), living water (Illustration 48b), and the rainbow, sign of the Covenant (Illustration 48c), are contemporary examples of biblical symbols.

The Last Supper has been portrayed by artists in every age, the most famous undoubtedly being the fresco by Leonardo da Vinci. Frescoes of Jesus and his disciples seated at a meal exist from as early as the second century in the catacombs (IIllustration 37b‡). Illustration 49 is a contemporary interpretation of the continuation of the Lord's Supper from the beginning throughout all time. The parament is worked in appliqué of materials ranging from blue violet to gray. The broken loaf is of suede leather with a chain stitch between the sections; the chalice is of deep irregular textured gold metallic fabric, resembling thickly raised gold.

New symbols necessitate bringing the major issues of our age into focus. The first Christians looked for an early establishment of God's kingdom at the Second Coming, and a reunion with loved ones who had gone to their reward. The medieval church was primarily concerned with salvation of souls through the sacraments and intercession of saints and a Last Judgment with the alternatives of heavenly bliss and eternal damnation. Attention has shifted in our time to Christ's mission in the world, and today's society forces a concern for the plight of people and our obligations of Christian commitment in ministering one to another. Also, scientific advances place at man's disposal instruments of great benefit to mankind or instruments for total destruction. These are issues that could be symbolized with reference to the mission and message for Christian congregations today. The Scriptures can be searched for guidance and portrayed in terms of today's situations and problems. At the same time, it must be remembered that the concerns of other times have been by no means set aside, and we still hold the same hopes for eternity with Christ that sustained our Christian forebears.

Symbolism as a language requires the use of good grammar. A combination of symbols often increases the depth of meaning in the same sense as a sentence which expresses more than a single word. An *alpha* and an *omega* alone represent only the first and last letters of the Greek alphabet. Unless another element is added, representing the Christ, the statement is incomplete. The sequence of colored paraments and vestments for the seasons of the Christian year provides an opportunity to express a variety of significant concepts relating to the Christian life and faith. Since the paraments are changed regularly according to the seasons, individual subjects may be singled

*P. 29. †P. 90. ‡P. 63.

47a

Marion P. Ireland

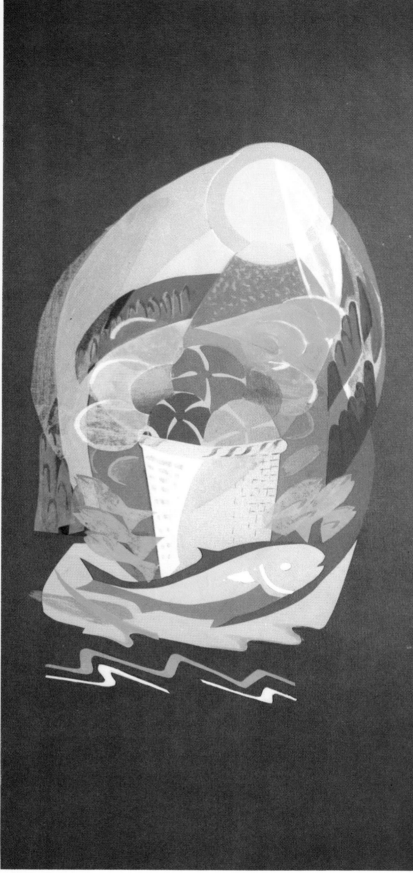

Marion P. Ireland

47 Parament designs by Marion P. Ireland,
for Geneva Presbyterian Church,
Laguna Hills, California; William L. Pereira architect
(a) Communion table antependium, "Creation";
(b) pulpit antependium, "Sermon on the Mount";
(c) lectern antependium, "Parable of the Sower"

Marion P. Ireland

Marion P. Irel[

48 Paraments, First Presbyterian Church, Concord, California, by Marion P. Ireland:
(a) Communion table antependium, "Worldwide Communion";
(b) pulpit antependium, "Rites and Sacraments," Communion, baptism, and matrimony;
(c) lectern antependium, "Covenant," the Word, chalice and crown, the rainbow, and circle symbolizing eternity

48b

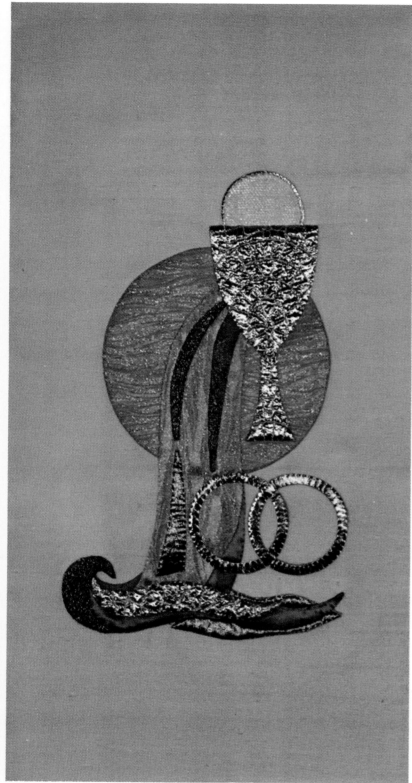

Marion P. Ireland

48c

Marion P. Ireland

Marion P. Ireland

49 Altar antependium, Marengo Avenue United Methodist Church,
Alhambra, California, by Marion P. Ireland: Lenten parament, "This Do in Remembrance of Me"

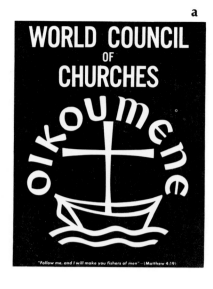

a

WORLD COUNCIL OF CHURCHES

"Follow me, and I will make you fishers of men" — (Matthew 4:19)

b

JESUS CHRIST

NATIONAL COUNCIL OF CHURCHES

DIVINE LORD AND SAVIOR

c

d

INTERNATIONAL CONVENTION CHRISTIAN CHURCHES

(DISCIPLES OF CHRIST)

"Building a Brotherhood Through Voluntary Cooperation"

50 Seals and emblems
of church organizations
and demonstrations

(a) World Council of Churches

(b) National Council of Churches

(c) Executive Committee,
Southern Baptist Convention

(d) International Convention
of Christian Churches

out for recognition on one piece or another of a set, with due regard for the occasions when the set is to be used. The communicative function of the symbol is of primary importance; the ornamentation of it is secondary.

Seals and Emblems

An examination of the various official and semi- or unofficial seals adopted and currently in use by different communions and organizations within the Christian church indicates some of the symbols which have been selected as most significant to the ideals, aims, and beliefs of each particular religious body.[20] Some were designed many years ago, and others newly acquired. The age of the various designs is usually quite apparent by their style and content. Some are heraldic shields, and others are symbols, both ancient and recent. In some cases, symbolic emblems are used to represent a denomination where no use is made of paraments and any form of symbolism is used sparingly. The use of seals in some of the latter churches, however, is an indication of an increasing interest in symbolism, which may eventually lead to a wider use, including paraments and the observance of the Christian calendar.

Using these fifteen examples (Illustration 50) as a sampling of current use

[20] The examples in Illustration 50 have been provided by the denominational headquarters of each, and when descriptive interpretation was included, it is described in the appendix.

50 (e) United Church of Christ

(f) American Baptist Association

(g) Reorganized Church of Jesus Christ of Latter-Day Saints

(h) Executive Council, Episcopal Church

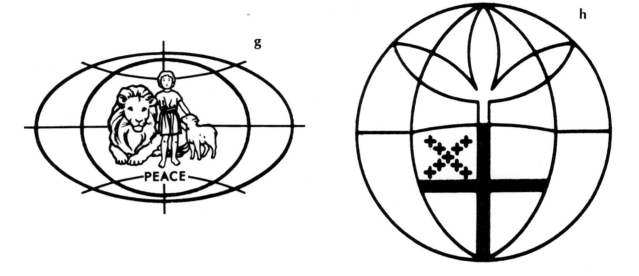

of symbolism to represent or identify particular communions or organizations, some interesting observations may be made. All but four emblems have at least one cross; some have several. Six have a globe, indicating worldwide spread of Christianity or relationship between the church and the problems or needs of the world. Five have an open book, representing the Word of God. The combinations of symbols say more than the individual symbols; for example, a cross, a globe, and a book symbolize the interrelatedness of the Church, the Word, and the world. The Ecumenical Seal of the World Council of Churches (Illustration 50a) goes back to the first centuries of the church, and the cross of the mast and yard of the ship.

Most denominational seals are typographical in nature and unsuited for direct copy for textile art. Some are suitable for use in embroidery of paraments and stoles, and others may be adapted or incorporated into a design. The emblem of the United Church of Christ (Illustration 50e) was adapted for embroidery for a pulpit marker (Illustration 13*), and the emblem of the Lutheran Church in America (Illustration 50m) was freely interpreted for a pulpit hanging (Illustration 126a†). Most emblems depend too much on lettering to be appropriate for embroidery, in which case the symbolism and general format may be used without the wording. The ship and *oikoumene* of the World Council of Churches (Illustration 50a) has been adapted to embroidery effectively, as has the Luther Seal (the rose, heart, and cross which appear in

*P. 36. †P. 230.

i

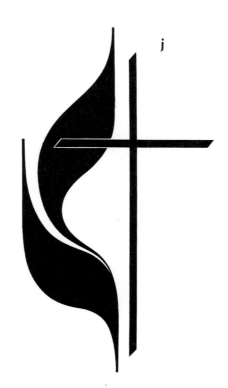
j

k

l

m

50 (i) Presiding Bishop,
     Protestant Episcopal Church

   (j) United Methodist Church

   (k) United Presbyterian Church in the USA

   (l) Presbyterian Church in the United States

   (m) Lutheran Church in America

   (n) Lutheran Church, Missouri Synod

   (o) American Lutheran Church

n

o

Illustrations 50n, 50o). The principal purpose in including these emblems in this discussion is not to provide designs to copy, however, or examples of good art, but to suggest a few symbols that may be appropriate at the present time.

New symbols for our day will depend on the insight of the artist and clergyman into the social, moral, and theological developments in the world and the ingenuity to find and express them.

Christian Art Through the Centuries

Man possessed art because he had religion.
—SARTRE

Church art has been energized again and again by notable events and leaders throughout the various eras of history. The art of the past reveals a limitless variety of ways in which Christian artists have portrayed the faith. The changing patterns of history, and particularly the history of the Church, both in the East and in the West, are reflected in both subject matter and artistic rendering of the designs: the curiously unrealistic figures of early Christian art as contrasted with the demand for realism in later centuries, the hypnotic gaze of the Byzantine icon, the elegance of the Renaissance, and the lavish display of the Baroque. The emphasis upon the saints and the Virgin Mary accounts for the predominance of personages in medieval art. The lavishly embroidered vestments of the Order of the Golden Fleece (Illustration 56*) and the Syon Cope (Illustration 55†) illustrate the heights attained by church embroidery in figure portrayal. The lessons to be drawn from the history of religious art would be incomplete without the inclusion of both East and West. In the West, peaks of artistic achievement were often associated with the leadership of a great individual, such as Charlemagne, whose era lasted for a few generations, or the Abbot Suger, the father of Gothic architecture. Some periods of religious art have been in terms of restoration or reconstruction of what was believed to have been closest to the religious life of the first-century Christians. In the Renaissance, the perfection of Classical

*Pp. 120-21. †P. 119.

107

art, as exemplified in the Golden Age of Greek antiquity, was the ideal for the highest possible means for expression of the Christian faith and for art in general. There is nothing in the history of the Christian East comparable to the Romanesque, Gothic, Renaissance, or Baroque periods and traditions. The East had its own traditions, and one can but stand in awe at the magnificence of the Byzantine cathedrals such as San Marco in Venice, a golden jewel of mosaic, shaped with domes and arches and adorned with colorful portraits of the saints. The two streams, East and West, followed their separate courses in a common goal: the dedication of their resources in the exercise of art, of which the church was the principal patron and recipient.

Origins of Textile Arts

The development of weaving and embroidery in Western culture stems mainly from the Middle and Far East. It is practical, therefore, to trace the origins and influences contributing to the development of textile art before considering its role within Christian churches, both Eastern and Western. Patterned fabrics, woven in tapestry weave, have been found in the tomb of a king in Egypt from 1400 B.C. Fabrics have been found in an excavated city of Anatolia (Turkey) woven in various weaves, coarse, medium, and fine, in the seventh millennium B.C. Wool weaving with woven designs was done in Mesopotamia as early as the sixth century B.C., and we know from the Old Testament that elaborate patterns of weaving, embroidery, and gold work were used for religious and royal garments and cloth curtains and coverings.

Homer wrote in the eighth century B.C. about the costume of the Greeks. They were draped, not decorated by weaving but probably painted or embroidered. Textiles of a high order were woven in Crete; typical patterns were borders, or "meanders." The Romans, two thousand years ago, were not skillful weavers. They imported, by way of the Mediterranean Sea route and caravans from the East, from China and Persia. Typical designs were garlands of leaves, the Greek key design, and meanders. Roman ornamentation and dress were based on the Greek, with extravagant materials.

Egypt, as well as India, made fine linens of flax; Babylon was known for its wool, and China for its silks. Before the Christian Era, the Chinese guarded the secret of silk production and enjoyed a lucrative trade with the Middle and Far East. The Japanese were the first to learn the secret in the third century A.D., and became adept in woven and printed textiles. India was next, and then Persia. By the sixth century, silk culture was known to the weavers of Byzantium.

The most important textiles at the beginning of the Christian Era were Coptic, Byzantine, and Persian, from the Sassanian dynasty. Coptic textiles, from the third to the seventh centuries, were of linen, wool, and silken twill, the designs woven in two colors, with fine geometric patterns of interlaced linen thread. In addition to Christian symbols, there were figures of Greek and Persian influence, such as animals in pairs, facing each other. A burial garment has been found with almost the same pattern in Peru. In the fifth century the Copts learned to dye their own yarns in bright colors, used mostly in tapestry.

The love of splendor and technical knowledge that led the Byzantines to create precious works of art from early times, including the color and light of their mosaics, also led to their most important art: their textiles. Silks, woolens, gold cloth, embroidery, and a lavish use of gold thread were included, in gaudy combinations of rich colors. Heavy embroidery was worked in huge designs sometimes one yard by two and a half yards to a repeat pattern, roundels, and medallions, large and small. Throughout the whole Near East roundels with paired animals—birds, elephants, lions, huge eagles (the most typical Byzantine design)—and scenes from the life of Christ were characteristic motifs. An Oriental influence on Byzantine textile art came from Persia and China where the silk raw materials originated. The Byzantines started their own silk culture around 550 under Justinian.

Mohammedanism, or Islam, originated at the end of the sixth century and spread through the whole Near Eastern world. It expressly forbade representations of living things, and textile artists wove quotations from the Koran into the textiles. Nonreligious stylized designs called "arabesque" concealed animal and plant designs. The Persians, who were opposed to Islam, continued to portray animals, plants, and personages. Kufic script became floral in Persia, more decorative and ornamented than the Islamic designs. Examples exist in Spain from the time of the Moors in the early eighth century. The Mohammedans conquered Spain in A.D. 711, and established weaving according to their dictates. The Arabs were not weavers, and so they made the conquered people work at the weaving.

When Sicily fell to the Arabs in the ninth century textile art flourished, and when the Arabs were driven out by the Normans in the eleventh century, weaving continued. Rich textiles with gold and silver thread were exported. The Byzantine style when the Arabs left included Christian symbols—crosses, crowns, etc. The earliest known Persian textiles were from the Sassanian dynasty. From the third to the seventh century, the most important art period, personages were displayed in the textile designs. At the end of the thirteenth century, when insurrection arose in Sicily, many weavers emigrated to Italy: Lucca, Florence, Siena, Genoa, and Venice. After the end of the thirteenth century, nothing of importance in textiles came from Sicily. Lucca and Sienna produced church textiles; Florence specialized in woolen fabrics with small designs; Genoa was noted for cut velvets. From the beginning of the thirteenth century, Venice held first place in rich velvets embellished with gold threads, large designs in an ogival frame of undulating branches, with the lotus flower a characteristic symbol within the frame. Venice traded with both Europe and the Near East, and was noted for individual designs and artistic specialties.

The technique of brocading had an important place in church vestments, allowing the loom to compete with the needle. Embroidery is done with a needle after the textile is woven; brocading is like embroidery on a loom. Unlike embroidery which may go in any direction, the design in brocading must go with the weft threads in horizontal rows. The intricate repeat patterns and saving in thread, as compared to the older damask and double weaves, made the art of brocade a great advance in textiles.

Gold thread was known in ancient China and the Mediterranean, and is described in the book of Exodus. There is a story, which may or may not be true, of finding the body of a Roman princess or queen who had been buried in a gold dress which, when melted down, produced fifty pounds of gold. We do know that ancient burial robes have been heavy with gold and have been melted to obtain the gold.

The Early Church

The Christians of the first two centuries were in a unique position: set apart from other religions and pagan cults, divided from the Jews by belief in Christ, and yet linked with the Jews by the Old Testament inherited from them but recast in the new light of fulfillment. The young church was rooted in the cultures of Greek and Roman civilization, emerging first as a sect within Judaism, in lands where paganism was firmly established and mystic cults existed side by side with the philosophies of Hellenism. Our knowledge of the contribution of the Roman world to early Christian art is increased by the existence of a wealth of pagan art buried at Pompeii and Herculaneum for centuries, by the eruption of Vesuvius in A.D. 79—perfectly preserved artworks believed to have been done in about 100 B.C.—and to the preservation of both Christian and pagan artwork in the catacombs around Rome mentioned in the previous chapter. Here the influence of the pagan world is apparent. The eschatological theme among first-generation Christians awaiting the Second Coming gave way to the development of a Christian iconography founded upon both the Judaic and the old motifs, but infused with new meaning. The art of the catacombs includes colorful scenes, floral motifs, portraits, mosaics, decorative domed ceilings, figures carved into the stone, and inscriptions—sometimes crudely done and sometimes with the greatest skill and beauty. An occasional statue in the round is to be seen, rare at the time among Jews and Christians because of a reluctance to make a "graven image." Seeing the colorful paintings, done eighteen centuries ago, one wonders how much more colorful they must have been during the centuries when the catacombs were in use. It is a mistaken notion that the presence of the first Christians worshiping in the catacombs was unknown to the Romans, and that they hid here secretly. All public burial grounds were outside the walls of the city, whether Roman, Jewish, or Christian, and burial places were respected even by the pagans. The Christians were allowed to give proper burial to their dead, and held services on the day and anniversaries of the death of their loved ones at the grave.

The first great turning point in the development of Christian art came about in A.D. 313, through the so-called "Edict of Milan," [1] which brought toleration and subsequent adoption of Christianity as the official religion by the

[1] This was not an edict, and was not issued at Milan, but was an agreement between the Emperors Constantine and Licinius.

Emperor Constantine. From this time onward, as the church emerged into the open, Christian architecture developed and the liturgy and arts were elaborated. In establishing a new capital, Constantinople, upon the old city of Byzantium at the heart of his empire, Constantine built a new Rome—relegating the old Rome to the role of repository of tradition and the past, though he built a church in Rome also. The emperor sought to surpass the glory of Rome and Greece by employing the finest artists to decorate the churches with sculptures of precious metals, marble pavements, mosaics, and tapestries. The imperial love of splendor extended to all parts of the empire.

Eastern Christendom

The development of Byzantine art had separate origins in the important cities, such as Alexandria, Antioch, and Ephesus, which yielded first place to the new capital of Constantinople as the center of artistic activity. While Italy remained part of the Byzantine state, Rome, Ravenna, and Venice employed the Byzantine style in their mosaics. This distinctively Oriental style is closely bound to the mystical and spiritual aspects of worship in churches of the East.

There were three separate periods of Byzantine art before the Empire fell under the Turkish yoke in 1453. The first began in the latter half of the fifth century and included Justinian's reign (527-65). St. Apollinare Nuovo in Ravenna was built just prior to this date by Emperor Theodoric (493-526), and is noted for the processions of figures in mosaic on both sides of the nave. The many figures are a valuable record of vestments worn at that time (Illustration 51). St. Vitale, also in Ravenna, was built by Justinian, and has splendid mosaics which include Emperor Justinian and Empress Theodora. A bishop and two priests are pictured with the emperor, wearing vestments.

The greatest monument of Byzantine architecture is without doubt the Church of St. Sophia, dedicated to the Holy Wisdom, at Constantinople, during the reign of Justinian. Upon its completion, Justinian, in a transport of enthusiasm, is said to have exclaimed: "Glory be to God who hath deemed me worthy to complete so great a work. I have outdone thee, O Solomon!" The concept of the circular building with a dome is the ideal among Eastern Christians, corresponding to the vision of the church as the Heavenly Icon: the cosmos with the cupola as heaven, the middle level as paradise, and the lowest level as earth. This concept underlies the Orthodox liturgy as well as architecture.

The features of the first period of Byzantine art, which lasted from the fourth until the seventh century, included monumental figures, movements restrained, saints gazing directly into the eye of the beholder, as part of an unchanging, eternal world. The vesture of kings and clergy was influenced by Persia with its love of splendor and ceremonial, heavily decorated textiles and artwork.

The first flowering reached its peak in Justinian's reign (527-65) during which the great churches and mosaics of Ravenna (Illustration 51) were made, as

Fratelli Alinari

well as other mosaics and frescoes in Rome and elsewhere in the empire, and the greatest Byzantine church of all, the Church of the Holy Wisdom (St. Sophia) at Constantinople. This period came to an end with the Iconoclastic controversy of 725-843. The second period or flowering began with the ending of the Iconoclastic movement and coincided with the Macedonian dynasty (867-1056), lasting from the middle of the ninth century into the twelfth. Until the eleventh century, the best work was done on the royal looms at Constantinople, where weaving reached its height, with rich textiles serving as royal gifts, examples of which are presently extant in the royal treasuries. During the iconoclasm, many artists traveled west, carrying their art with them, and the Byzantine style was not confined to the capital of the Empire; therefore, the collapse of the Empire did not bring about an immediate end to the art of this second period. The famous coronation mantle of King Roger (1134, now at the Schatzkammer at Vienna) was from Sicilian looms and is Byzantine in style. These royal costumes were not only woven into patterns, but profusely adorned with jewels.

The Sack of Constantinople by the Crusaders (1204) interrupted the development of Byzantine art, and the last great period, the fourteenth and fifteenth centuries, came as the Empire finally fell to the Turks in 1453. The Great Saccos of Photius (1414-1417?) is a fine example of the textile art of this

51b

51c

51 Mosaics, Ravenna: (a) Basilica St. Apollinare Nuovo, right wall of the great nave;
(b) group of martyr saints (section of mosaics at St. Apollinare Nuovo); (c) Church
of St. Vitale, the Emperor Justinian offering gifts for the temple; at his left, the
Archbishop Maximinianus, and assistants. One of the oldest and finest illustrations
of early vestments for the church. The archbishop is wearing a dark green paenula
over a white dalmatic with purple clavi. Around his neck is the omophorion or
pallium. The assistants also wear dalmatics with clavi.

52 The Great Saccos of Photius, Museum of the Moscow Kremlin: (a) the Saccos, composition of Greek crosses and circles, with scenes and personages embroidered with stitches and pearls; (b) detail of bottom border, showing the Grand Prince Dmitrievitch and Princess Sophia Vitovtovna, with Greek inscriptions; (c) portrait of the Metropolitan Photius (detail)

last period (Illustration 52). Textiles played an important role in the spread of the Byzantine style, and served as models for painters and sculptors, as they were easily carried about. Motifs, especially Islamic, were transmitted by the weavers and appeared side by side with Christian texts. During the first few centuries linen and wool were used for tapestries, the linen for the background and the wool for the embroidery. By the middle of the sixth century silk weaving had come to Egypt, Constantinople, and Persia.

The traditions of East and West have gone separate ways through the centuries in spite of efforts toward reunion. The East at the Council in Trullo (692) condemned some of the Western customs. At this council it was for-

bidden to represent the Holy Spirit symbolically as a dove, except in a painting of the baptism of Christ; likewise, it was forbidden to depict Christ as a lamb—the persons and events of sacred history were to be portrayed directly, not by symbols. The triumph over iconoclasm in 850 had the result that, in the Byzantine Rite, art of a very specific kind was fully integrated into the liturgy of the Church. It is difficult for a Westerner to comprehend the religious aesthetics of Eastern art, as there is nothing directly corresponding to the place which icons occupy in the life of the Eastern Orthodox Christian. An icon is more than a picture; it is made according to symbolic formula and transformed by grace. It is an offering to God, and at the same time an encounter with God through his descent into our midst.[2]

[2] See Nicolas Zernov, *Eastern Christendom: A Study of the Origin and Development of the Eastern Orthodox Church* (New York: G. P. Putnam's Sons), p. 276; Leonid Ouspensky and Vladimir Lossky, *The Meaning of Icons* (Boston: Boston Book and Art Shop, 1952), p. 37; and A. A. Vasiliev, *History of the Byzantine Empire*, 2 vols. (Madison: University of Wisconsin Press, 1961).

Western Christendom

While the Byzantine Empire was at its height, the fortunes of the West sank to a state of decay, to be rescued and restored by Charlemagne, who was crowned Holy Roman Emperor in A.D. 800. Seeking to revive the ideals of classical and Byzantine antiquity, Charlemagne brought together scholars and artists to form an academy and workshop, and at Aix-la-Chapelle a cathedral was built, modeled after St. Vitale at Ravenna.

Charlemagne's theologians were Augustinians, with a Neoplatonist attitude toward pictorial representation and an inadequate grasp of Incarnation. With an anti-Byzantine political bias, they opposed both parties in the iconoclastic controversy, and approved images for didactic but not for devotional purposes. The results were: (1) the West never integrated art and liturgy, never acquired canonical style, and could abandon Romanesque for Gothic, Gothic for Renaissance, etc., and (2) a great development of *symbols* took place in the medieval West, a tremendous body of which has come down to us for the ornamentation of our churches and vestments.

Romanesque

The Carolingian Renaissance, extending from Charlemagne's accession in 768 to the death of Charles the Bald in 877, began as a movement toward liturgical reform. The models studied by the Carolingian churchmen were the patristic writers of the fifth and sixth centuries—Augustine, Ambrose, Jerome, and Gregory the Great. The products of the Carolingian workshops included manuscript paintings, metalwork, and ivory carvings. Famous manuscripts of this period include the Utrecht Psalter, the Ebbo Gospel Book, the Breton Gospel Book, and the Vivian Bible.

The lowest ebb of the church and of the Western world was reached after the death of Charlemagne, and was relieved by the Benedictine monastic system in the tenth century and by the Crusades, which left a new religious enthusiasm in their path to the Holy Sepulchre in Jerusalem. Pilgrimages to Rome, Spain, and Jerusalem influenced the spread and development of the Christian art of the Romanesque period, which extended from the ninth to the end of the twelfth century, in the countries of Western Europe which had been under Roman rule. Islamic art also influenced that of the West, through Muslim invasion and warfare.

The Norman period (1066-1198) in England corresponded with the Romanesque on the Continent, and had its own distinctive architectural style: bold and massive, with semicircular arches, ponderous piers, and flat buttresses. The Norman Conquest has been chronicled by the famous Bayeux Tapestry (Illustration 53), dated between 1066 and 1077, in Normandy. It is one of the most celebrated works of embroidery in existence, not only because of its size and artistic merit, but because it records a historical event. Durham Cathedral is a fine example of the Roman style in England, and Dunfermline Abbey in Scotland (see p. 67) reflects the spread from England to other parts of the British Isles. Scottish and Irish architecture had their own heritage, influenced by the Continent, in the Middle Ages.[3]

[3] See Banister Fletcher, *A History of Architecture on the Comparative Method,* rev. by R. A. Cordingley (1st ed. 1896; New York: Charles Scribner's Sons, 1961).

TEXTILE ART IN THE CHURCH

Jean Bessé

Jean Bessé

The Gothic Period

The Gothic style, beginning in the early twelfth century in France, spread to Germany, Italy, and Spain in the same century, lasting until the sixteenth century. Whereas the Carolingian Renaissance had taken place in the royal courts, and the Romanesque style developed in the monasteries, the Gothic period began in the cathedrals of towns and cities. The era of the guilds and artisans brought new patrons of the arts, and many of the great Gothic achievements were commissioned by the guilds.

CHRISTIAN ART THROUGH THE CENTURIES   117

A new figure comes into prominence, gathering the finest artists and craftsmen of his time to revitalize the art of the church; this is the Abbot Suger (1081-1151), creator of the first Gothic building, patron of the arts, theologian, and statesman of France. His fame is assured through his own written account of the circumstances and details of the rebuilding and transformation of the ancient Abbey of St.-Denis, a few miles outside of Paris, the account entitled *"De rebus in administratione sua gestis."* [4] As a patron of the arts, the abbot employed stonemasons, carpenters, painters, and goldsmiths to create the windows, sculpture, furnishings, and jeweled objects which could all help in the visualization of the celestial hierarchies.

A religious philosophy that had a profound influence upon Gothic art was the Neoplatonic concept, which held light to be the source and essence of all visual beauty. The Abbot Suger was an ardent follower of this Pseudo-Dionysian philosophy, which was also embraced by Thomas Aquinas (c. 1225-74). It is this reverence for light that spiritualized the Gothic windows, so that the buildings became walls of glass, expressing the emotional mysticism of the age.

From the standpoint of textile art, certain monumental works have survived which reflect the art of the Gothic period and the high level of attainment in tapestry and embroidery. The famed Parament of Narbonne was done in 1374-75 during the rule of Charles V. It is a painted altar cloth, the design composed in three sections and painted in a monochromatic color scheme on silk. The authorship is uncertain, but the artist is believed to have been related to the School of Paris miniaturists and influenced by Northern, Byzantine, and French painters.

A tapestry that was destined to have great effect upon one of the greatest tapestry artists of the twentieth century, Jean Lurçat, was the Apocalypse Tapestry of Angers, designed by the Flemish artist Jean de Bruges and woven by Nicholas Battaille for the Duke of Anjou in 1382 (Illustration 54). One of the masterpieces of the Gothic age, it consisted of ninety pictures, of which seventy still exist.

The most important single movement involving Christian textile art was known as *Opus Anglicanum*, lasting from the eleventh century to the close of the medieval period, the end of the fifteenth century. Its peak was from 1270 to 1330, when it was renowned throughout Christendom. The term referred to the ecclesiastical embroidery done in England, universally esteemed for its beauty and richness. Many fine examples are to be found in English cathedrals and abbey churches, and some of the finest specimens are found abroad, sent there either as work commissioned by foreign dignitaries or in order to avoid destruction at the time of the Reformation. Probably the most famous vestment of *Opus Anglicanum* is the Syon Cope (Illustration 55), now in the Victoria and Albert Museum. Its date is between 1300 and 1320, during the peak of the movement.

The Syon Cope is embroidered throughout in gold, silver, and colored silk threads on a double layer of linen and completely covered with figures in quatrefoils. The subjects include the Coronation of the Virgin, Crucifixion, St.

Originally in Latin and available in parallel texts prepared by Erwin Panofsky, *Abbot Suger on the Abbey Church of St.-Denis and its Art Treasures* (New Jersey: Princeton University Press, 1946).

Archives Photographiques, Paris

Victoria and Albert Museum. Crown Copyright.

54 Apocalypse Tapestry (section), Angers, France;
designed by Jean de Bruges, woven by Nicolas Battaille
for the Duke of Anjou

55 Syon Cope, Victoria and Albert Museum, London

56 Mass vestments of the Order of the Golden Fleece, Netherlands,
Kunsthistorisches Museum, Vienna:
(a) mantle of Christ; (b) altar antependium of Christ

56a

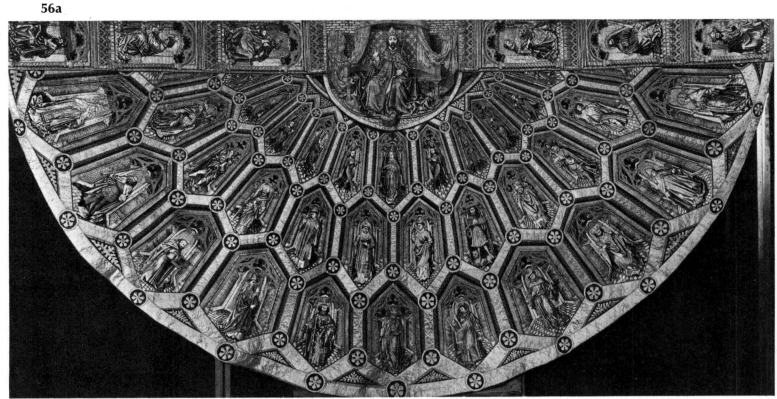

Michael, scenes from the lives of Christ and the Virgin, apostles, six-winged
seraphim, and priests. The cope was originally a chasuble; the orphreys, morse,
and outer border were added later, probably when it was made over into a
cope. The colors are paler than one might expect them to be, but it is probable
that six and a half centuries ago, when it was made, it was more colorful. The
background of the quatrefoils is gold, and the background between the
quatrefoils is soft green. There is continuity throughout the surface as a result
of this quatrefoil pattern through the repetition of flesh tones on the many
figures and repetition of the winged seraphim. The various figures are an interesting record of vestments worn at that time. Although the quatrefoils are
joined at right angles throughout, the figures within them radiate so that they
all stand upright when the cope is worn. Interlaced quatrefoils also appear in
a twelfth-century imperial alb, of the reign of William II in Palermo, in the
Islamic style. It is a favorite motif of the times.

Another popular motif, first appearing in textiles in the twelfth century
and of great importance in the design of Renaissance velvets, is the
pomegranate, an ancient symbol of fertility and eternity in Classic, Jewish, and
Christian tradition. In the twelfth century it replaced the lotus flower as a
motif in Sicily. As new types of patterns emerged in textile centers such as
Venice, in the beginning of the fifteenth century, the pomegranate attained an
increasingly important role. Early Renaissance painters designed fabrics with
delicate pomegranates, pine cones, and thistles, amid undulating stems and
branches or within curvilinear lattices. A confusion arose in the nineteenth
century, where the name "pomegranate" was applied to a figure with a center

© Kunsthistorisches Museum, Vienna

like a pine cone or artichoke. The French name was *pomme de pin,* or "pine cone." The name "pomegranate" was probably a transliteration of the French, a logical error since the pomegranate was so frequently employed as a design, and anything resembling it in shape, in a stylized form, could easily be mistaken for one.

A copious use of saintly figures is particularly identifiable with the *Opus Anglicanum* period, when saints' days filled the calendar—a system that has been greatly curtailed in recent years as a part of liturgical reform movements.

The art of embroidery reached an unexpected height in the fourteenth century, and Austria, Bohemia, and France became the main centers, taking the lead from the *Opus Anglicanum.* The types of embroidery were silk and needle-painting, which followed very closely the models of the painters of the times. This was the beginning of a movement which came to maturity a hundred years later, and achieved its highest perfection in the Burgundian-Netherlandish vestments made by the Order of the Golden Fleece. A complete set of Mass vestments for a chapel of the Netherlands, made by the Order of the Golden Fleece in the middle of the fifteenth century, is now in the Kunsthistorisches Museum, Vienna (Illustration 56). The embroidery is worked on a linen ground, and includes gold thread, pearls, topazes, sapphires, and colored silks in a great variety of shades. The frames of the pictorial panels are of red velvet with gold bands. The subject matter consists of an array of figures, each within its own architectonic framework. The Flemish love of figures draped in elegant fabrics is evident in these vestments, as it is in the paintings of the same period.

CHRISTIAN ART THROUGH THE CENTURIES

The close association of the arts of painting and embroidery resulted in many instances where the design was first rendered by a painter and translated into embroidery or tapestry, such as the works of Antonio Pollaiuolo, Botticelli, Raphael, and others. Tapestry weaving was carried out on a large scale in Western Europe from the eleventh and twelfth centuries onward, and it was the Brussels weavers who obtained the order from Pope Leo X for the reproduction in tapestry of the Raphael cartoons intended for the Sistine Chapel in the Vatican (Illustration 57).[5] The Flemish weavers were given the work

[5] The original cartoons by Raphael are in the Victoria and Albert Museum. A set of tapestries woven from the cartoons is at the Vatican. The pictures are reversed in weaving.

TEXTILE ART IN THE CHURCH

57 Cartoon for tapestry "Miraculous Draught of Fishes," by Raphael

of reproducing the cartoons of Van Eyck, Roger Van der Weyden, Thierry, Steuerbout, and Hugo Van der Goes. A French weaver, Nicholas Bataille, reproduced the cartoons by Jean de Bruges in the oldest French tapestry preserved today, the Apocalypse at Angers, in the fourteenth century (Illustration 54).

The Renaissance

The new age of the Renaissance, which started in Italy in the fifteenth century, spread its influence over the Western world. The spirit of humanism and rediscovery of antiquity, modified to serve the new spirit, brought changes in architecture, painting, and sculpture, as well as literature and other forms of scholarship. The spiritual elements in art became materialized, and religious emotions were mingled with aesthetic charm and sensuous beauty.

The Renaissance was marked by an advance in science and mathematics. Perspective and third dimension in art were carried to a high state of development, and in fact, became the preoccupation of painters such as Paolo Uccello (1396-1475). The Flemish painters, observing the new movement which had taken root in Italy and joining into it, carried the effects of perspective into the use of colors, using warm, advancing colors and cool, receding colors to achieve the appearance of foreground and distance. Geometric forms were used in combining architectural elements with human figures, thereby uniting the design with the idea of the picture.

Venice, as we have already observed, held first place in the production of elegant textiles. The same city also drew artists from other parts of Europe for its reputation in the use of color, led by the master-colorist Titian (1487/90-1576) and followers such as Tintoretto. The great Flemish painters, beginning with Jan van Eyck, as well as the Italians, contributed greatly to the art of textile design for Venetian production, and in turn, artists found the Venetian fabrics a rich source of inspiration from which to copy. Weaving held the status of a major art in the development of its versatility. Velvet pile, sometimes cut and sometimes uncut, provided various levels of thickness for background and subject, and a brocaded pattern of gold introduced in various ways added further variation in height and texture. The Venetians invented and exploited all manner of techniques for the enhancement of their art, utilizing the characteristics of the medium, such as the effect of light against the pile of the velvet and on satins, and the textures of various weaves. These developments in the art of weaving and embroidery progressed out of the realm of painters into an autonomous art, and finally invaded the field of architecture, wherein classical architectural ornaments were incorporated into wall hangings and tapestries, and cloth was made to look like stone.[6]

Architecture was one of the chief areas of Renaissance preoccupation. The basilica in the form of a Latin cross, representing Christ crucified, gave way in some instances to the Greek cross and the square church with a central dome. The Roman triumphal arch and colonnades were borrowed from antiquity, and the objectives were artistic perfection and balance. In the sixteenth century, under the patronage of the Popes, Rome became the art center of the Christian world. The art of the High Renaissance was classic, formal, and majestic.

The Reformation and Counter Reformation

The High Renaissance came to an end with Mannerism, a trend toward exaggerated emotionalism and distortion, and with anti-classical tendencies. Conflict in the world of art was symptomatic of conflicts in the world in general

[6] There are numerous examples abroad where draperies are painted on the walls over and around the altar; a particularly objectionable example is in a church in Scotland, where curtain rods and riddel curtains are painted on each side of the altar. Elevated pulpits, ornately swathed in painted stone drapery, may be found in many churches of Western Europe and the British Isles. Cloth in the likeness of stone, or stone in the likeness of cloth, can be equally dishonest and objectionable.

—a situation that is being paralleled in our own day. Luther's burning of the papal bull was both a symbol and a symptom of the changing climate, initiating a new era at the time of the Reformation.

The role of the church in the arts was divided in two directions from 1520 onward: the Protestant Reformation and the Roman Catholic Counter Reformation. Artists found little patronage among the Protestant Reformers, whose attitudes toward religious art ranged from tolerance to violent opposition. The Roman Catholic Church turned, on the other hand, to the Baroque, which asserts itself in spectacular splendor and overstatement. The church did not create the Baroque style, but it did use it and influence its contents. Artists were commissioned by the church to conform to canonical law in representing dogmas and increasing the piety of the faithful in the veneration of images. The artists of this period were restricted by the decrees of the Council of Trent (1545-63).

Although the Puritan Reformers had little use for art as decoration, there was a need for finding a new architecture in keeping with the revised liturgy and emphasis upon preaching. The altar had become a table removed from the wall and brought forward among the congregation. William Laud, Dean of Gloucester and later Archbishop of Canterbury, returned it to its former position against the east wall and protected it with altar rails set up on three sides. There was immediate and intense reaction on the part of the Puritans, who refused to initiate the Laudian reforms.

The room plan or auditory church was popularized by Christopher Wren, who was appointed after the great fire in London, 1660, to rebuild St. Paul's Cathedral and London's fifty-one parish churches. Such a large-scale restoration within a short period established the Christopher Wren style for a long time to come.

There was little Christian art produced in the eighteenth century, with the possible exception of the Georgian church architecture in England. By now the divorce between the church and the artist was all but complete, and the nineteenth century witnessed a progressive degeneration toward realism and sentimentality interpreted by mediocre artists.

The Roman Catholic Church of the nineteenth century allowed the use of cheap plaster toy-shop saints, paper flowers, tinsel, and chromo-lithographs to produce a sort of folk-art atmosphere that was near and dear to the people. There were also cheap Virgin Marys enthroned in roses and blood-trickling Sacred Hearts. . . . The Protestant Church rejected these tawdry things, but while she white-washed her walls and swept her temple clean, she accepted the dreamy-eyed veiled Virgin of "The Annunciation" by Arthur Hacker and the scent of roses and violets in melodramatic Madonnas of William Bourguereau. . . . The Protestant Church also rejected the harshness of the crucifix and the Man of Sorrow, but accepted the sentimental, weak, unreal Christs of Ary Scheffer, Plockhorst and Hofmann.[7]

Liturgical Revival

Obviously, there was need for reform. In England, the reform was led by Augustus Welby Pugin in the first decade of the reign of Queen Victoria. By this time persons of good taste had grown tired of Classical art, and "Gothick"

[7] Katharine Morrison McClinton, *Christian Art Through the Ages* (New York: The Macmillan Co., 1962), p. 123.

had become fashionable among the avant-garde—a "Gothick" that was a far cry from anything that had existed before the Reformation. "England was waiting for the voice of one crying in the wilderness, so that all mankind could see the saving power of true Christian architecture, i.e. medieval Gothic. This new John the Baptist, Augustus Welby Pugin, was born in 1812 and died in 1852." [8] The son of a Low Church Anglican mother, Pugin turned toward the Catholic Church in search of an ideal worship and found tawdriness instead. He was convinced that drastic changes in the externals of worship were imperative, and devoted himself to the restoration of that which he regarded as the perfect expression: true Gothic. His great work is a monumental encyclopedia, *A Glossary of Ecclesiastical Ornament and Costume . . . with extracts from the works of Durandus, et cetera,* first published in 1844. Included with the origin, history, and significance of the various emblems and symbolic colors peculiar to Christian design in the Middle Ages are many pages devoted to the decoration of vestments and altar furnishings. This contribution alone toward better furnishings of places of worship entitles Pugin to grateful remembrance more than a century after his death.

On the continent of Europe, a similar movement was going on at the same time among the medievalists. In France there were Charles René, Dom Prosper Guéranger, and Eugène Viollet-le-Duc. The early Gothic revival in Germany was closely bound up with the Romantic movement, the chief prophet of which was J. A. Moehler (1796-1838).

The ecclesiological movement in England was the outcome of the Cambridge Camden Society founded by John Mason Neale and Benjamin Webb, who brought out a translation of the first volume of a medieval treatise on Christian symbolism, the *Rationale Divinorum Officiorum,* written by William Durandus, who was Bishop of Mende between 1285 and 1296. The aims of the society drew fire from the Low Church or Evangelical Anglicans, as being dangerously close to Rome. *The Ecclesiologist,* the journal of the Society, was being widely read.

> The ladies in many a country parsonage, so Dr. Pusey had made clear to Dr. Hock, the Vicar of Leeds, as early as 1839, badly need "a holy employment" in their spare time. It was essential to direct their zeal, "which will otherwise go off in some irregular way, or go over to Rome." . . .
> No holier employment could be found for the early Victorian virgins than the making of altar frontals and church embroidery.[9]

The effects of the Cambridge Camden Society are still very much in evidence, the style of furnishings advocated and established by this movement being used in Anglican churches all over the world to this day. Nevertheless, by the end of the nineteenth century, the work of the Society of the 1840's had lost its impetus and the Anglican Church was in need of another housecleaning. The majority of Anglican churches were Low Church or Central (middle-of-the-road) and would make little or no use of devotional *objets d'art:* the popular item was the stained-glass window. During the last fifty, and more particularly the last twenty-five, years there has been a great leveling up of churchmanship, but the decor of the average Anglican church is still restrained,

[8] Anson, *Fashions in Church Furnishings, 1840-1940,* p. 21.
[9] *Ibid.,* p. 61.

and this, of course, is now liturgically up-to-date. The object of Percy Dearmer, the Warham Guild, and the like was to "clean up" Anglo-Catholic churches, but their influence here was temporary and limited. Their main effect was on cathedrals and large central town churches, where an "English" ceremonial and furnishing tradition was established in place of little or nothing before.

A new concern for proper ornaments at the end of the nineteenth century meant a closer look at the *Book of Common Prayer,* which contained specific directions for the Ornaments of the Church:

And here is to be noted, That such Ornaments of the Church, and of the Ministers thereof at all times of their Ministration, shall be retained, and be in use, as were in this Church of England, by the authority of Parliament, in the second year of the reign of King Edward the Sixth.

No one was quite sure *what* "Ornaments of the Church" had been in use in the second year of Edward the Sixth between January 28, 1548, and January 27, 1549, and everything depended upon those twelve months more than three hundred years ago. A new society was formed to remedy the situation with a succession of tracts and publications: the Alcuin Club. The most prominent spokesman for the society was Percy Dearmer, the author of *The Parson's Handbook,* first printed in April, 1899. A thirteenth edition, revised and rewritten by Cyril E. Pocknee in 1965, is evidence that Dearmer's word is still authoritative, at least in some circles. In fact, in some narrow cliques such is the weight of his influence that one need look no further than Dearmer for the true facts. A few years ago, I had occasion to send questionnaires to churches of Great Britain, Western Europe, and the United States with reference to the present use of liturgical color sequences. In one reply, three pages of questions brought a single response: "See Percy Dearmer's *Parson's Handbook.*" With Dearmer's word already published, there was no need, in that writer's opinion, to send questionnaires or write a thesis on the subject.

It was not enough for Dearmer and others simply to write about the correct interpretation of the Ornaments Rubric. It must be carried out in actual practice. Therefore, the Warham Guild was established, with the help of liturgical experts, to give valuable advice toward the designing and making of the ornaments. The Warham Guild is still in active service, making and directing the making of ornaments and vestments in accordance with the rubrics. The organization has taken note of the changes affecting liturgical worship in both the Roman Catholic Church and the Church of England, on the Continent and in Great Britain. *The Warham Guild Handbook,* first published in 1932 and now in a second, fully revised, edition of 1963, contains a number of photographs of fine design in vestments and furnishings. Illustration 58 shows examples of the guild's work in contemporary design.

Despite the fact that the Church of England often fell short of the goals set by its leaders in liturgical reform, the Anglican Communion deserves credit for doing something very special in the liturgical revival. All churches with any sense of fitness have tried to do something to redeem themselves from the awful conditions prevalent after the eighteenth century, but nowhere was there such determined and devoted effort as in Anglicanism. Nor did any other

58a

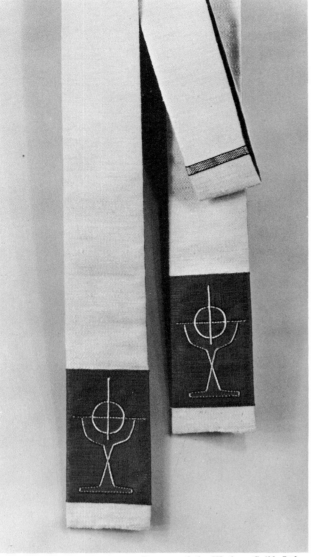

58 Contemporary designs by the Warham Guild, London:
(a) stole; (b) burse

58b

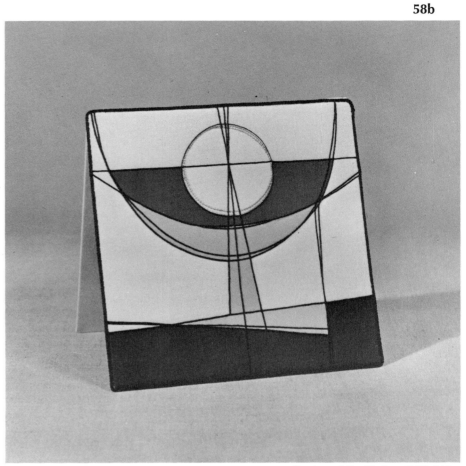

Courtesy of the Warham Guild, Ltd.

Courtesy of the Warham Guild, Ltd.

church have such extensive influence over others in the matter. No other church saw so clearly the importance of reform; nor did any (except Rome) understand the value of ancient liturgical heritage. The Oxford Movement, the Tractarian Movement, and the Ritualist Movement had tremendous impact not only on the Anglican Communion, but on the Presbyterians, the Methodists, the Congregationalists, and scores of other churches. Just what would Protestantism have been like but for the nineteenth-century Anglican liturgical zeal, such as it was? There were many mistakes, to be sure, but our churches would be poorer and uglier today if such a movement had not taken place.

Sacred Art Movement in France

Church art in France during the nineteenth century was in as deplorable a state as in England and elsewhere. In a chapter entitled "Decadence and the Dominicans," William S. Rubin describes the increasingly sentimental and bourgeois character of cheap and gaudy ornaments called *Kitsch,* a German term that for good reasons has passed into other languages.[10] A symptom of the post-Renaissance decline in sacred art was the spread of *Kitsch* ornamentation, some of the modern forms springing from fussy and flamboyant Baroque and Rococo churches. Only one important church decoration was

[10] William S. Rubin, *Modern Sacred Art and the Church of Assy* (New York: Columbia University Press, 1961), p. 9.

TEXTILE ART IN THE CHURCH

59 "Saint-Sulpician" Christ

realized in the entire nineteenth century, according to Rubin, and that by the atheist Delacroix: the Chapel of the Holy Angels in the Church of Saint-Sulpice in Paris. When finished in 1861, it was roundly condemned. Ingres, who had become the model for liturgical art, when asked his opinion of the Delacroix frescoes, replied: "Rest assured, my dear Curé, there *is* a hell."[11] A type of art called "art of Saint-Sulpice" is a brand of *Kitsch,* and received its name by being sold in religious stores in the neighborhood of Saint-Sulpice.

The attitude of the church toward the wholesale reproduction of these sentimental pieces was paradoxical. The objection of Vatican authorities to this art was not primarily in terms of style, quality, or character, but because it was manufactured. Canon law 1399 forbids the decoration of churches with images reproduced in series on the theory that the spark of genius can be present only in unique artistic creations. Rubin points out that the handmade *Kitsch* prototypes are indistinguishable from their serial duplications.

The average churchgoer prefers sentimentality to suffering and sacrifice, and prefers what Rubin calls a *Kitsch*-like "Coca-Cola" Christ, derived from stereotypes of advertising and "popular" art (Illustration 59), to the more profound art of Rouault (Illustration 71*). H. A. Reinhold devotes a full chapter of *Liturgy and Art* to "The Enemy Kitsch," comparing it to trash and then making

[11] *Ibid.*
*P. 148.

a distinction. Trash, he says, is without ambition, not intending to be taken for true art. *Kitsch,* however, pretends to be true art, and has wormed its way into the hearts of many people.[12]

The Sacred Art Movement in France was led by the Dominicans, and received new impetus at the close of the Second World War through the efforts of Père Couturier, O.P., and Canon P. R. Régamy, O.P., who endeavored to foster a spirit of openness to new ideas in an attempt to reanimate sacred art. An artist whose work was destined to be copied at that time was Maurice Denis, a member of the Nabis, a group of young artists who had abandoned the principles of the *École des Beaux Arts,* in order to follow a new style composed of flat, unmodeled surfaces. The name "Nabis" comes from a Hebrew word meaning "prophets" and the credo was expressed by Maurice Denis (1870-1943): "A picture—before being a horse, a nude, or an anecdote—is essentially a flat surface covered with colors assembled in a certain order." The Nabis abandoned the principle shortly, due to its limitations, but the credo has remained. From the time of the first showing of a religious painting, *Le Mystère Catholique,* by Maurice Denis in 1890 until his death in 1943, a tradition of modern sacred imagery was established. The *Atelier de l'Art Sacré* was founded by Denis with the help of Georges Desvallieres, under the patronage of the Catholic Institute of Paris.

The Catholic modernist movement had produced no outstanding works on the eve of the Second World War, and it was through the review *L'Art Sacré* that Fathers Couturier and Régamy hoped to give the necessary impetus. The practical occasion arose for putting into action the hopes of the Dominican modernists in 1939, when Father Couturier invited his friend Canon Devémy and the architect Maurice Novarina to collaborate on the decoration of Notre-Dame-de-Toute Grâce at Assy. The plans were suspended until after the end of the war, but what followed was one of the unique accomplishments in twentieth-century church art.

This backward glance at history has brought to light the trial and error, the shortcomings, and the glorious achievements in religious art throughout the centuries of Christianity. There are lessons to be learned from the complacency of indifference, and from the zeal of the reformers. The purpose behind this review of the past is to recognize what has caused periods of decline, and upon what foundations a new and vigorous Christian art may be built throughout all Christendom.

[12] H E.. Reinhold, *Liturgy and Art,* XVI (New York: Harper & Row, 1966), pp. 79-80.

Textile Art in the Church Today

The art of our time and of all peoples and countries should have in the Church full liberty of expression, provided it preserves due honor and reverence for the requirements of sacred buildings and rites.
—CONSTITUTION ON THE SACRED LITURGY

Textile art is the stepsister of contemporary art forms. Of all the arts employed in today's churches, textiles probably receive the least recognition. Too often they are regarded as items of furnishings to be found in religious supply catalogs, or else a pleasant hobby or pastime for sewing circles. The result is a pedestrian repetition of stock designs of usually mediocre quality.

In some cases, works of textile art are so outstanding that they are famous in their own right. Such are the tapestries of Lurçat and Sutherland. Usually, however, one must search among a multitude of sources to find the exceptional examples and artists. One might expect to find really creative paraments and vestments wherever the church building itself is exceptional. It is disappointing indeed to find occasions where the high regard for good art and architecture has broken down at this point, and barren furniture appears to have been forgotten, or—even worse—a token gesture of mediocrity has been made. Few attempts have been made to survey this particular branch of art on a broad scale, and the examples included here are necessarily far from complete. Many fine works have been accomplished, and a continual search will turn up more and more artists whose work has not reached the attention of the public. Examples have been selected for illustration in this

131

book from churches of many denominations in various parts of the Western world to represent the scope and originality of some of today's art for church furnishings, tapestries, and vestments.

Efforts toward revitalizing religious art in general, including textile art, are being made through guilds and organizations, religious orders, periodicals devoted to the arts, and exhibitions. The most prominent and influential periodicals are *Liturgical Arts,* published by the Liturgical Arts Society, *L'Art Sacré,*[1] and *L'Art d'Église.*[2] All three promote and encourage contemporary art in vestments, and from time to time, *L'Art d'Église* has included patterns for making vestments and embroidery designs to be copied. There is no journal devoted to the arts in the Protestant churches comparable in scope to these three which serve the Roman Catholic Church. Examples of paraments, vestments, and wall hangings in churches of the various communions in the United States are found in architectural and religious journals, such as *Christian Art,* a nonsectarian publication. Magazines dealing with techniques and design, although not devoted exclusively to church art, include *Craft Horizons, Handweaver and Craftsman,* and a British publication, *Embroidery,* the journal of the Embroiderers' Guild. The latter contains many fine articles and examples of embroideries in Anglican churches.

Contemporary church art and architecture are closely associated with recent liturgical developments, generating an extensive literature on the subject.[3] Professional organizations such as the Guild for Religious Architecture and the American Society for Church Architecture hold annual conferences to study and compare new trends, problems, and solutions, and in 1967 the First International Congress on Religion, Architecture, and the Visual Arts met in New York, sponsored by thirty-five organizations in nineteen nations. The subject of a contemporary style of art and architecture in keeping with the changing pattern of urban society, was the prevailing theme of lectures, exhibits, and tours of religious buildings and art galleries. Among the vestments exhibited, many were hand woven by members of religious orders. Symbolism of design gave way to the symbolism of the vestment itself, in many instances, and the ornamentation was purely decorative, but dignified and restrained.

Serious artists are encouraged to direct their talents toward church art and the public is given the opportunity to see works of merit through the sponsorship of juried competitions and exhibitions by organizations such as the Guild for Religious Architecture,[4] the Liturgical Conference, and Christian Arts Associates. A religious banner and hanging exhibition titled "Signs in Cloth" was conducted by the Christian Arts Associates. The banners selected from the entries for their high standard of artistic achievement were placed in a traveling exhibit so that they could be seen in all parts of the United States. A similar event took place in England on the occasion of the Diamond Jubilee of the Embroiderers' Guild in 1966. The exhibition was attended by 23,000 people, and 1,200 entries were received, of which 200 were selected by the judges to be displayed.

[1] Directed by RR. PP. Couturier and Régamey, O.P. from 1937 to 1954, published in Paris.
[2] Published at Abbaye de Saint-André, Bruges, Belgium.
[3] See bibliography.
[4] The set of Pentecost paraments shown in Illustration 15 (p. 37) was awarded first prize in textile arts in the Ecclesiastical Arts Competition at the annual National Conference of the Guild for Religious Architecture held in Miami in 1968.

Progress is now being made toward healing the breach between artists and churches. There are responsibilities on both sides: churchmen cannot expect the best artists to produce masterpieces comparable to those in the days of church patronage if they continue to furnish their sanctuaries with mediocrity, and artists cannot hope for acceptance of works that are merely the particular fad of the moment. The Constitution on the Sacred Liturgy adopted at the Second Vatican Council expresses the Church's respect for art and for the freedom and responsibility of the artist:

> The Church has never kept as its own any particular style of art. Rather, according to the character and the condition of the various countries and the demands of the different Rites, she has admitted the artistic forms of every age, thus creating in the course of centuries an art treasury that should be preserved with all care. So too the art of our time and of all peoples and countries should have in the Church full liberty of expression, provided it preserves due honor and reverence for the requirements of sacred buildings and rites. In such wise it will be able to add its own voice to the marvellous symphony of praise which in times past great men have raised to the Catholic faith.[5]

The Church Abroad

Great Britain

One contributing factor toward originality and creativity in English ecclesiastical embroidery is the coordinated endeavor of the Embroiderers' Guild. Another factor is the ingenuity of the individual artists. Unlike the situation in the United States, where the most progressive works are usually found in relatively new church buildings, some of the finest works in England, such as the John Piper tapestry at Chichester Cathedral (Illustration 4*), are designed for centuries-old churches.

During the sixty years since its inception, the Embroiderers' Guild has moved from the Art Nouveau to the variety of methods employed today, including the introduction of the use of the machine in embroidery. Although the machine was previously scorned as an inferior shortcut to handwork, it has been discovered that spontaneous effects are possible by this medium that become labored and stiff when wrought by hand.

One of Britain's leading textile artists, Beryl Dean, showed a dossal hanging entitled "The Crowning of the Virgin" at the Diamond Jubilee exhibition of the Embroiderer's Guild. The hand-embroidered design, measuring four yards by three yards, utilizes brilliantly-colored silks applied to a lurex cloth-of-gold background (Illustration 60). The complete plans call for a matching altar frontal and a row of six tall candles to stand in front of the bottom of the hanging. It is fortunate that the entire project was planned at the beginning, as otherwise the candles—when they are obtained—would obscure a part or at least the balance of the design. This is a common fault in a great deal of church planning; each addition tends to cancel the last, unless precautions are taken to avoid it.

A new form of embroidery represented among the works at the exhibition

[5] Constitution on the Sacred Liturgy, 123.
*P. 29.

60 Dossal, "The Crowning of the Virgin,"
by Beryl Dean

61 Altar frontal, Epiphany Chapel, Winchester Cathedral,
   by Margaret Kaye

From *Embroidery*, Diamond Jubilee Issue, 1966; courtesy of Winchester Cathedral

is the use of freehand stitchery and collage, an approach that calls for constant experimentation in design, color, and technique, and offers particular scope for large pieces. The freehand and collage technique are used on the Elisabeth Hopper cope and also on the very dramatic frontal (Illustration 61) by another capable English embroideress, Margaret Kaye, for the Epiphany Chapel of Winchester Cathedral. This frontal is adorned with fabrics of widely different textures, applied to a background of dull sheen. Bouclé wool, chenille, gold and synthetic metal threads are used for the couching, chain, and straight stitches of the embroidery. This very contemporary design is shown against a background of massive pillars and arcading of Norman architecture. The Dean of the Winchester Cathedral says: "It is indeed a most imaginative and effective piece of design and craftsmanship and we are very proud to have it in this Cathedral where it is much admired."

TEXTILE ART IN THE CHURCH TODAY

62 Chasuble designed by Susan Riley,
embroidered by Beryl Dean

The embroidered chasuble (Illustration 62) designed by Susan Riley and embroidered by Beryl Dean is a magnificent example of contemporary English embroidery. On a background of off-white Thailand silk, the design is worked in various golds, some raised, with braids and threads couched down, and including black and white chenille. The whole effect is radiant and splendid, in keeping with the festal occasions for which the white vestment is intended.

A banner (Illustration 63) embroidered by Beryl Dean for Stoneleigh Church, Warwickshire, is of laid work, couched gold on cloth-of-gold, and quilted. The background textures are tapestry-like, and the gold figure suggests a monumental brass effigy. The craftsmanship is exquisite and the effect is jewel-like, revealing the artist's familiarity with historical brasses and illuminated manuscript paintings and her ability to turn these to a new and fresh use.

A lavish set of vestments was presented to His Holiness Pope Paul VI in 1965 by a party of pilgrims en route to the Holy Land, led by the Bishop of Exeter. The vestments were designed by Laurence King and embroidered by Sister Kathleen of the Anglican Society of St. Margaret, St. Saviour's Priory,

TEXTILE ART IN THE CHURCH

63 Banner, Stoneleigh Church, Warwickshire,
   by Beryl Dean

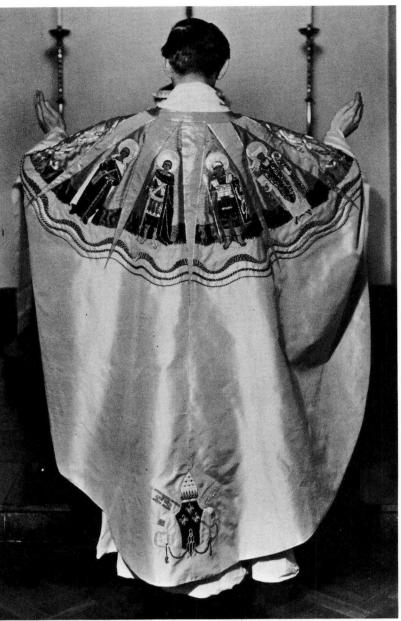

64 Chasuble for His Holiness Pope Paul VI

From *Embroidery*, Diamond Jubilee Issue, 1966; courtesy of Sister Kathleen S.S.M.

Haggerston (Illustration 64). The conical-shaped chasuble of cream satin-backed wild silk, lined with taffeta, is embroidered with figures of saints associated with Great Britain before the coming of St. Augustine. The embroidery is done with applied fabrics and overlay of transparent or semitransparent fabrics, and worked with surface stitchery. The colorings of the design are introduced with green paper-soft taffeta, pale lime nylon crepe, grotta straw, and organza; the sun's rays are worked in gold lurex fabric.

England's most monumental work of modern textile art is the famous tapestry of "Christ in Majesty" by Graham Sutherland, at Coventry Cathedral. It is fitting that textile should be the crown of all arts combined in this new cathedral, since the prosperity of the city, extending from the medieval guilds, depended upon wool and cloth manufacturing in large measure, for a considerable length of time. A momentous occasion in the history of England's great cathedrals was the building of St. Michael's Cathedral at Coventry to replace one destroyed by fire through an air raid in World War II. This new edifice was to be a twentieth-century cathedral, a religious proclamation of our own times, an artistic triumph of the finest work in architecture, sculpture, stained glass, and—particularly relevant to the subject of this book—textile art. The enormous tapestry was an original concept of the architect, Sir Basil Spence, almost from the moment he went to visit the ruins of the old cathedral for the first time (Illustration 65).

The architect's concept was a tapestry over the entire wall behind the altar.

65 Coventry Cathedral; tapestry by Graham Sutherland, "Christ in Majesty,"
woven by Pinton Frères in Felletin near Aubusson

The preconceived ideas of the architect would seem to restrict the creativity of the artist, but it is part of Sutherland's genius to be able to grasp the architect's vision and bring it into being. Sir Basil Spence had recently visited an exhibition of tapestries by famous British artists, all made at the Edinburgh Tapestry Company. The brilliance of colors and the nonreflecting quality appealed immensely to the architect, who felt that an altar is to be seen and appreciated as an invitation to Communion, and that a bright window behind it would make it difficult to see the altar. A tapestry, on the other hand, illustrates and emphasizes the concept of the Eucharist.

Spence was particularly impressed by a tapestry of Wading Birds by Sutherland at the exhibition of tapestries, and also greatly admired his painting of the Crucifixion at Northampton. He vowed that if he should be so fortunate as to win the competition to rebuild the cathedral, he would insist that Sutherland be asked to do the tapestry. When this came about, and his request was approved, he took the committee to an exhibition at the Tate Gallery to see samples of Sutherland's work. The reaction of some of them, including the chairman of the committee, was "stunned incomprehension." So it was up to the architect to proceed at his own risk. He was convinced that his faith had been rewarded, in finding that the artist fully comprehended what was asked of him.[6] Many people who have seen the tapestry share the committee's reaction to their preliminary viewing at the exhibition and find it disconcerting, because of the cocoon-like figure of Christ reminiscent of some ancient time and the pronounced geometric outlines encasing the figures of the winged evangelists.

The tapestry is designed to be the climax of the building, and is unequaled in its scale and size of the figure of Christ. The colors of the surroundings are muted in order to enhance the effect of intense green background of the tapestry. The figure of Christ in a white garment and surrounded by a *mandorla*, an almond-shaped aureole, was obviously inspired by early Christian mosaics in the Byzantine style. Sutherland was also impressed by Egyptian royal figures from the Valley of the Kings and Egyptian mummy pictures—bound, coffined figures.[7] The total effect is a curious blend of Romanesque and mid-twentieth-century styles. The framework within the composition links the tapestry to its architecture, securing the whole of the figure-work to the walls and roof. The tremendous size of the tapestry, 78 feet high by 38 feet wide, fills the entire wall like a mural; it is presumably the largest tapestry ever woven in one piece. The texture of wool appears soft and warm against the polished wood and stone around it, and the dullness is in striking contrast to the highly polished floors. It is a magnificent undertaking, whether or not one finds the composition pleasing.

The making of the Coventry vestments was entrusted to the firm of Louis Grossé Ltd., under the supervision of J. Doneux, Director. The Bishop's Procession in the Cathedral (Illustration 66) is led by the provost's verger in cassock and gown, followed by the great cross, with two lights; then three priests in copes; then the banners of the See of Coventry. The style of the

---

[6] The architect has written an account of the Cathedral project: Basil Spence, *Phoenix at Coventry: the Building of a Cathedral* (New York: Harper & Row, 1962).
[7] Douglas Cooper, *The Work of Graham Sutherland* (London: Lund Humphries, 1961), p. 36.

66 Bishop's Procession, Coventry Cathedral,
vestments by Louis Grossé

67a

67 Guilford Cathedral:
(a) high altar;
(b) sanctuary carpet

67b

Courtesy of Guildford Cathedral

dalmatic is an innovation exclusive to the Coventry vestments. In place of the conventional orphreys, two box pleats were made with contrasting fabrics.

Two remarkable Anglican cathedrals were consecrated within a year: Guildford in May, 1961, and Coventry in May, 1962. The physical setting of each was quite different, Guildford situated on a hill in a town surrounded by rolling hills and green countryside, and Coventry in the center of an industrial city. An open competition for the design of the new Guildford Cathedral was held in 1932, and the plans of Sir Edward Maufe were chosen. In 1933 the land was given—the summit of Stag Hill, about a half mile northwest of the center of town—and from this hill the cathedral dominates the town and its surroundings. Building came to a standstill during the war, and it was not until twenty years after its beginning that the Cathedral of the Holy Spirit was consecrated. This is the first Anglican Cathedral to be built on a new site in the south of England since the Reformation.

Stag Hill provided the theme for many of the embroideries for the new cathedral, which were designed principally by the architect, Sir Edward, and his wife Prudence Maufe, or under their supervision. A conventional road sign of a steep hill was adopted for all of the kneelers (Illustration 112*). The lower

*Pp. 214-15.

TEXTILE ART IN THE CHURCH

68 Lectern fall, Guildford Cathedral

Courtesy of Guildford Cathedral

left corner of a triangular division of each kneeler was worked in a dark blue background, representing the hill; the upper right triangle was white to represent the rolling clouds of the Surrey skies.[8]

Textiles have an important role in the furnishings. A predominantly blue carpet (Guildford's color) designed by the architect and worked on a hand loom at the Royal Wilton Carpet Factory proceeds up the center aisle and steps to a long altar completely covered with "Laudian" altar cover, and folds of cloth cover the wall behind the altar by means of a dossal curtain 45 feet high with seven widths of Lurex material (Illustration 67). The first frontal for the high altar had been designed by the architect, "a noble piece of gold embroidered, couched and appliquéd embroidery," and a frontlet was also designed which was intended to be used on all future high altar frontals. The cathedral authorities later asked that all future frontals should be of a Laudian design, not requiring frontlets.[9]

The lectern fall (Illustration 68) is an eagle, designed by Alix Stone and embroidered by Mrs. Russell at the Royal School of Needlework. Much gold couching and technical skill are evident, worked on a background of damask in a traditional manner. Although the cathedral and its furnishings are still quite new, the character is more Neo-Gothic than contemporary, with the exception of the building materials of light brick in place of stone. Undoubted-

[8] Prudence Maufe, "Embroideries at Guildford," *Embroidery*, XIII (Summer, 1962), 44.
[9] *Ibid.*

ly, the long timespan of its construction, from planning time to completion, is responsible for its conservative style, which certainly does not diminish its stately beauty.

The long tradition of needlework guilds in English cathedrals is exemplified in Lady Prudence Maufe's account of a banner designed and embroidered by one of the members:

> It is a remarkable achievement and is the result of twenty-five years of patient, skilled and devoted labour. It has, of course, been remarked that this banner is not in character with any of the other embroideries in the Cathedral; the reason is that the architect had no part in it. This makes the difference understandable, but the beauty and integrity of the work remain as an example of wonderful embroidery and it was accepted by the Cathedral authorities.[10]

These words of praise for the twenty-five years of labor are an indication of the high value placed upon the effort required to execute a work. Artistic merit is not measurable in time and effort as much as in the talent and skill of the artist. If the design is good, the length of time required to carry it out has little significance; if the design is bad, no amount of time will save it. Mrs. Stephanie Holt, former curator of textiles and costumes at the Los Angeles County Art Museum, once remarked to me that when she showed a particularly fine example of textile art, the two most frequent questions asked were: "How long did it take to make it?" and that most vulgar of questions, "How much is it worth?" Neither question has much bearing on the quality of the art.

France

The practice of selecting "great men for great tasks" was initiated under the leadership of Canon P. R. Régamey, O.P. and Père Couturier, O.P. who set a precedent which was to leave its mark on the period following World War II. This was the Art Sacré Moderne movement which had been interrupted by the war. For the first time in centuries, great artists were assembled to direct their talents toward art for the church. A revolutionary situation struck the keynote of a new evangelical spirit, as works of the pious Rouault were seen side by side with those of non-Christians, including atheists, Communists, and Jews.[11]

Whereas each work of art selected for Coventry Cathedral was planned for, and the artist was selected by the designing architect to fulfill the total concept, the situation was reversed in the Church of Notre-Dâme-de-Toute-Grâce at Assy. Here the acquisition of a Rouault stained-glass window in 1939 set in motion a plan to select works from the greatest living artists. The consecration of this Dominican-inspired church at Assy in 1959 marked the commencement of a Renaissance of sacred art, in which the Dominicans in France sought to rescue the Church from the mediocrity and sentimentality into which church art had degenerated.

Père Couturier stated that he trusted genius above piety, and his trust was rewarded with the beautiful Chapel of the Rosary for the Dominican nuns at Vence (Illustration 69).[12] Complete unity was accomplished in the new chapel, designed and decorated by Henri Matisse, starting in 1951 at the age of seventy-

[10] *Ibid.*, p. 46.
[11] William S. Rubin, *Modern Sacred Art and the Church of Assy*, p. 2.
[12] See Illustration 22, p. 43, regarding the Stations of the Cross.

69 Chapel of the Rosary, Vence, France, designed by Henri Matisse

eight. The artist had never been devout, and this, his last great work, was not the result of a conversion experience. "At last," he said, "we are going to have a gay chapel!" He declared his work in the chapel to be "the conclusive achievement of a whole life of labour and the flowering of a huge, sincere, and difficult striving."

Matisse was a painter and not an architect, although he directed the building of the chapel. His intention was to create a "religious space" [13] to be decorated with painting. The most outstanding accomplishment, in my opinion, has been in the use of color in a seemingly all-white space. The first impression one receives on entering is that the whole chapel is white: plastered walls of white, set off at the right by white ceramic tile. Black line drawings on the white tile increase the feeling that there is no color here. When we regard the stained-glass windows at the left, with their strong, gay colors in contrast to the walls, we note that it was the genius of the artist to use the sun itself to decorate the chapel. In the ever-changing light, the reflections cast new patterns and colors on the white surfaces. Sir Basil Spence, after his visit to the chapel, remarked: "What bowled me over was the quality of light that played on those

[13] "Ce que j'ai réalisé dans la chapelle, c'est la création d'un espace religieux"—Matisse, quoted by M. A. Couturier in Les Chapelles du Rosaire Vence par Matisse et de Notre-Dame-du-Haut à Ronchamp par le Corbusier (Paris: Les Editions du Cerf, 1955), p. 7.

white surfaces. It was like walking into a pearl." [14] Between the stained-glass windows on the left and the painted ceramics on the right, between color and design, is the heart of the picture bathed in living light. Here stands the altar, and the priest moves about the altar wearing vestments designed to echo and repeat the colors and motifs of the windows (Illustration 70).

The colors in the glass are taken from nature, an emerald green background interjected with deep blue and scattered with bright yellow flowers. The simplified flower form, a favorite figure in the paintings of Matisse, appears in the vestments which he designed. A number of these sets of eucharistic vestments are now owned by the Museum of Modern Art in New York. Illustration 70a shows a white silk set from their collection, consisting of a chasuble, stole, maniple, burse, and veil. The design of gay flower forms surrounding a bold central panel is worked in yellow and green appliqué. The chasubles are made of silk and decorated with appliqué shapes of silk, satin, and velvet. Matisse worked his designs with gouache on cut and pasted paper (Illustration 70c), and the contours of the shapes of the sewn pieces retain the character of scissor-cuts of the original art work. Some outlines are emphasized with raised gold cord. Others are accented with a solid line or a series of stitches at right angles to the figure (Illustration 70b).

The artistic triumph of the chapel does not depend only upon the use of color and reflections; even in late afternoon when there is no sunshine, and

[14] Spence, *Phoenix at Coventry,* p. 39.

TEXTILE ART IN THE CHURCH

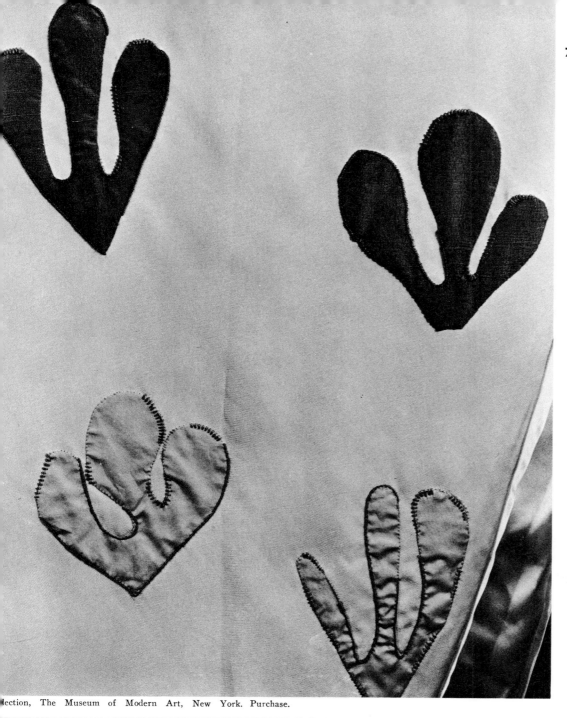

70 Chasubles by Henri Matisse:
    (a) white silk chasuble, stole, maniple, burse, and veil;
    (b) chasuble detail;
    (c) designs for red and yellow chasubles

71 Tapestry, "The Holy Face," designed by Georges Rouault and woven by J. Plasse-LeCaisne; Chapel of St. Thérèse, Hem, France

at night, the chapel is radiant as a jewel, with clusters of little lights in delicate chandeliers sparkling like stars. The greatness lies in the complete unity throughout the entire planning of the small chapel and the vestments which become a part of the whole plan through their liturgical function. A lesson that may be learned from this chapel is that a masterpiece of a church need not be a cathedral. Like all true creativity, Matisse's chapel still appears fresh and new and will remain contemporary for some time to come.

A third example of outstanding textile art is the compelling tapestry of Christ, the "Holy Face," designed by Georges Rouault, at the Chapel of St. Thérèse at Hem (Illustration 71). The tapestry hangs over an altar of the same width. Quite unlike the overwhelming drama of Lurçat's Apocalypse (Illustration 21*), The Rouault "Holy Face"—visually linked with the similarly proportioned altar by means of a slender long-armed cross—creates a profoundly religious effect. A deeply devout man and perhaps the greatest master of Chris-

*P. 43.

TEXTILE ART IN THE CHURCH

Courtesy of Renate Gruber

72 Paraments designed by Pastor Johannes Jourdan
and Professor Helmut Lortz, artist:
(a) green set, Cross Church, Darmstadt-Arheiligen;
(b) white set, Paul Gerhardt Church, Mannheim

72b

From G. E. Kidder-Smith, *The New Churches of Europe*

tian art in the twentieth century, Rouault felt that art should enter the church
"kneeling and in silence." The church was given to this textile community by
a local industrialist.

Germany

Distinctive sets of paraments were made for the Cross Church of Darmstadt-
Arheiligen, designed in collaboration with the pastor, Pfarrer Johannes
Jourdan; a member of the congregation, Professor Helmut Lortz; and the
architect, Reinhold Kargel. About the same time (1963), the Paul Gerhardt
Church in Mannheim was built, and since the paraments of Darmstadt-
Arheiligen fitted so perfectly the conception of the Paul Gerhardt Church in
Mannheim, permission was given by Pastor Jourdan and Professor Lortz to
have them made for this church also (Illustration 72).

TEXTILE ART IN THE CHURCH TODAY

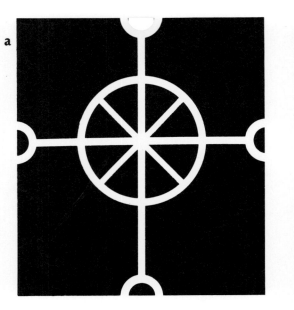

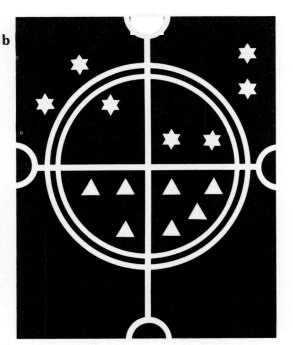

73 Paraments for Cross Church,
Darmstadt-Arheiligen,
and Paul Gerhardt Church,
Mannheim, Germany: (a, b) violet set;
(c, d) green set; (e, f) red set;
(g, h) white set; (i, j) purple set.

The paraments were made in the Deaconesses' Houses of Darmstadt and Mannheim of linen dyed in the colors of the Church year and embroidered with white floss. The linen was handwoven and dyed in their own workrooms, and the embroidery was done by hand. The symbols (Illustration 73) chosen by the artist, Professor Lortz and the pastor, were planned to the last detail and were drawn with compass and ruler—not freehand. The prominence of the cross in each design was planned as the main symbol for the Cross Church congregation.

A darker purple is used for the Lenten set than for Advent. The lighter color for Advent indicates the lights and joy of Christmas, as the candles lighted each Advent Sunday are enjoyed in preparation for Christmas. The light of Easter also spreads its rays over the Lenten time. This light is closer to us than the darkness of Good Friday. The darker purple for Lent comes very close to black, which is used in many churches in Germany on Good Friday, and points to the light of Easter. Good Friday and Easter cannot be separated, as the Bible indicates in the victorious words of Jesus, "It is done." The theme of each design is given by Pastor Jourdan in a booklet, "*Evangelisch-Kreuzkirchengemeide, Darmstadt-Arheiligen,*" for the paraments shown in Illustration 73.

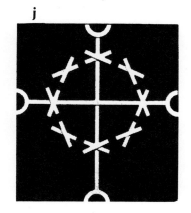

The ceiling of the Paul Gerhardt Church in Mannheim, by architects Gerhardt Schlegel and Reinhold Kargel, is unquestionably the most prominent architectural feature (Illustration 72b). A hint of late Gothic is seen in the space-frame of white tubing against a blue ceiling. The pews of wood and steel, the freestanding steel and Macassar ebony altar, and the pulpit and font on either side, show a slim, linear effect closely related to the ceiling structure. The embroidered designs of the rectangular altar and pulpit cloths (Illustration 72a) carry out a similar character, with geometric precision. Another version of the space-frame ceiling exists in Christ Church, Leverkusen-Bürig, by architects Hentrich and Petschnigg.

Christ Church in Bochum, designed by architect Dieter Oesterlen, is distinguished by its unusual roof structure, the diamond-shaped planes of the roof, as they ring the periphery of the church, suggesting the symbolism of the crown of thorns. The simple slab altar and the pulpit are furnished with

TEXTILE ART IN THE CHURCH TODAY 151

74 Christ Church,
Bochum, Germany

From G. E. Kidder-Smith, *The New Churches of Europe*

rectangular paraments (Illustration 74). G. E. Kidder Smith remarks: "The church, one of the finest in Germany, has only one trouble: like too many Protestant churches, it is almost invariably locked." [15]

Sweden

Some of the finest creative textile art for the church is done in Sweden. The national Church of Sweden is Lutheran, and vestments, paraments, and dossals are used extensively. Furthermore, the country has a long and notable tradition in art, and is one of the most progressive countries in the world of art today. This combination of national characteristics is bound to result in a place of leadership in contemporary textile art. Weaving and embroidery are important in the arts, and the number of large, handwoven tapestries and wall hangings in public buildings of all sorts, as well as handwoven rugs, is most impressive.

One of Sweden's foremost textile artists of the twentieth century was Sofia Widén (1900-1961). Following her famous predecessor, Agnes Branting, at Licium, where weavers and embroiderers are trained, first as artistic collaborator and later as chief, Miss Widén opened her own studio along with Alice Lund, who now directs the studio since Miss Widén's death. Sofia Widén was the first to revive the old Swedish Lenten colors, blue and gray, and in the

[15] *The New Churches of Europe*, p. 136.

75 Wall hanging by Sofia Widén,
Kung Karl's Church, Kungsör, Sweden

30's she made blue vestments for the cathedral in Strängnäs and Västerås. In later years she became more and more interested in indigenous materials, such as wool and linen. These simple stuffs demand more of the creative artist but adapt themselves better to many Swedish churches than more costly materials would do. Sofia Widén made probably a thousand church textiles, spread over the whole of Sweden. Her last works were for Växjö and Gotebörg cathedrals and St. Ansgar's student chapel in Uppsala.

A variety of techniques has been employed by Sofia Widén and Alice Lund, her successor. The handwoven wall hanging suspended from the canopy over the pulpit in Kung Karl's Church, Kungsör (Illustration 75) is the work of Sofia Widén. The geometric design, in an ever-changing pattern, gives stability and variety at the same time, and harmonizes well with the surroundings. There

Courtesy of the Swedish Institute for Cultural Relations

is an interesting contrast between the air of repose in the parallel lines of the hanging and the entwined design of the pulpit carving, reminiscent of illuminated manuscripts. Among the vestments designed by Miss Widén are block printed and appliqué chasubles (Illustration 136*).

The carpet designed by Alice Lund for Härlanda Church, Göteborg (Illustration 76) is done in *röllakan* technique, woven in different shades of gray, dark red, and green. The handsome altar antependium is by Folke Heybroek. The geometric design of each blends beautifully with the pattern of bricks on the wall behind the altar. The series of steps and the triple division of kneelers, altar, and altar-piece accentuate the rhythmic pattern of rectangles.

Another outstanding Swedish textile artist is Anna-Lisa Odelqvist-Kruse, who was an artistic collaborator at Licium from 1948 to 1952. She is now manager and artistic director of the firm Libraria, an important ecclesiastical art studio of Stockholm and a subsidiary of Verbum, a corporation connected with the Board of Deacons of the Swedish Church. An interesting variety of work is done under the supervision of Mrs. Kruse. At the time of my visit to the studios, large wall hangings were being embroidered on huge frames, the designs worked according to small watercolors; rare old vestments were being restored; fabrics for future vestments were being woven on the looms; and a number of completed vestments were on display. A particularly interesting set of chasubles was designed by Mrs. Kruse to meet an unusual lighting situation in a church built in 1968 (Illustration 77). There are no windows in the

*P. 242.

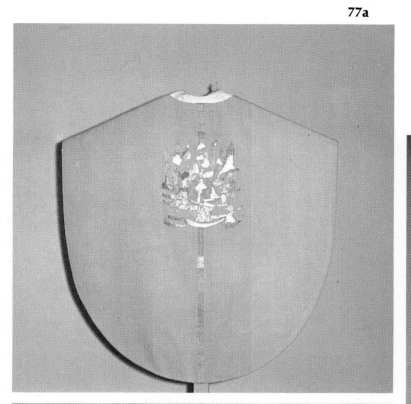

77 Chasubles by Anna-Lisa Odelqvist-Kruse, Libraria, Stockholm:
   (a) gold-embroidered ship design;
   (b) gold flame-cross for Pentecost;
   (c) crown of thorns design

77b

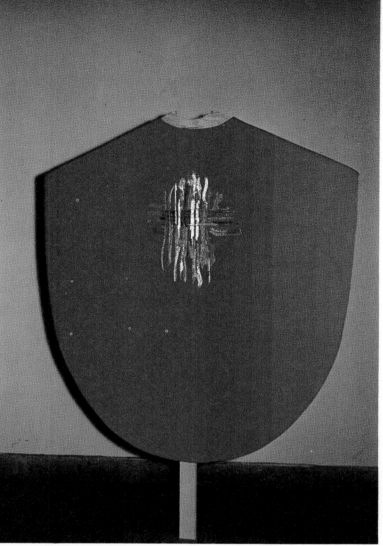

77c

Photos by Marion P. Ireland

brick walls, and all of the light comes through a dome in the ceiling, over the altar. The sun's rays enter on a slant, and the cloth was woven to accentuate the direction of the beams of light, shading from dark on one side of the vestments to light on the other. The embroideries are abstract designs worked in metallic and colored threads on a fabric of spun silk and spun wool. The white chasuble (Illustration 77a) is shaded from pale blue to white, with sailing ships in silver and gold. The red chasuble (Illustration 77b) is variegated from red to pink and red-orange. The design is an abstract cross and flames. The symbolism on the blue chasuble (blue is used instead of purple in Sweden) is a crown of thorns, in light and dark silver (Illustration 77c).

78b

78 Chasubles by Anna-Lisa Odelqvist-Kruse,
Libraria, Stockholm:
(a) white, with center design in blues;
(b) grayish-black wool, with inscription
INRI (*Iesus Nazarenus Rex Iudaeorum*,
or "Jesus of Nazareth, King of the Jews")

78a

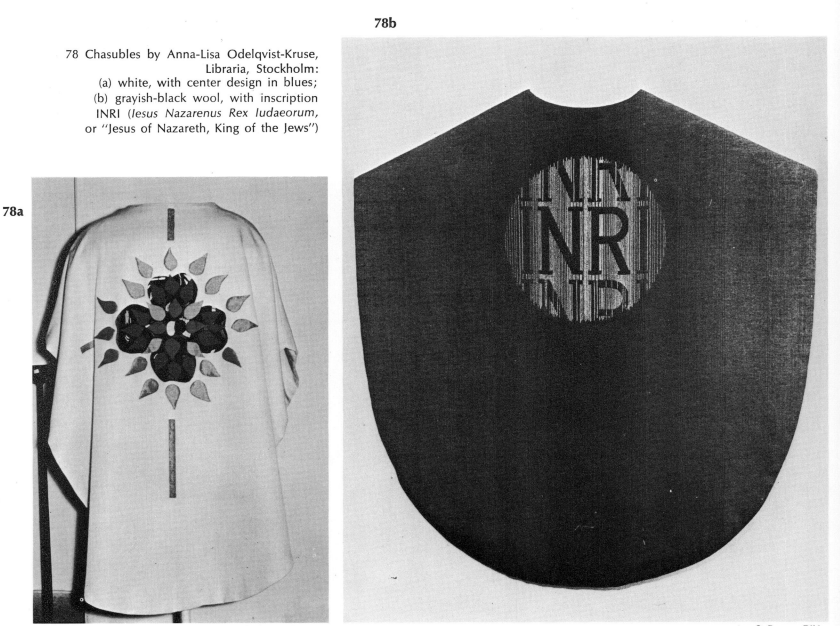

Marion P. Ireland

© Dagens Bild

Two quite different chasubles designed by Anna-Lisa Odelqvist-Kruse are a white one (Illustration 78a) with appliqué of rich shades of blue and gold, for festal use, and one of grayish-black wool (Illustration 78b) for Good Friday. Her work includes many styles and techniques, including the burse with couching and a variety of decorative stitches (Illustration 79), the appliqué wall hanging at Raus Church-house (Illustration 117*), and the abstract hangings worked in linen embroidery (Illustration 111a†). A representative example of her present work is a large wall hanging for the new Lutheran School of Theology in Chicago, Illinois (Illustration 111b‡). This is of woven wool, and the design is a blend of soft pastel shades of red, gold, blue, and green, on a black background. It was presented as a gift through the Swedish section of the Lutheran World Federation. Other works by Anna-Lisa Odelqvist-Kruse are owned in the United States, and her works have been exhibited at the Museum of Contemporary Crafts in New York and in traveling exhibitions.

*P. 222. †P. 213. ‡P. 213.

79 Burse by Anna-Lisa Odelqvist-Kruse

80 Chasuble by Hans Krondahl,
Licium, Stockholm

A number of different artists prepare designs in color for Licium, a firm with about thirty employees, directed by Inga Johansson who is a designer in her own right. Much of the weaving is done on the premises, and other hand-woven fabrics are purchased, mostly silk and wool blends, to be made up into vestments. Many tapestries are also made for public buildings. The variety work in progress on the looms and on display is impressive, and represents the work of several capable designers and craftsmen. Most of the designs are hand woven, but an interesting chasuble in red with black and white appliqué is shown in Illustration 80. An unusual shape is used for a series of chasubles woven in the same pattern but with different combinations of colors: a green background shading to blue on each side of a central panel in white with gold, and a white chasuble with metallic gold, each combination producing very different effects (Illustration 81). The stole for the green vestment has a white contrasting pattern running the full length (not shown), whereas the

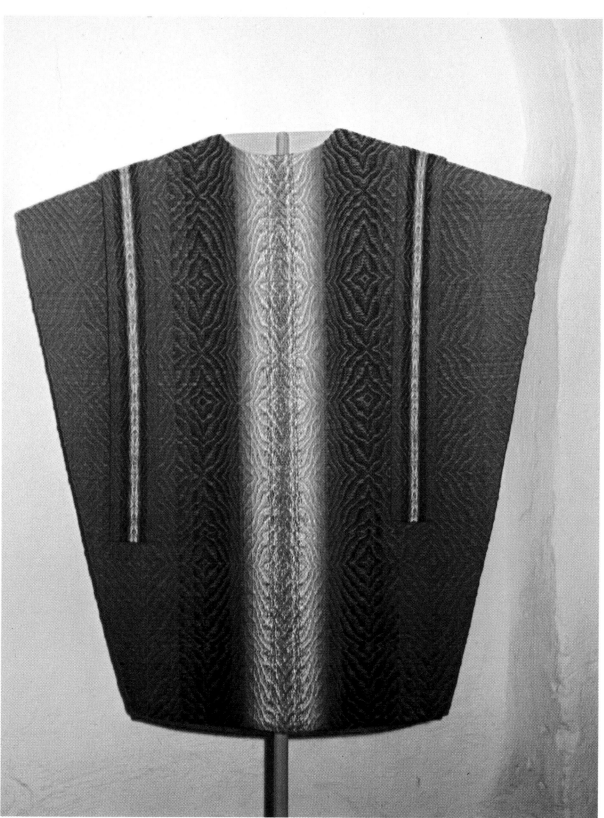

81 Chasuble by Eva Robertsson,
Licium, Stockholm

82 Chasuble and stole by Inga Johansson,
Licium, Stockholm

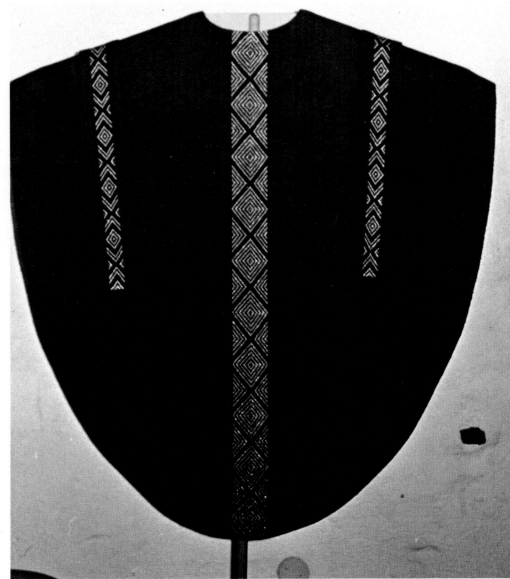

82 Chasuble and stole by Inga Johansson,
Licium, Stockholm

Marion P. Ireland

ends of the white stole have a woven pattern. The stoles woven at Licium are
narrow and of equal width throughout, and the chasubles are cut on various
patterns, generally not very full. A chasuble and stole by Inga Johansson (Illustration 82) are woven in variegated shades of purple for the background
and metallic silver for the geometric design. A red fabric with a Pentecost design of flames, by Eva Robertsson (Illustration 83), had not yet been made up
into a chasuble at the time of my visit, but shows the close relationship between the weaving pattern of the symbol and that of the background material,
an effect that cannot be attained as fully with embroidery.

One of Sweden's finest workshops for weaving tapestries and carpets is the
firm of Märta Måås-Fjetterström at Båstad. The firm was founded in 1941 to
carry on the remarkable work of its originator, Märta Måås-Fjetterström (1873-

83 Red fabric woven for a chasuble by Eva Robertsson, Licium

1941), whose lifework has been recorded and illustrated in a recent book by Tyra Lundgren.[16] At the time of her death, the number of weavers in her company had grown to twenty and had produced 662 *flossa* carpets, *semi-flossa* carpets, *rya* rugs, *röllakan* tapestries, draperies, and various other rugs. The first manager of the firm, after the founder's death, was Mrs. Barbro Nilsson, who carries on with a select group of talented artists. The greater part of the work of this firm is for places other than churches, and some of their tapestries and rugs are on a large scale for important public buildings. A particularly fascinating project in a thoroughly contemporary design is a series of seven tapestries for the electric company. The symbols of the seven panels

[16] *Märta Måås-Fjetterström och vav-verkstaden in Båstad* (Stockholm: Albert Bonniers Förlag Ab, 1968).

84 Markus Church, Stockholm:
    (a) two tapestries designed by Robert Nilsson and woven by his wife, Barbro.
Frontlet for altar by Marin Hemmingson, Märta Måås-Fjetterström AB;
    (b) tapestry detail

Courtesy of Märta Måås-Fjetterström AB

represent the sun, lakes, waterfalls, steam power, atomic power, network of clouds, rain, sea, and light switches, combined. A legendary horse is in each panel.

One of the most outstanding collections of contemporary textile art that I have seen in any single church is at the Markus Church in Stockholm-Björk-hagen, Sigurd Lewerentz, architect. A magnificent pair of tapestries reaching from the altar to the ceiling (Illustration 84) sets off altar frontlets and pulpit antependia. These, and chasubles, are the work of the Märta Måås-Fjetterström firm and its chief designer, Barbro Nilsson. One can only realize the perfect harmony between the rich colors of the tapestry and the dark-colored Hälsing-borg bricks by seeing it personally. The thick, warm texture of wool tapestry

TEXTILE ART IN THE CHURCH TODAY　　　　　　　　　　163

weave is complemented wonderfully by the brick, which is a work of art in itself. The architect selected these deep purplish bricks, which had been popular around 1910 and since fallen into oblivion, to blend and harmonize with the birch grove in which the church is situated. Only whole bricks could be used, and the individual way that each bricklayer worked shows through. A great deal of mortar is used between bricks, giving the surface an unusual pattern and texture. A golden relief sculpture of Christ, designed by Robert Nilsson, appears as a jewel, linking the two tapestries and crowning the altar. The tapestry panel on the left, starting at the top, has scenes of the Nativity, the teachings, the triumphal entry into Jerusalem, the agony in the garden, and the Crucifixion. The panel on the right shows the Resurrection, the Holy Comforter, Pentecost, flaming heart, martyrdom, and the Church. The textiles for the altar and chasubles (Illustration 141*), dealt with in the final chapter, are of exceptional beauty. All the textiles are woven in the same technique, a variation of tapestry technique. There is a set for each of the seasons of the Church year.

Large tapestries treated as a part of the whole architectural concept are used more widely abroad than in this country, I believe. They are frequently seen in hotels, banks, and all sorts of public buildings as well as in churches. Hand weaving is costly, and tapestry weaving is particularly so because each warp thread is dealt with separately rather than throwing a shuttle across the full width. The results, however, are lasting and well worth the investment. The tapestry by Sten Kauppi at the Theological Seminary at Lidingö[17] is a major feature of the chapel and enhances it so much that it might even be called a necessity to the total interior.

Norway

The American Lutheran Church in Oslo, dedicated in 1964, is an American church on Norwegian soil, built during the pastorate of the Rev. Myrus L. Knutson of Los Angeles, who served there from 1962 to 1966. The architects were the firm of Sövik, Mathre, and Madson of Northfield, Minnesota, and the stained glass was the work of the Willet Stained Glass Studios of Philadelphia, Pennsylvania. The building of an American church on foreign soil provided an opportunity to demonstrate abroad the achievements in contemporary architecture and stained glass that are taking place on this side of the Atlantic Ocean.

At the dedication of the new church, the American clergy wore cassocks, surplices, and red stoles; the Norwegian clergy wore the black gown and ruff—the traditional preaching attire in Norwegian churches. The red kneeling cushions, flags, and the glorious stained-glass windows, spreading their reflections across the floors and pews, add color to the setting in addition to the liturgical colors of the paraments. Divided altar cloths are used (Illustration 10†), consisting of two separate cloths side by side, carrying out a relationship to the separated pedestal of the altar. Parallel cloths on the altar have been used effectively by this architectural firm in churches in this country as well.[18]

[17] See pp. 254-55 and Illustration 148.
[18] See Illustration 9, p. 33.
*P. 246. †P. 34.

The Church at Home

Admirable achievements have been made in the combined use of contemporary architecture and the allied arts in various parts of the United States. An outstanding example is St. Paul's Cathedral (Episcopal), Peoria, Illinois. The architect was Frederick Wallace Dunn of St. Louis, and the stained glass was the work of the Emil Frei Studios, St. Louis, designed by Robert Harmon. The drama of the architecture and stained glass is immediately apparent when one views the simple, long rectangular-shaped building set off by a tall campanile. The drama reaches a climax with the large stained-glass window, which constitutes the entire front with the exception of the doors. The towering figure of St. Paul, the patron saint of the parish, dominates the window.

Textile art predominates in the interior of the church (Illustrations 85, 114, 135*). A specially designed carpet, hand woven in Puerto Rico, extends the entire length of the nave, and surrounds the square railing around the high altar. The entire north wall (the chapel end) is covered with a silk-screened

*Pp. 218, 242.

85 St. Paul's Episcopal Cathedral, Peoria, Illinois: reredos of silkscreened fiberglass by Zelda Strecker; handwoven carpet designed by William Donaldson

86 St. Mark's Episcopal Church,
New Canaan, Connecticut:
reredos by Clark B. Fitz-Gerald;
paraments designed by Leah Fitz-gerald

Annette D. Kynaston

fiberglass reredos. Needlepoint kneeling cushions in richly contrasting colors extend completely around the four sides of the altar. The eucharistic vestments include sets made by Louis Grossé Ltd. of London, and by Zelda Strecker, who also made the reredos. The entire project shows a high regard for contemporary textile art in its various forms.[19]

Contemporary arts and architecture are coordinated in St. Mark's Episcopal Church in New Canaan, Connecticut. The angular planes and arches of the walls and ceiling of this church, designed by architects Sherwood, Mills and Smith, present a contrast with the swirling pattern of the unique sculptural reredos, designed and executed by Clark B. Fitz-Gerald. The drama of redemption is portrayed in this remarkable work, which contains 184 key figures (Illustration 86). The stained glass, designed by Odell Prather and executed by the Willet Stained Glass Studios, is best described in the words of Henry Lee Willet as "an entire fenestration of pure color, unfettered by figures and symbols which destroy the majesty of the Almighty—just glass and God's

[19] Each of the forms of textile art is dealt with in other chapters. See the index for pages.

TEXTILE ART IN THE CHURCH

D. Jones

87a

87 (a) St. Patrick's Church,
Kansas City, Kansas

sunlight, expressed in its ultimate." [20] The iconography chosen was God's creations, expressed with glorious movement and evolution of color.

The paraments for the high altar and pulpit were designed by Leah Fitz-Gerald, wife of the sculptor who created the reredos. The designing and hand embroidery of needlepoint kneeling cushions was an ambitious project requiring the combined efforts of sixty-seven embroideresses, over a period of ten months, to complete the eighty-five feet in length. [21]

The striking canopy above the tabernacle at St. Patrick's Church (Roman Catholic), Kansas City, Kansas, Shaughnessy, Bower, and Grimaldi, architects, is a modern adaptation of the ancient custom of surrounding the holy places with cloth curtains and canopies. In this case, four banners are mounted to a square frame forming a canopy high above the tabernacle (Illustration 87). The artist, Janet Kuemmerlein, describes her work and the theme of the banners in a letter:

The technique used in producing the banners is primarily machine-sewn stitchery on fabric ranging from wool, felt and velvet to pure silk and transparent organza. Some areas are stuffed to produce a three-dimensional effect. The subjects of the banners are (1) Eucharist, (2) Resurrection, (3) Four Evangelists, and (4) Trinity.

[20] Booklet, *St. Mark's Episcopal Church, New Canaan, Connecticut,* text on stained glass by Henry Lee Willet (published under supervision of the Reverend Grant A. Morrill, rector).
[21] The projects of the paraments and kneeling cushions are discussed in separate sections. See the index for pages.

87b

87c

87 (b) Canopy banners by Janet Kuemmerlein for St. Patrick's Church, Eucharist;
(c) Resurrection; (d) Four Evangelists; (e) Trinity

88 Chancel hanging by Janet Kuemmerlein;
Faith Lutheran Church,
Prairie Village, Kansas;
Hollis and Miller architects

The set of banners is an outstanding accomplishment for its decorative value with regard to color, design, and embroidery technique, and for the fresh, new use of symbols, interpreted with originality and understanding. A spirit of life and animation pervades the designs, heightened by angularity of lines and richness of colors against a black background. Great use of contrasts is made: in intense colors with black and white; in intermingled linear patterns and solids; in dimensional effects by means of padding and textures; and in the bold decorativeness of the canopy against the brown wood of the ceiling, which literally surrounds the canopy.

The symbols of these banners are *interpretations* drawn from the traditional vocabulary of Christian symbolism. The Eucharist is represented by the Host, a white circle embroidered with the head of a lamb, with a blood-red pattern

TEXTILE ART IN THE CHURCH

Art Waldinger

89 First United Methodist Church
of Garden Grove,
Garden Grove, California;
paraments by Marion P. Ireland

and radiant gold and blue flowing around it. The Resurrection is readily recognized: Christ, encircled in pure white, the figure achieving an effect of transparency by its linear design. A gold halo and the gold outline of the circle symbolize the radiance and holiness of the Lord, and set apart the theme of the banner from the leaflike pattern beneath, worked in a subtle and somber color harmony of grayed tones of red, violet, brown, and green. The banner of the Four Evangelists shows the four traditional symbols, winged figures representing Matthew (man), Mark (lion), Luke (ox), and John (eagle), balanced in the four corners around the circle representing eternity. In the Trinity banner, symbols of God the Father (the eye), the Son (fish), and the Holy Spirit (the dove) are arranged in a pyramid of triangles and circles as a base pointing to eternity.

A handsome chancel hanging by the same artist, Janet Kuemmerlein, was made for Faith Lutheran Church, Prairie Village, Kansas (Illustration 88). The colors move upward from dark to light, with black and red predominating at the base and progressing to shades of gold and white at the top.

The First United Methodist Church of Garden Grove, California, Hal C. Whittemore, architect, presents a setting for unique design of paraments, suggested by the abstract bronze sculpture of J. E. Thompson, and stained-glass windows by Jos Maes, as well as the architecture itself (Illustration 89). The sculpture consists of a baptismal font, a series of candle holders mounted on the wall behind the altar, the legs of the altar and face of the pulpit, and the chalice. The stained glass, lining an entire side and large areas of each end of

Art Waldinger

the church, combines symbolism and abstract design in sweeping lines and forms of color. The architect conceived a series of textures: stone, sculpture, glass, and fabric. An asymmetrical plan balances large areas: windows, exposed organ pipes, grill-covered organ chamber, and pulpit. A centrally placed altar encircled by a communion rail is elevated upon a trapezoidal-shaped dais with rounded corners. This same shape is repeated for the opening of the organ chamber. The elevation of the building is in the form of a truncated arch.

The unique features of this church, and the free rein allowed in designing the paraments, led to experimentation with new shapes and effects. The white set, used during the Christmas and Easter seasons, is the festal set and reflects the joyous air of celebration by means of rich texture of fabric and embroidery, harmonizing with the faceted bronze sculpture. A textured fabric with some metallic threads in the weave to blend with the bronze and cut stone was chosen. The large rectangular cloth for the altar (Illustration 90a) extends down front and back, since the communicants approach the altar rail from all sides. The embroidery design is a collage of appliquéd fabrics, layers of semi-transparent net, gold mesh, and gold kidskin with accents of hand embroidery. A freeform dove enveloping a stylized replica of the church façade and steeple symbolizes the presence of the Holy Spirit in the life and ministry of that particular congregation.

The pulpit design (Illustration 90b) is based upon a covenant theme represented by a rainbow, the Lord's sign to Noah. The Old Testament covenant is

Art Waldinger

90 White paraments,
First United Methodist Church of Garden Grove,
by Marion P. Ireland:
(a) altar antependium;
(b) pulpit antependium

Art Waldinger

91 Purple paraments,
First United Methodist Church of Garden Grove,
by Marion P. Ireland:
(a) pulpit antependium;
(b) altar antependium

Art Waldinger

expressed by an olive branch, and the New Testament is the promise of eternal life, symbolized by a golden crown: "Be thou faithful until death, and I will give thee a crown of life" (Revelation 2:10). The shape of the pulpit antependium is unique, designed to enhance the bronze panel rather than to cover it. To reflect the sweeping lines of the stained-glass windows, the arches of the walls, and the ranks of exposed organ pipes on the opposite side, a curved line was extended down each side of the parament to form an arc around the bronze pulpit front.

The purple paraments were designed to represent the seasons of Advent and Lent, and to express the somber character of these penitential periods. The architect remarked that it is unfortunate that cloth is so seldom allowed to look like cloth, showing the natural qualities of draping. Instead, paraments are expected to hang flat. Therefore, this unique characteristic of fabric was deliberately emphasized by extending the pulpit cloth down in a deep curve to a point at the right, and balancing it by draping a short curved portion in folds at the left (Illustration 91a).

The symbolism on the purple set consists of a chalice and Host encircled by a rude crown of thorns worked in hemp and leather. The purple altar cloth (Illustration 91b) is the same shape as the white one, but the background of the composition is a trapezoidal form used by the architect as a basic motif. An analogous color harmony ranging from blue-violet to red-violet and crimson relates to the purple background. The main fabric is rough textured, with a pronounced slub.

TEXTILE ART IN THE CHURCH TODAY   175

92 Altar antependium for the Chapel
of the First United Methodist Church of Garden Grove,
by Marion P. Ireland

The chapel of this church was built at the same time as the church, on a smaller scale but completely related. The same sculptor made the bronze pulpit front and cross and candles for the altar. In keeping with the small scale of the chapel, a strong relationship needed to be established between the altar and pulpit. This was done by creating a "sculpture" of gold kidskin on the altar cloth (Illustration 92). The border of bands of various shades and textures of gold complements the design and further relates the altar and pulpit.

A distinctive feature of the Queen Anne Lutheran Church of Seattle, Washington, Durham, Anderson, and Freed, architects, is the series of dossals for the seasons of the Christian year. Each curtain is designed for its own seasons. The red one shown in Illustration 93, is used at Pentecost, and the center portion, on which flames are embroidered to symbolize the seven gifts of the Holy Spirit, hangs relatively flat with deep folds on either side. The purple

TEXTILE ART IN THE CHURCH

Courtesy of Durham, Anderson, and Freed

93 Queen Anne Lutheran Church,
Seattle, Washington:
red dossal for Pentecost

dossal is without folds and has a band of deep velvet at each side. Parallel traverse rods carry each dossal on its own track, concealed in the recessed area, so that only one is seen at a time. This is an effective way of mounting such a series, making it a simple matter to change from one dossal to another. It is a splendid use of the color sequences of the Church, particularly in a communion where the tradition of liturgical color use is strongly established.

Daniel Schuman

Although this book has concentrated primarily on Christian art, we should note that splendid work is being done in some of the synagogues and temples. A most unusual and spectacular use of needlepoint is the Torah curtain (Illustration 94) at Temple Israel in Tulsa, Oklahoma. The panels, designed by Hans Moeller, contain contemporary rendering of the ancient Hebrew

Daniel Schuman

94 Torah Curtain, Temple Israel, Tulsa, Oklahoma; Percival Goodman, architect;
with sculpture, "The Fruitful Vine," by Seymour Lipton;
(a) the Torah Curtain, designed by Hans Moeller;
(b) detail.

symbols, defined in heavy black lines of varying widths and enriched by glowing colors against a sparkling fabric of white. The strong, bold, angular lines are wonderful in relation to the "Fruitful Vine" sculpture above, and the Menorah and Eternal Light, by sculptor Seymour Lipton. The making of the Torah curtain is described by Rabbi Norbert L. Rosenthal as a cooperative venture—the artist directing and the lay people executing. Eight panels are involved; they were finished by the women of the congregation. The design was worked in needlepoint, a combination of both gros and petit point depending on the material used. The material is both wool and silk. Regarding the intensity and brilliance of the colors, Dr. Rosenthal says, "In some ways they seem to become more vivid with the years."

A great deal is being accomplished, both here and abroad, in the creation of fine church art and architecture, and the examples presented here are but a glimpse. A great deal of bad art and architecture is also being done in the name of religion. It is in the hope of encouraging an appreciation and use of art that is worthy that these examples are presented—not only in this particular chapter, but throughout the book.

Principles of Art and Design

Forms are but symbols; we should never rest in them, but make them the stepping stones to the good to which they point.
—EMMONS

Liturgical art in the service and adornment of the church is subject to the same principles which underlie works of art in other media. A work of art is of value when it stimulates and directs an aesthetic experience. In this sense, art is a practical activity which has played an important role in all religion and has been inspired by religion. Art is a necessity for the life of the church, since we are so constituted that we require stimulation and help in our aesthetic experience. The church uses art for her own enrichment, and must stimulate her religious intuitions for the continuance of her life. Geddes Mac-Gregor warns us that if the church should lack the vigor necessary to gain access to good art, she must use inferior art, such as Saint-Sulpice or its many equivalents.[1]

The standards by which works of art are judged today seem very far removed from the standards which dictated the art of the early Christian basilicas and the intervening ages. In every age, however, the role of art has been to *express:* the object may be expression of *feeling* or *understanding.* Susanne K. Langer defines all art as the creation of "expressive forms" or *"apparent forms expressive of human feeling."* [2] The important point with reference to our discussion is that good art requires something worthy of expression. The artist

[1] *Aesthetic Experience in Religion* (London: Macmillan & Co., 1947), p. 209.
[2] *Problems of Art* (New York: Charles Scribner's Sons, 1957), pp. 108-9.

181

must first feel and understand something of value to religious experience in order to transmit it in his work.

One of the greatest detriments to good art in all times is public response. This has often had a most depressing effect upon art in the church. Nowhere is art judged more subjectively or with more prejudice. We cannot hope to raise the level of church art without raising the level of appreciation and understanding on the part of the people who have a voice in its selection.

If genuine works of art are to be procured for the church, we must be trained to see beyond the styles of a particular time and place, and determine whether the deeper and more profound requirements for aesthetic experience in religion are present.

Principles of Aesthetic Form

Good design, if it is to be a work of art, is a discipline. It may appear to be a "happening," a spontaneous outpouring of the artist's vision and ingenuity, but there are certain underlying principles of art which the artist cannot ignore when carrying out this inspiration. Virtuosity cannot remedy a poor design, nor is technical proficiency enough by itself. At the same time, a fine design can be marred or negated by crude craftsmanship. How often we hear people say, "I know what I like," as though that were sufficient basis for forming a judgment as to the quality of a work of art. Taste is not infallible; there is such a thing as *bad taste,* and it is not scarce.

A work of art may be compared to a musical masterpiece, magnificently structured as in a Bach fugue—balanced, proportioned, with theme and variations skillfully composed and performed by an artist. DeWitt H. Parker describes six principles of aesthetic form which can be applied as criteria of good design. The first is organic unity, or unity in variety. The others are the principles of theme, thematic variation, balance, hierarchy, and evolution.[3] I would add the principle of rhythm, which Parker classifies as a variation of thematic repetition and balance. In some works of art, one of these principles predominates, and in others, another, but each is singularly important.

Organic Unity

The principle of unity dictates that each element of a design is necessary to its value, and the work contains no elements that are unnecessary. In the case of church needlework, many a design would be improved if the embroiderer knew when to stop! Once the design has achieved a successful organic unity, further embellishments tend to place a screen or obstruction between the work and the observer. The impact of the design may be weakened, and this is important in the case of church embroideries which are to be seen from a distance.

Theme and Variations

The principle of the theme refers to a dominant character which runs through the whole of the work. In every complex work of art, the characteristic value

---

[3] "The Problem of Aesthetic Form" in *Problems in Aesthetics,* ed. Morris Weitz (New York: The Macmillan Co., 1959), pp. 175-84.

Marion P. Ireland

95 Lectern antependium,
   Geneva Presbyterian Church,
   Laguna Hills, California,
   by Marion P. Ireland

of the whole is identified by some pre-eminent shape, color, line, melodic pattern, or meaning. If the design is intended to represent Pentecost, for example, the *spirit* of Pentecost should be present whether a particular symbol is used or not. This underlying character unites the various designs used on paraments and vestments. For example, the theme of Pentecost may be represented by flames, suggesting the appearance of the Holy Ghost to the apostles on the day of Pentecost: "And there appeared unto them cloven tongues like as of fire, and it sat upon each of them" (Acts 2:3). Flame colors rather than actual forms of flames may carry out this theme. The red paraments for the chapel at Occidental College, Los Angeles (Illustration 20*) illustrate this, with the form of a dove in variegated flame colors as a background for the symbols, and various layers of semitransparent materials overlapping to create the illusion of flickering light. A related example (Illustration 95) employs the flame theme with its characteristic of semitransparency as it mingles with the dove. Most of the fabrics used are opaque, but the transparency here is achieved by different colors, shades, and textures.

The theme may be an architectural motif, such as the trapezoid form which

*Pp. 40-41.

PRINCIPLES OF ART AND DESIGN

is repeated in a variety of ways in the First United Methodist Church of Garden Grove (Illustration 89*). The sloping walls form a trapezoidal shape or truncated arch, which is repeated as a theme in a series of levels leading up to the one upon which the altar is placed, and again in the opening for the sound chamber for the organ. The purple altar cloth reflects this theme in areas of red-violet and blue-violet, as a foundation for the symbols, (Illustration 91a†). A theme of sweeping curves is established by the exposed ranks of organ pipes, and repeated with a dramatic curve in the cut of both the white and the purple pulpit hangings (Illustrations 90b, 91a‡). The tubular framework on the ceiling of the Paul Gerhardt Church, Mannheim, Germany, establishes the theme which is repeated on the furnishings—the pews, altar, pulpit, and front. Each of the sets of designs for the paraments is based upon this theme (Illustrations 72b, 73a-j§).

Thematic variation is so closely related to the principle of the theme that I would not elect to classify it as a separate principle. The theme is not stated and restated always, but elaborated and embroidered (literally and figuratively, in the case of needlework), or repeated in a variety of ways. The "theme with variations" is familiar to all, but how often poor compositions in art or music are actually variations *without* a theme!

Balance

Balance is one of the most fundamental principles of design and is necessary whether there is symmetry or not. In designing paraments, balance must be achieved within the design and also in relation to the architectural design, particularly with reference to the chancel as a total design. Balance in color as well as form or line must be observed also, within the composition and as a part of the whole setting, especially when the paraments are seen in conjunction with stained-glass windows.

Chancel design includes the shapes, proportions, and placement of the furnishings—altar, pulpit, lectern, dossal, etc. Balance is of great importance to this total design. Perfect symmetry has found favor in the past as an assurance of a well-balanced arrangement, but some of the factors that contributed to a symmetrical arrangement have changed. The centrally located pulpit has all but disappeared, and the altar—which never lost its favored place at the center, in most settings—has come back to create the central focal point in most cases. A center altar often creates its own symmetry, with pulpit and lectern at either side, the simplest form of balance. The A-frame church, which has been popular in recent decades, tends to become static if symmetry is carried too far in the placement of furnishings and style of decoration. Some variation which achieves balance is often more interesting and satisfying. Good balance must be planned: symmetry may be a shortcut and moderation may appear to be the safest way. The most skillful artists and architects of our day, however, are not looking for the obvious solutions to balance; instead, they are achieving balance through diversity, and some of our finest churches are the result.

Some very effective innovations in the placement of the altar have been conceived by the architectural firm of Sövik, Mathre, and Madson. A very

*P. 171. †P. 174. ‡Pp. 173, 174 §Pp. 149, 150-51.

96 Cover designs, *Worship*, by Frank Kacmarcik, staff artist:
  (a) life-giving waters;
  (b) a Holy City;
  (c) the Community of Believers: Pentecost

96b

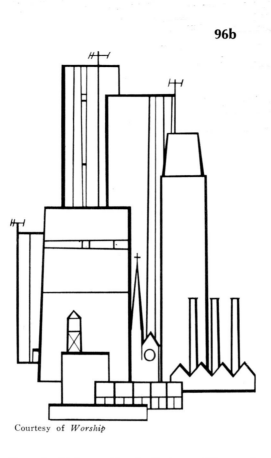

Courtesy of *Worship*

Courtesy of *Worship*

Courtesy of *Worship*

long altar in Trinity Lutheran Church, Lisbon, North Dakota (Illustration 9*) is placed at the far left of the chancel, with three antependia and a pair of tall candles placed at the left end of the altar. A tall vertical pulpit balances at the right. Overhead, a Trinity symbol establishes a central axis and stability for the whole chancel. A long, off-center altar is also used at Our Saviour's Lutheran Church in Austin, Minnesota (Illustration 11†), with well-proportioned altar covering, and at Olivet Lutheran Church in Fargo, North Dakota, where a long, vertical hanging on the pulpit balances a long, horizontal cloth on the altar at the opposite side (Illustration 132‡).

Churches designed by Hal C. Whittemore and Associates are also notable for their excellent balance. The First United Methodist Church of Garden Grove and the First United Methodist Church of Escondido (Illustrations 89, 16§) each exhibit a complex balance of shapes, lines, and textures.

Rhythm

Rhythm is a fundamental principle of classical Greek architecture, as well as in architecture and art of the present. A uniform repetition is pleasing to the senses, and adds stability upon which variations can be played. Recurring patterns, like the motion of waves or the columns of a colonnade, set up a rhythm of balance within a composition. Three effective examples are found in contemporary cover designs from the periodical *Worship* by Frank Kacmarcik (Illustration 96). The first represents the life-giving waters that flow

*P. 33 †P. 34 ‡P. 239. §Pp. 37, 171

Art Waldinger

from the side of the risen Lord, sending his spirit to gladden the city of God, enlivening, refreshing, and consoling men. The next shows a rhythmic pattern of buildings depicting the spirit of the Risen One working in the church and in the hands of man to build a holy city, a new community prepared to serve the Lord. The third, a rhythmic repetition of flames, illustrates thematic variation and balance.

A rhythmic character marks the abstract design of the pulpit fall made for the Trinity United Presbyterian Church of Santa Ana, California (Illustration 97b). The series of graphlike vertical lines of the embroidery is related to similar rhythmic series of lines in the wood carving on the face of the pulpit, and further carried out in the streaming lines of the stained glass. A series of rhythmic lines is used on a stole which is designed to suggest the Incarnation (Illustration 98)[4]: light penetrates darkness in a transition of colors from light (gold, yellow, and orange) to dark (violet and blue, the comple-

[4] Made for Dr. R. E. Palmer, Westminster Presbyterian Church, Lincoln, Nebraska.

Art Waldinger

97 Trinity United Presbyterian Church, Santa Ana, California:
stained glass by Jos Maes; paraments by Marion P. Ireland:
(a) interior;
(b) pulpit antependium

ments). The sacred monogram *Iota Chi* (Jesus Christ) proclaims him Light of the world.

A rhythmic treatment of a figure by means of the folds of a garment has long been a favorite of artists and sculptors. The thousands of sculptured figures on the great cathedrals of Europe carry out this rhythm in the lines of their garments, and in the rows of figures themselves. The frontal at St. Thomas Church, Stockholm-Vällingby, shows a regularly of rhythmic repetition (Illustration 8*), divided into seven draped panels. Two separate rhythms form a counterpoint at the Shepherd of the Hills Lutheran Church, Edina, Minnesota, by architects Sövik, Mathre, and Madson (Illustration 150†): the faceted planes of the brick wall and the row of sheep on the long tapestry by Jan Yoors. The shadowed and lighted planes form a pleasant background for the curved linear patterns of the tapestry.

Hierarchy

Hierarchy refers to the relative importance of the elements within the artwork. This is of particular consequence in the designing of church embroideries which are intended to convey a meaning. It should not be necessary to provide a printed description in order for the congregation to find the most significant elements of the design. The ornamentation may be of such delight to the embroiderer that the symbolism or theme is obscured.

Another kind of hierarchy is employed in the portrait iconography of Eastern Orthodox churches, and that is the traditional placement or progression of personages in the church in accordance with the Orthodox liturgy, and the concept of the building as an image of the cosmos.[5] The cupola represents the heavenly vault and is reserved for a picture of Christ Pantokrator (ruler of the universe). The Mother of God is shown in the eastern apse, and the story of the Incarnation is shown on the walls, beginning with the Old Testament patriarchs and prophets and including the apostles and evangelists, saints, doctors and teachers, etc., in prescribed order.

Matisse employed his own plan for portraying the Stations of the Cross (Illustration 22‡), breaking with tradition and arranging the various steps in a hierarchy with Christ the culminating figure. The figure of Christ on the cross is the obvious center of the sacred drama.

The theme of redemption through the birth and death of our Lord is portrayed in a pair of designs for the pulpit and lectern of the First United Methodist Church, Santa Monica, California (Illustration 99). The principle of hierarchy is observed in the prominence of a central, distinctive cross in each composition: a cross with upraised arms signifying birth for Advent, and a cross with arms sagging from its burden signifying death for the Lenten season. Subordinate to the crosses are symbols suggestive of the events—a manger with a star for the birth, and a crown of thorns and stormclouds with the hand of God pointing to the cross representing death.

An enthusiasm for symbolism often leads to a jumble of ideas competing for attention and endangering the prominence of a central theme. This zeal

[5] See Nicolas Zernov, *Eastern Christendom* (London: Readers Union, Weidenfeld and Nicolson, 1963), p. 279.
*P. 33. †P. 256. ‡P. 43.

98 Stole, "Incarnation," for Westminster Presbyterian Church,
Lincoln, Nebraska, by Marion P. Ireland

98

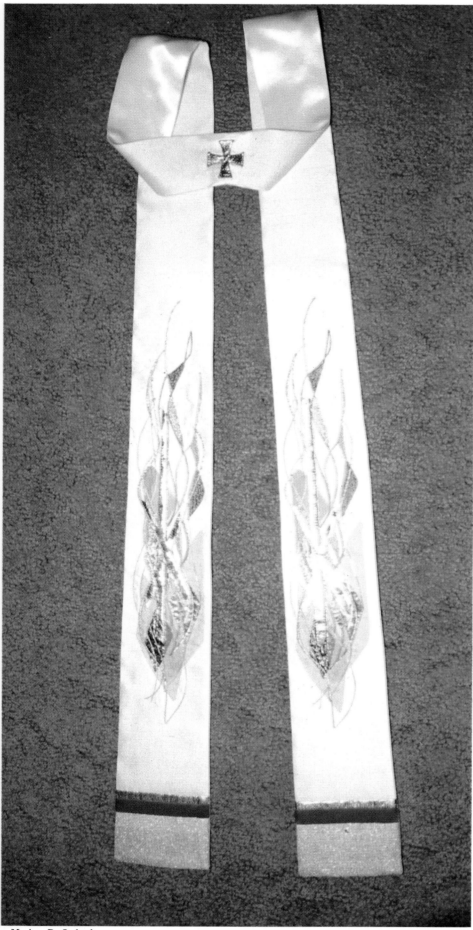

Marion P. Ireland

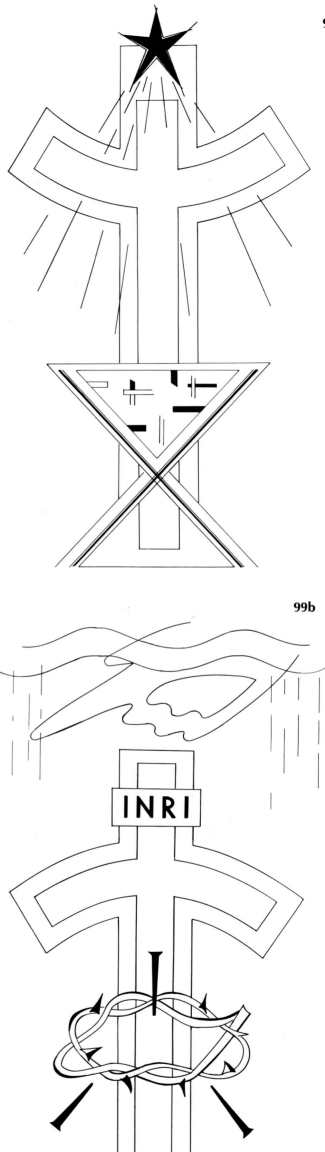

99b

99 First United Methodist Church, Santa Monica, California:
drawings for pulpit and lectern antependia by Marion P. Ireland:
(a) Advent; (b) Lent

often needs to be curbed. For example, in one conference with a minister and altar guild, after discussing various possibilities, ideas began to come forth like wildfire. One recalled that this was the oldest church of one of the oldest communities in the region, and therefore something of the historical element should be shown. Also the New England heritage of the denomination might be represented. Then too, since this was a coastal city, ships would be appropriate; groves and vineyards were also significant to the congregation. All very interesting ideas, but they obviously must be subordinate to a specific point bearing upon the liturgical purpose of the paraments.

Evolution

The principle of evolution in design involves a progression to a goal, wherein the eye is led to the climax or focal point through a series of lines, shapes, patterns, or colors. The goal toward which the arts and the liturgy progress is the altar, surrounded by the pulpit, lectern, font, stained glass, and other dominant features of the architecture. The direction proceeds from the nave to the altar. The wall behind the altar provides the setting for the Lord's table, which should be the most dramatic and compelling sight in the entire church.

This progression is represented in the tapestry by Marijke Neyens-Wiegman for St. Nicholas Church, Limburg, Netherlands (Illustration 149*). It provides the only focal point against a wood-paneled wall. Small figures are balanced in groups around the large central figure with upraised arms. The colors, mainly blue and purple, range slightly darker toward the bottom, and the eye is guided upward to the large figure.

Creating the Design

The artist who is trained in contemporary art is usually a long way ahead of the general public in his understanding and appreciation of what constitutes "good" art. By the time the public has learned what it is all about, the artist has gone on to something newer. This is also true of the trained church musician, who is requested (or ordered) to "use something we know"—a counterpart to the dull repetition in so much of church art. It is a real problem to bridge the gap between artist and congregation. It is also crucial to avoid faddishness and sensationalism in the search for art that is alive. A constant goal of reverence and dignity will safeguard the art from this impiety and eccentricity.

Effective steps may be taken to condition the congregation (and the artist) to a gradual and continuous process of learning to understand a form of art that is meaningful today. A new church building, of course, affords a direct and immediate experience. Before the building committee can become equipped to allow an architect the freedom to create a fine new church, the members must make an acquaintance with today's architecture and its relationship to the religious life of today. One enterprise that has helped admirably

*P. 255.

100 Sunday bulletins, by Sacred Design:
    (a) "This is my son";
    (b) "Come; for all is now ready";
    (c) "At your word I will let down the nets";
    (d) "According to his promise we wait for new heavens and a new earth."

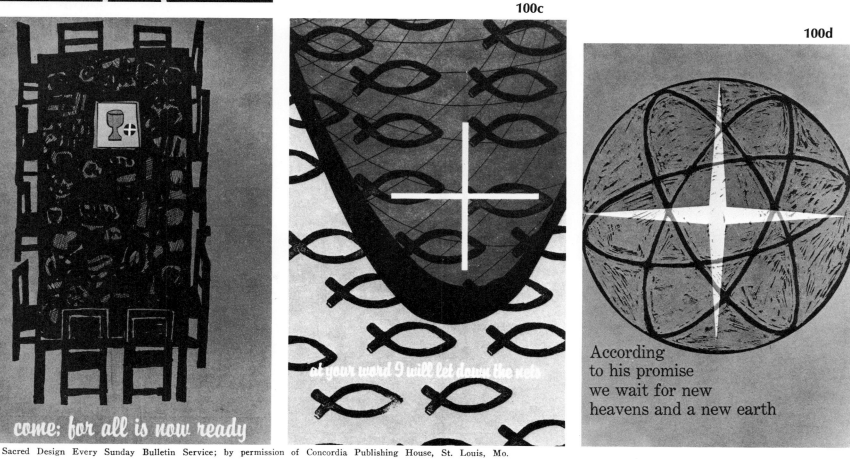

Sacred Design Every Sunday Bulletin Service; by permission of Concordia Publishing House, St. Louis, Mo.

in week-to-week education is the work of Sacred Design Associates Incorporated, a major segment of which is devoted to designing Sunday bulletins, with an interpretation of the design printed on the back cover. A sampling of their work is shown in Illustration 100. Their aim is to make each bulletin more than an order of service and calendar of events; they seek to put into visual form the *meaning* of the scriptural reference rather than simply the *setting,* relating the gospel to life, worship to mission, and the Church to the world.

    In addition to the success of this venture in attaining these goals, there is an added advantage in the changing progression of designs based upon sound principles of art and theology. The question does not arise as to whether an individual likes a particular design; therefore, it is not rejected before it ever gets off the ground. It becomes a prelude to the worship service, and each week the reader looks forward to more. The adoption of such a plan is to be recommended to any congregation that anticipates a new church building or the acquisition of items of liturgical art.

The aforementioned reference to the *meaning* rather than an illustration of the *setting* points directly to the difference between symbol and representation. We must search for the *essence* of that which we wish to portray, rather than a likeness of some particular object. How is the Lord's table different from some other table? How is an empty tomb to be his tomb? Is a dove a bird with outstretched wings, or does it lead to a conception of the Holy Spirit? What kind of fruit grows upon the Tree of Life? There are no easy answers to these questions.

The artist has two fields of responsibility in designing and creating paraments and vestments for church use: an understanding of the liturgical function and theological content required, and a working knowledge of the principles of good art. The former demands an appreciation of the use of decorative textiles for vestments set apart for a unique purpose. Both the liturgical use of the cloth and the subject matter of the design make demands upon the artist.

Many a devout churchwoman is well versed in the symbolism of the church and the use of vestments, but is unaware of the principles of art. In this case, the result is usually a slavish copying of traditional symbols without regard for their transplanting into a particular church setting, or their relationship to one another artistically, or the dominance of an underlying theme, aside from the theme of symbolism. Once glanced at and recognized, they are either dismissed and forgotten or are admired for their needlework.

Works that have fulfilled both the liturgical and the artistic qualifications with a fresh and creative approach will be looked at again and again, bringing forth a newer, deeper response each time. Often a work that lacks immediate appeal is one which grows upon the beholder and requires more participation on his part. This is an important part of creating a religious environment conducive to meditation and response.

Color Harmony

The purest and most thoughtful minds are those which love color the most.
—JOHN RUSKIN

The skillful use of color is partly intuitive and partly acquired knowledge. Tastes differ in what is pleasing and what is not, and there are so many variables involved that hard and fast rules cannot be set down that meet each situation. In the course of the past century and more, however, color has achieved the status of a science, which can be classified and measured. Colors, for example, have certain attributes or qualities that are recognized and that form the basis for all color harmony. Some colors are called "primary," such as red, yellow, or blue, any two of which produce another color when mixed together, and "secondary," such as orange, green, or violet, which are produced by mixing two primary colors.

Leonardo da Vinci was probably the first great color theorist; his *Treatise on Painting*, a collection of his notes which included advice on the use and characteristics of color, was first published in 1651. Isaac Newton designed the first of all color circles in the latter part of the seventeenth century, and in 1730 a German engraver, Jacques Christophe Le Blon, discovered the primary nature of red, yellow, and blue in the mixture of pigments.[1] Da Vinci had written of four primary colors, including green, although he surely would have known that it was compounded of blue and yellow. Several names stand out as contributors to the development of color harmony systems, but

[1] Faber Birren, *Color: A Survey in Words and Pictures, from Ancient Mysticism to Modern Science* (New Hyde Park, N.Y.: University Books, 1963), p. 143.

193

the greatest predecessor to the present best-known systems is believed to be M. E. Chevreul (1786-1889). He was director of the dye department of the famous Gobelin tapestry works, and his findings were based on exhaustive experiments in color research. His famous work, *The Laws of Harmony and Contrast of Colours*,[2] on the laws of simultaneous contrast, the harmony of adjacents, complements, split-complements, and triads, was published in 1839. During his 103 years, Chevreul influenced and inspired many artists, including the Impressionists, and his book sold in large numbers for over sixty years, translated into several languages and reprinted in many editions.

The two leading systems of color now in use are those developed by Albert H. Munsell (1858-1918) and a contemporary, Wilhelm Ostwald (1853-1932).[3] The serious artist will wish to understand each of these systems and principles of color harmony for the benefit of his art.[4]

Attributes of Color

Color is more than a name, such as red, blue, or yellow, and it must be regarded more specifically than simply light or dark, bright or dull. Furthermore, even the name of a color becomes unclear as it lies somewhere between two names. It is obvious, therefore, that these various characteristics or attributes of color must be organized into a working knowledge or system. A. H. Munsell based his system of color notation on three attributes by which colors can be measured and classified: hue, value, and chroma or intensity (Illustrations 101, 102). *Hue* is the name of the color; *value* refers to the lightness or darkness of the color (the white content called "tint" and the dark content called "shade"); *chroma* or intensity indicates the saturation of color.

Some colors have greater attention value than others, and they influence the part of the picture where they are applied. Full intensity occurs in a lighter value in some hues than others. The colors in the spectrum are at full intensity, and it is easily seen that yellow and yellow-green appear much lighter than red or purple at opposite ends of the spectrum. This is attributable to the relative sensitivity of our eyes to various wave lengths. We have a tendency to see blues and reds as dark, and yellows and yellow-greens as light. The most luminous point is almost in the very center of the spectrum: in dim illumination, the center moves over into the blue-green.

The Munsell system takes this into account as shown in Illustration 101: the chroma scales radiate in equal visual steps from the neutral axis (0 chroma) outward to the most saturated chroma (10, 12, 14, etc.) obtainable for a specific hue on a specific value level (Illustration 102b). The fractions indicated on the hue circle in Illustration 101a show the comparative values at which the various hues have their strongest chroma and the number of

[2] Recently republished in a new edition with introduction and explanatory notes by Faber Birren: M. E. Chevreul, *The Principles of Harmony and Contrast of Colors and Their Application to the Arts,* based on the first English edition of 1854, trans. from the first French edition of 1839, *De la Loi du Contraste simultané des Couleurs* (New York: Reinhold Corp., 1967).

[3] Munsell was American; Ostwald was born in Latvia, died in Germany, known as a German physical chemist and philosopher, winner of the Nobel Prize in chemistry (1909).

[4] See bibliography.

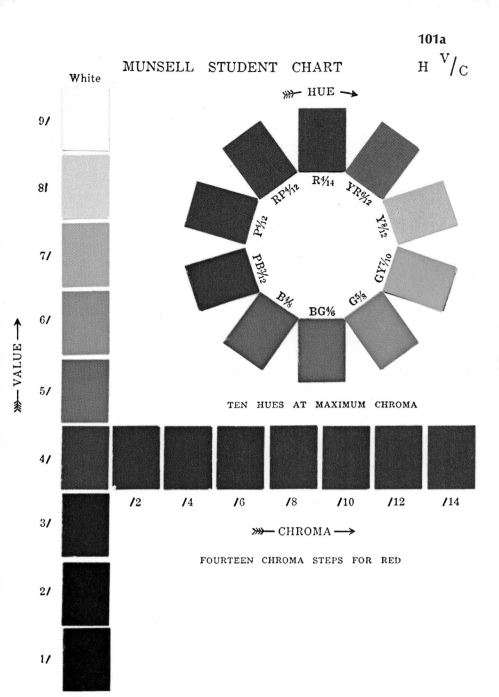

MUNSELL STUDENT CHART

White

VALUE →

9/
8/
7/
6/
5/
4/
3/
2/
1/

Black

HUE →

R⁴/₁₄
RP⁴/₁₂
YR⁶/₁₂
P⁴/₁₂
Y⁸/₁₂
PB⁵/₁₂
GY⁷/₁₀
B⁴/₈
G⁵/₈
BG⁶/₈

TEN HUES AT MAXIMUM CHROMA

/2 /4 /6 /8 /10 /12 /14

→ CHROMA →

FOURTEEN CHROMA STEPS FOR RED

Munsell Color Company, Inc.

101 Munsell Color System:
(a) Munsell Student Chart: hue, value, and chroma;
(b) Munsell Color Tree, showing yellow, red, and purple-blue

101b

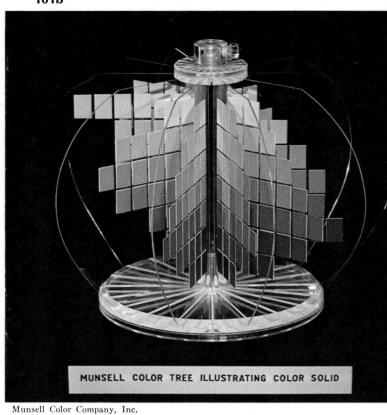

MUNSELL COLOR TREE ILLUSTRATING COLOR SOLID

Munsell Color Company, Inc.

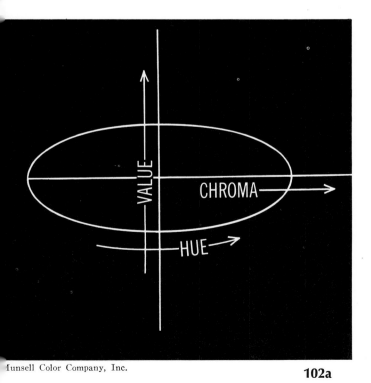

VALUE

CHROMA →

HUE →

Munsell Color Company, Inc.

102a

102b

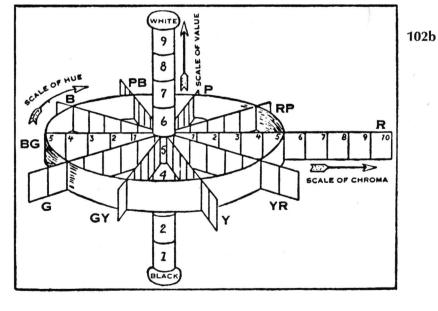

WHITE
9
8
SCALE OF VALUE
7
6
SCALE OF HUE
PB   P
B   RP
BG   R
5 4 3 2 1   1 2 3 4 5   6 7 8 9 10
5
4
SCALE OF CHROMA
G   GY   Y   YR
3
2
1
BLACK

SCALES OF HUE, VALUE AND CHROMA
IN RELATION TO COLOR SPACE

Munsell Color Company, Inc.

102 Munsell Color System:
(a) hue, value, and chroma;
(b) scales of hue, value, and chroma in relation to color space

103 Ostwald Color Tree

steps to the most saturated chroma: for example, red has the highest chroma (14) obtained at 4 on the value scale; blue-green has the lowest chroma (6), also at 4 on the value scale. The maximum chroma of yellow (12) is at 8 on the value scale. The Ostwald color tree (Illustration 103) places a maximum color saturation at 5 on the value scale, which has been equalized for every hue. An advantage to the Munsell system is that if a more saturated color for any hue is ever made, it can be accommodated into the system. In the case of the Ostwald system, the whole system would have to be revised. Since it is not possible to duplicate with pigments the purity of hue that we perceive in viewing a spectrum, Ostwald referred to his system as a system of semi-chroma (half colors).

Another comparison to be made between the two systems is with regard to the division of colors in the hue circle. Munsell divides the circle into five basic hues and five intermediate: (R) red, (YR) yellow-red, (Y) yellow, (GY) green-yellow, (G) green, (BG) blue-green, (B) blue, (PB) purple-blue, (P) purple, and (RP) red-purple. Ostwald based his system on four basic hues: red, yellow, green, and blue, and added intermediate hues to total twenty-four: yellow (1, 2, 3), orange (4, 5, 6), red (7, 8, 9), purple (10, 11, 12), blue (13, 14, 15), turquoise (16, 17, 18), sea green (19, 20, 21), and leaf green (22, 23, 24). One of the differences that arises between the two divisions of hues is in determining the complements of each; according to the Munsell hue circle, yellow is opposite, or the complement of, purple-blue, whereas the Ostwald hue circle has yellow opposite ultramarine blue, etc.

In applying the attributes of color to use, it is essential to consider each color individually and in its interaction with the others. The sunshine-shadow series is of great importance in determining the range of values within which to work. This is the variation produced on a single color surface: (1) in direct sunlight, (2) in daylight (skylight), without direct sunlight, and (3) in the shadows. The maximum interval our vision will accept and call hue and color constancy starts at a middle point (skylight or daylight), ranging from direct sunlight to shadow. Sunlight adds yellow as it lightens the value, and sky shadow adds blue as it darkens the value. Another aspect of the sunshine-shadow series is that a shadow is darker at the source than farther on. A greater range than the normal span from direct sunlight to shadow will separate; a narrower range will harmonize. Hence license plates are intended to have a great contrast in value, while interior decoration of a room calls for less. Accents, of course, require greater contrast. This is an important principle in designing paraments and vestments, depending on whether one wishes the colors to blend or to stand out. The values of the composition might well be kept within the sunshine-shadow series, and the principal symbolism might go considerably lighter or darker in order to separate it from its background.

Some colors are called warm (red, orange, and yellow) and have a tendency to advance. Others are called cool (blues) and tend to retreat. This is a generalization and depends on other factors, such as full intensity against a grayed background: the full intensity tends to advance over the grayed color. An important point to remember is that we seldom use just one single color in art, and therefore everything (hue, value, and intensity) is relative to the other hues, values, and intensities with which it is associated. We must speak of relative hue, relative value, and relative intensity when we consider color harmony.

Color is three-dimensional, and each dimension acts upon the other two. An optical illusion causes a dark, cool color to appear to advance when placed on a field of its own hue; a dark, warm color will appear to recede on a field of its own hue. Dark blue lettering on a light blue ground will stand out; light blue lettering on a dark blue ground will look like holes.

Complementary colors carry an after-image of each other. If we look closely at a strong color on a white paper, and then look away to another place on the paper, we will see the opposite or complementary color. When we wish to use a pair of complementary colors, they should not be of equal value and equal saturation, or there will be contrast in hue only. If we separate one from the other with a strong neutral, the optical conflict is resolved. This is what makes stained-glass windows effective: black separates the strong colors.

A restricted color range with respect to brightness value produces a feeling of unity, quite apart from hue. A scene done in saturated colors with high reflectance has spontaneity and gaiety, whereas a dark, low saturation scene has dullness and depression. As a relative area increases in size, its color is seen first. If the color is strong, a small amount will suffice; if weak, the area will need to be increased if equal attention is desired. The background, foreground, or surrounding area—any of these—could be the reference in relation to which the other colors are seen, and all hues, values, and chroma are influenced by this. In the case of liturgical paraments, the background materials (with the exception of white) are usually strong, in accordance with the colors of the Church year, and this must be reckoned with in the planning of the design and color scheme. Marc Chagall faced a similar problem in designing the stained-glass Jerusalem windows, symbolizing the twelve tribes of Israel, color-keyed to the text of Exodus 28:15-21.[5] The background colors of the windows are in groups of three each, in blue, red, yellow, and green, in the same order used by Jacob to designate the tribes. Chagall's solutions in handling this situation are worth studying by church textile artists.

Texture is not actually a color quality, but it is so closely related to these attributes that it should be considered, particularly in a discussion of textile art, where stitches and fabrics are the materials that bear the colors. A shining satin will have more attention value than wool, and a thick, dimensional, or raised area will advance more than a flat, dull one. There should be a consistency in texture, with variations and contrasts that are intentional for a certain desired effect.

Organization of Colors

Harmony of colors is often compared with harmony of music, both made up of measurable wave lengths—one of light and the other of sound. A particular musical note takes on its special character when sounded with others, forming a chord. A combination of colors also becomes a chord. A harmonious combination of color or musical sound has certain properties that can be identified: a relationship between parts; regular intervals within the hue circle or scale; form or direction; and balance (complementary colors, or tonic and dominant in music, for example). Dissonant and shocking combinations are the legitimate tool of the artist when he uses them intentionally and judiciously, in both color harmony and in music. A knowledge of color theory does not make a work of art, any more than a knowledge of grammar makes a poem. Color is a means of expression to the artist, as words are to the poet, to know and to select according to the desired effect. "It is analogous to familiarity with the grammar and vocabulary of a language, which makes speech possible but does not in the least guarantee that anything said will be worth listening to." [6]

Color harmony depends upon an orderly plan, whether the plan is extremely simple or complex. The spectrum is orderly, and from its structure we may select a plan. To ensure the success of our plan, we should determine what constitutes harmony. Something that is familiar is more apt to be harmonious to us than that which is strange. We must gradually become conditioned to

[5] Marc Chagall, *The Jerusalem Windows,* text and notes by Jean Leymarie, trans. by Elaine Desautels (New York: George Braziller, rev. ed., 1967), pp. xiv, xv. The step-by-step preliminary studies of Chagall for each window are valuable to the artist who plans to incorporate symbols into a contemporary composition.

[6] Albert C. Barnes, *The Art in Painting* (New York: Harcourt, Brace and Company, 1937); quoted by Egbert Jacobson, *Basic Color, An Interpretation of the Ostwald System* (Chicago: Paul Theobald, 1948), p. 102.

new ideas. Nature is our first model, and its colors are pleasing to us. If we are to accept the colors of nature as an ideal harmony, we must go beyond naming the hues and see the gradations of sunlight and shadows reflecting upon the colors of the objects, and we will find infinitely more variety than we see at first glance. Another natural phenomenon to which we are accustomed is the order of proceeding from dark ground to light sky. We find it difficult to visualize a picture that is dark and heavy at the top and light and airy at the base.

Harmony also exists when there is some quality that is held in common. To refer again to nature, blue exists in the sky and in the green of foliage. The blue of the sky is also reflected in the shadows that cling to each object out-of-doors. This common quality of some blue reflected in all colors out-of-doors gives us a clue to harmonizing even unrelated colors: a small amount of one common hue mixed with each of the hues creates harmony. Harmony also occurs if value is the quality held in common. We must not let our search for harmony lead us to dullness, however. Harmony is balance, and balance is the avoidance of excess.

In selecting a color harmony, it is necessary to consider the relative size of the area involved. A color scheme that would be pleasing on a relatively small pulpit fall might be overpowering in a huge tapestry behind the altar. In church textiles it is particularly important that the color scheme should be appropriate for the subject. A Crucifixion scene or symbol would be more suitable, perhaps, in low values and color saturation, while a Resurrection might be more effectively portrayed in colors high in value and chroma.

Before a project is begun, the general effects should be planned: whether warm or cool colors should predominate, whether the general effect is to be light and lively or dark and somber, whether the hues should be intense or weak. There should also be a predominant hue, the soloist around which the supporting harmonies are orchestrated. Liturgical embroideries start out with a predominant hue—the liturgical color of the season. In addition to this given condition, the principal colors of the chancel area must be taken into account, because these colors will be seen in large areas around the particular piece that is being planned.

The light source is crucial to whatever color combinations are used. Many a work of art looks splendid in the studio and turns drab when placed within the chancel. Not only will the colors of artificial light affect the colors of the cloth and embroidery, but also the light that comes through stained-glass windows. Insufficient light or a yellowish cast can rob a fine parament of its beauty. A white light of daylight quality will cause the least distortion of the various colors that might be used.

Monochromatic Color Scheme

A single hue is occasionally called for in church embroideries, and it need not be dull. Illustrations 97b* and 104 are two examples of gold on an off-white background. The creamy hue of the fabric is actually a close relative of gold in a high value, low intensity. The abstract design in Illustration 97b employs several variations of hue within the gold range and variations in chroma.

*P. 187.

Texture is also varied to a considerable degree, to lend depths of shadow and highlights. The materials which are appliquéd are allowed to ripple, and are padded in some places. Gold fringe was included at the request of the architect, to repeat the linear character of the abstract design and the wood carving on the pulpit. The abstract design worked in gold leather (Illustration 104) is also a monochromatic color scheme, worked almost entirely in a single shade of gold. The shapes and the method of applying them provide contrasts and accents through the reflective quality of the leather. The general character of the fragments of leather appears to be faceted.

It is possible to introduce subtle hints of analogous and complementary colors and still stay within a monochromatic scheme. Since the background of a liturgical hanging is strong and symbolic, a single dominant hue is sometimes desired. The artist must find other ways of introducing contrast and strength into the scheme.

Analogous Color Scheme

Colors that are adjacent on the color circle share a particular hue and are closely related. When combined in an analogous color scheme, one hue should dominate and the others support. While three, four, or even five hues may be grouped together, it is wise to keep the range within one third of the color circle or the analogy becomes lost because there is no longer a common hue. Red, orange, and yellow are related, since orange contains some of each, but when the range is extended to green, it has reached a complement and the relatedness is destroyed. The supporting hues should vary in value and saturation (chroma) from the dominant hue. The very fact that an analogous harmony is so closely related tends to make it monotonous or weak, unless the artist introduces contrasts in value, chroma, and even possibly in texture.

Analogous Scheme with Complementary Accents

This is a particularly satisfying color scheme for liturgical furnishings, because the background can be a part of the analogous harmony and the symbolism can be forcefully emphasized with a complementary hue. I find this color scheme appropriate for a Pentecost theme of flames on a red background, accented with blues, some of which have a high value and low intensity. Illustrations 20b and 20c* show the adaptability of this color scheme to the emotional quality of a Pentecost design.

Green liturgical hangings are also effective in an analogous color scheme with complementary accents, the strong green of the foundation color harmonized with shades and tints of blue, blue-green, and yellow-green. A rust or red-orange accent is effective here.

Complementary Color Scheme

A harmony of opposites, or complements, is preferred by many who find contrast especially satisfying. Although complementary colors are opposite on the hue circle, as far apart as they can be, there is a close relationship, proven by the fact that each hue creates the after-image of its opposite. Used together,

*P. 41.

104a

Marion P. Ireland

104 Contemporary stole in gold leather, by Marion P. Ireland;
(a) full length;
(b) detail

104b

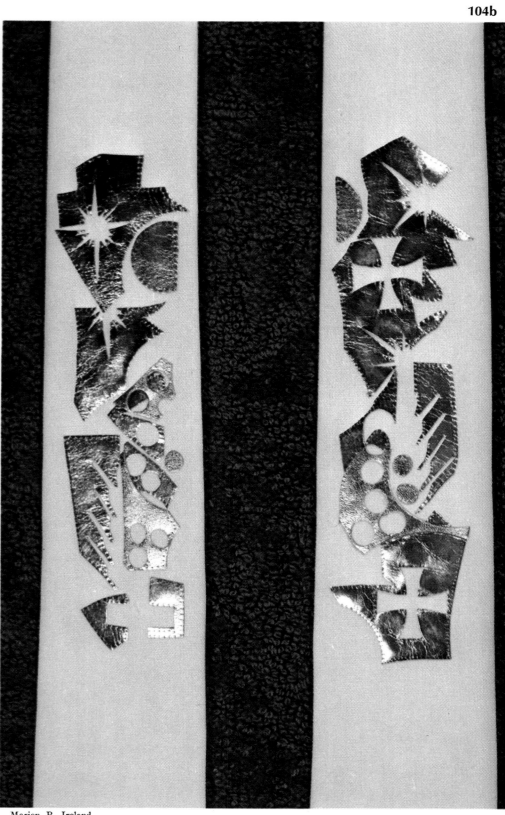

Marion P. Ireland

105 Paraments for Grandview Presbyterian Church,
Glendale, California, by Marion P. Ireland:
(a) pulpit antependium, Christmas theme:
the birth of the Christ Child;
(b) Communion table antependium,
Easter theme: Christ as victim and victor

105b

105a

Marion P. Ireland

Marion P. Ireland

they lack the unifying influence of any common hue. The fallacy of assuming that complementary colors are always harmonious lies in the fact that value and chroma are ignored. When complements are combined, they should not both be of full intensity, or in equal areas. Complements of full intensity, placed next to each other, cause a blurred image that is distracting. Furthermore, two complements of equal value, when mixed together in paint, produce gray. In unequal areas and strength (value and chroma) they work well, one serving as a foil for the other.

Variation

A variation of the analogous scheme is the use of adjacent relatives of one hue with adjacent relatives of the complement. In this case, one set of hues should be subordinate to the other. In any event, one set is bound to be predominantly cool colors while the other is warm. There should certainly be contrast in values or saturation. An example of this variation is the set of white paraments (Illustration 105) in which the predominating hue shades are blue and turquoise, with accents of pale rust, beige, red, and gold. The accents are in small areas and subdued, but being light in value, they advance from the darker background of the cross.

The white paraments for the First United Methodist Church of Garden Grove (Illustration 90*) are done principally in blues and orange, but adjacent accents were borrowed in small amounts of hot pink and gold. In the overall color scheme, however, the large expanse of very dark green carpet was

*Pp. 172-73.

106 Banner by Norman Laliberté

taken into account, thus relating the blue and green and resulting in an analogous use of complements. This variation is a "near complement" rather than a "true complement."

Split-Complement

Variety and richness can be obtained by the use of a split complement, a term which is self-explanatory. Instead of selecting the hue exactly opposite, the adjacent hues on each side of the opposite are used. Thus, blue-violet and red-violet would be used as the split complement of yellow. Norman Laliberté, without doubt one of the most adventurous and exciting modern colorists, exploits the possibilities of complementary variations to the full. His banner (Illustration 106) uses the whole family of orange and red-orange relatives in strong chroma, accented with an intense turquoise blue. This would appear to break all of the rules, but the results are exciting. The artist intersects the vivid colors with black lines to produce a glowing effect, and in some places uses orange-red and orange in equally full chroma to cause a vibration where the hues meet. Subtle accents of pink and lavender in a high value soften the effect with a strangely gentle quality. The strong black outlines and glowing character of the predominantly full chroma in orange produce a unity and harmony, enhanced by suggestions of the complement, blue, and by white.

Triads

Three hues equally spaced on the color circle form a triad. The triad of red, yellow, and blue consists of primary colors, and the alternate triad is of secondary colors. Since every hue can be made of the primary colors, there is plenty of room for error unless one of the three hues is selected as the dominant hue and the others are subordinate. Rivalry can be prevented between basic colors of the triad by using semitransparent net or nylon organza, lace, or stitchery over certain areas to screen colors.

With each of the major color schemes outlined above, it is helpful to analyze the color schemes of our own and others to increase our understanding of the strange and marvelous things that can happen when working with colors. Sometimes it seems that none of these plans was used, and in fact I have only suggested the most frequently used systems. Usually, concealed by variations and subtleties, an order and harmony appear *if it is a genuine work of art*. Otherwise, there is chaos.

People largely react to color with their *emotions* rather than their *minds*. The *mood* character of any given project may be anticipated by the general color quality planned. Joy, sadness, repose, anticipation, strength, are some of the moods a religious embroidery might need to depict or reflect. It is generally accepted that red, orange, and hot pink are vibrant, exciting, and generally positive; lavendar and purple are sad; blue and green, reposed, quiet, and unworried; yellow, a happy color, optimistic—and so on. These suppositions are not foolproof, and mood objectives might be obtained through surprisingly different directions. However, a definite *mood* should be agreed upon in the beginning and all color sketches should be judged on how well they achieve the desired *mood*.

Textile Arts: The Needle and the Loom

To cultivate the sense of the beautiful is one of the most effective ways of cultivating an appreciation of divine goodness.
—BOVÉE

An awareness of the unique possibilities inherent in threads and fabrics enables the artist to see potentials in other media and times which may be applied to textile art. Medieval manuscripts, for example, are an abundant source of decorative invention, from which to launch a refreshingly new and exciting design. The very fact that it is to be transformed into textures and stitches prevents it from resulting in a copy of a flat, painted surface. The special character of stained glass, involving pieces of color, suggests new ideas for the appliquéing of pieces of cloth. The important point to remember is that a work of art must be true to the character of the particular medium that is to be used. Let cloth be cloth, glass be glass, and paint be paint. If the design is better suited to stained glass, it should not be imitated in embroidery. It may well *suggest* stained glass as a part of the intended psychological effect of the design; it need not *imitate*.

There are so many effects that can be obtained in fabric and threads that cannot be done as well in other media that the artist must consider and exploit these special features if he is to make the most of his art. Fabric is essentially thread, and there is an endless variety of textures and gradations: rough, smooth, silky, coarse, fine, dull, shiny, bulky, metallic. The threads may be combined in any number of ways: woven or pressed into fabric, embroidered or woven into design. Dimension is one of the features of contemporary stitchery—the texture obtained by the use of thick, bulky threads or piling up of fabrics and stitches to strengthen and accent the composition. Texture is also possible in weaving, a quality that lends itself well to a harmonious relationship with the whole church: the walls, wood, sculpture, glass, etc.

Textiles have a unique character of pliancy—the rise and fall, or draping quality—not found in other media. A textile may be sheer and almost transparent or thick as a carpet. In fact, carpets are important decorative features in the combined textile art of some very outstanding new churches, such as the carpet of abstract design, hand woven for St. Paul's Cathedral, in Peoria, Illinois (Illustration 85*) and the blue figured carpet leading to the high altar of Guildfold Cathedral in Surrey, England (Illustration 67b†).

Color effects can be achieved in special ways in textile art, as a part of the background fabric and pattern in weaving. The colors may be mixed as paints are mixed, by combining threads of various shades and hues, so that the resulting colors are seen as an optical mixture similar to the style of painting developed by the Neo-Impressionists, called "divisionism" or "pointillism." The leading exponent of this style, Georges Seurat (1859-1891), evolved a system of placing his paint in small dots of contrasting colors, breaking down the colors into their component parts, so that the bright yellow-green of grass, for example, containing reflections from the sky, is juxtaposed with reddish-purple in its shadows. The weaver or embroiderer might well explore this discovery in relation to threads, which blend optically while still retaining their individual hues. The whole process of creating a work of textile art involves a threefold approach: design, color harmony, and technique. It is this third approach which is to be found among the varieties of textile ornamentation.

Textile arts may be broadly classified in two groups: (1) ornamentation applied to a ground fabric, and (2) ornamentation woven as a part of the fabric. In the first group, various techniques are included such as stitchery, appliqué, a combination of the two, collage, and textile paints or dyes, including stenciling, batik, printing, etc. The second group includes weaving of fabrics, tapestries, and carpets. All these methods are employed in church textiles; a selection of examples is presented here to illustrate some of the many possibilities for contemporary use and the imaginative and skillful use that various artists have made of these techniques.

Applied Ornamentation

There is a new interest in textile art through the growing popularity of stitchery and collage. Although the term "stitchery" really means embroidery, it implies a greater freedom for creativity. All types of traditional stitches are used, plus a great deal of invention. The difference between today's creative use of stitches and that of the past is the lack of limitation on regularity of stitches, varieties of threads and materials used today. The same stitch may be

*P. 165.   †P. 142.

sometimes large and sometimes small, even or irregular, all within the same area or line. Texture is often attained by piling up threads, materials, or stitches one upon another. This freedom of invention and spontaneity tends to give a designer a false sense of security and misleads the hobbyist into feeling that no particular knowledge of basic embroidery is necessary. This may result in poor design and clumsy rendering.

True artists who have successfully executed contemporary needlework are marked by a discipline, skill, and knowledge of good design. They are instilled with creativity and originality. It is to these artists that the church must look for a satisfactory expression of religious textile art in our time. Many books have been written in recent years to guide the artist in the basic skills of needlework and also to suggest new, creative ways to employ these techniques, some dealing with embroidery in general and others with emphasis on a particular phase.[1]

Fortunately church embroiderers are no longer under pressure to use only the so-called "liturgical" brocades in making paraments and vestments, and to finish them off with the inevitable fringe. As a matter of fact, it is relatively seldom that these materials are used now, and when they are it is for a particular reason, such as the desire for a figured background as part of the composition, or for a relationship to other art within that church—stained glass, carvings, etc.[2] The artist is now at liberty to compose a total design, selecting the materials and textures that will be most effective, rather than to impose a figured pattern upon the design simply because it has come to be regarded as traditional.

Basic Embroidery Stitches

Embroidery stitches may be classified broadly into two groups: (1) flat, looped, knotted, and chain stitches, and (2) couching, or the laying of one thread or yarn by means of overlapping it with another. Couching is particularly useful in ecclesiastical work, not only for outlines and fill-in, but also for covering the edges of appliquéd pieces of material and separately embroidered pieces attached to the background fabric. A variety of stitches including appliqué is used in the joyous banner "His Name Shall Be Called Emmanuel" by Sister Helena Steffens-Meier, Alverno College, Wisconsin (Illustration 107). A spatial effect is attained by the use of intricate patterns of stitches in the foreground and subtle shading in the distance. Illustration 108 shows a more formal use of embroidery stitches on altar frontals and pulpit hangings for St. Mark's Episcopal Church in New Canaan, Connecticut, by Leah Fitz-Gerald. The row of wheat embroidered on the green frontal is surmounted by an *Iota Chi* (Jesus Christ), signifying his reign over all nature. The fabric of the green set is linen. The red woolen frontal represents Pentecost with a "mighty rushing of wind," with swirls of gold cord converging on a triangle of gold leather in the center, signifying the Trinity. The passion flower, crown of thorns, and nails are worked on the purple set, which is of a synthetic material.

[1] See bibliography.

[2] In studios I have visited abroad, where contemporary vestments are being made by fine artists, the possession and occasional use of "liturgical" brocades were a source of some embarrassment, as though it were a reproach to their positions as pioneers of a new day.

AND HIS NAME SHALL BE CALLED EMMANUEL
GOD WITH US MIGHTY ONE

Courtesy of the artist

107 Banner, "His Name Shall Be Called Emmanuel," appliqué and stitchery by Sister Helena Steffens-Meier, O.S.F.

108a

108 Frontals for High Altar,
St. Mark's Episcopal Church,
New Canaan, Connecticut,
designed by Leah Fitz-Gerald:
(a) green frontal;
(b) purple frontal;
(c) red frontal

108b

108c

109b

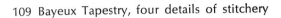

109 Bayeux Tapestry, four details of stitchery

109a

Jean Bessé

Jean Bessé

Crewel Embroidery

Crewel is primarily an embroidery done with wool on a linen or canvas ground. The name "crewel" (or "crule" or "cruell") was associated with the techniques, motifs, and traditions of sixteenth- and seventeenth-century England, but applied also to any technique where a two-ply yarn was used. The Bayeux Tapestry[3] represents an example of wool on linen that precedes the term "crewel" but may be included in that style "after the fact." Various stitches are employed, one being called the Bayeux stitch because of its effective use in this important work.[4] The Bayeux stitch covers the ground quickly and economically, the wool threads being laid on the face of the fabric and not worked as satin stitch, where an equal amount of thread lies underneath. The surface yarns are couched down with stitches at right angles to the surface threads, or they may be couched at an angle or in a geometric

[3] (1066-1077). See Illustration 53, p. 117.
[4] Jacqueline Enthoven, *The Stitches of Creative Embroidery* (New York: Reinhold Publishing Corp., 1964), p. 171.

TEXTILE ART IN THE CHURCH

109c

Jean Bessé

109d

Jean Bessé

pattern. Details of the embroidery of the Bayeux Tapestry (Illustration 109) show some of the various uses of embroidery stitches, which include chain, stem, split stitch, and couching. Plied woolen thread in yellow, green, red, blue, and black is worked onto a white linen ground. It is an excellent source of ideas for the modern embroiderer.

110 Canvaswork hanging, "Mother and Child," by Bucky King

Canvas Embroidery

One of the most durable forms of embroidery is canvas work, the distinctive feature of which involves the counting of threads. The stitches may cover the entire ground including the pattern, or parts of the background may be left exposed. A background material of even weave such as linen or canvas is used. A canvas embroidery by Bucky King (Illustration 110) illustrates several kinds of stitches, covering the entire background in a handsome contemporary design. The wool embroidery threads have been repeated in a knotted fringe, and the embroidery has been mounted to a fabric background.

The stitches for counted thread and canvas embroidery fall into three main groups: flat stitch, cross stitch, and embroidery stitches which are adaptable to this technique for special effects. Flat stitches—called tent or needlepoint or,

111 Wall hangings designed
by Anna-Lisa Odelqvist-Kruse:
(a) embroidery worked in flax;
(b) tapestry for the Lutheran School
of Theology in Chicago

111a

111b

when stitches are diagonal, petit point—include a number of variations, such as
Gobelin, named for the Gobelin tapestry-weaving technique which it resembles. Two fine canvas embroideries worked with flax by Anna-Lisa Odelqvist-Kruse are shown in Illustration 111.

TEXTILE ARTS: THE NEEDLE AND THE LOOM

112a

112 Kneelers, Guildford Cathedral:
(a) Guildford Diocesan Arms;
(b) St. John;
(c) music;
(d) shipbuilding

112b

Canvas work, or needlepoint, is particularly appropriate for communion kneeling cushions because of the durability of this type of embroidery—wool solidly stitched to a sturdy backing, with no long stitches to pull out or snag. The kneelers for Guildford Cathedral were made by volunteers, both men and women, under the direction of Lady Maufe, who made most of the designs herself or supervised the designing. Illustration 112 illustrates

TEXTILE ART IN THE CHURCH

112c

112d

the diagonal division which is the central theme of each design, using the Guildford colors, blue and white, to portray earth and sky, with the hill on which the cathedral stands. In addition to designs pertaining to the church and its religious life, many secular occupations and trades have been symbolized, such as ship building.

TEXTILE ARTS: THE NEEDLE AND THE LOOM   215

113 Kneelers, St. Mark's Episcopal Church,
New Canaan, Connecticut, designed by Erica Wilson and Ruth Noble:
(a) needlepoint cushions for high altar, corner design, thorn tree;
(b) needlepoint wedding cushion;
(c) kneeler for high altar steps

113a

The needlepoint cushions for St. Mark's Episcopal Church at New Canaan, Connecticut (Illustration 113), were designed by Erica Wilson[5] and Ruth Noble. The designs for cushions on the high altar steps were adapted by Millie Holmes. An 85-foot length of kneelers around the high altar rail was worked by 67 women of St. Mark's over a period of ten months. The project is described in a booklet, "St. Mark's Episcopal Church," published by the church:

These cushions were designed by a professional designer to be in harmony with the contemporary feeling of the architecture, reredos and windows. The concept of a flowing background with superimposed designs is unique to this church. To enhance this unbroken effect, the work was mounted on cushions each of which reach from one altar rail opening around a corner to the next opening.

The four corners show the tree grown from a mustard seed, the thorn tree, the fig tree (Illustration 113a), and the barren fig tree.

[5] Author of *Crewel Embroidery* (New York: Charles Scribner's Sons, 1962).

TEXTILE ART IN THE CHURCH

Scutti Photography

Scutti Photography

114 Needlepoint kneelers, high altar
of St. Paul's Cathedral,
Peoria, Illinois

Photo by Jim Walker

A centrally situated high altar set within a square, enclosed by a communion railing, is greatly enhanced with contemporary kneelers at St. Paul's Episcopal Cathedral, Peoria (Illustration 114). The kneeling cushions were done by the women of the parish, and the designs represent many of the occupations and work of man, along with the symbols of the Eucharist—wheat and grapes. They were designed by William Donaldson, who also designed the hand-woven carpet.

A coordinated plan for the vestments, paraments, and kneelers for St. Thomas-in-the-Fields Episcopal Church, Gibsonia, Pennsylvania, is described in an article "The Work of My Hands, Wherein I Glory" by Bucky King.[6] The designs were the joint endeavor of Eliza Miller, artist-sculptress, who also designed the pulpit, lectern, font, and sanctuary candlesticks, and Janet de Coux, sculptress, who designed the black pearl Canadian granite altar, carved wooden Christus Rex, and other artworks for the church. A creation theme is carried out on sixteen rail kneelers, for three sides of the communion rail, approximately 53 feet in length. The unifying symbol on each kneeler is a tongue of flame, symbolizing the Holy Spirit in the New Testament and the Law of Moses in the Old Testament. Each kneeler has its own design in addition. Over twenty kinds of stitches were used, including tent, Hungarian, Florentine, Gobelin, mosaic, rice, straight cross, and others, the Parisian stitch being used for the background. The work was done by the combined efforts

[6] *Christian Art*, III (February, 1966), 4-5.

of women from St. Thomas with the assistance of Presbyterians, Roman Catholics, and Lutherans—a coordinated effort in more ways than one.

Machine Embroidery

Machine embroidery has now achieved respectability as a legitimate technique in the art of embroidery, because of its own particular merits—its versatility, spontaneity, and practicality. Prejudice on the grounds that only hand embroidery is proper for church use is quite as unfounded in this day and age as the insistence on only hand-hewn logs for modern church architecture. People often greatly admire an embroidery and then ask, "Is it all hand embroidered?" When told that an embroidery machine was used, the work is given a scornful glance and dismissed as cheap and unworthy (or even worse, "commercial").[7] Fortunately, this reaction is not universal, for many opportunities for creativity would be closed without this valuable asset.

The possibilities and versatility of machine embroidery are just beginning to be explored, and even within the industry the full scope is not realized.[8] There are not only household sewing machines but also industrial machines made specially for certain types of embroidery which depend on professional skill for satisfactory results. Bonnaz is basically a chain stitch, and is useful for outlines, filling, cording, chenille, and a wide variety of other results. The industrial monogramming machine (a zig-zag or satin-stitch machine such as the Singer or Meistergram) is capable of far more flexibility than the domestic machines which are designed to do double duty with straight sewing. Both hands are free to guide the cloth, as the width of the stitch is controlled by the knee and the speed is operated by a foot pedal. There is no feed under the cloth, so the operator may make the embroidery as thickly raised or as flat as desired, and the width of stitch can be varied gradually or abruptly without taking a hand from the work. A number of the embroideries illustrated on these pages were done, at least in part, on these machines, as indicated in the text (Illustration 115).

There are several kinds of home-type domestic sewing machines which are designed for embroidery as well as straight stitching, using both pre-set and variable widths of stitch as well as freestyle stitching. Some wonderful effects have been obtained in the hands of ingenious artists. Everett K. Sturgeon used machine embroidery for his experimental burse (Illustration 116). The burse appears to be handwork, but the artist says: "I *do not* try to get a hand-worked look with the machine; that would be false. The pleasure of

[7] Those who believe that there is a special virtue in painstaking toil required for hand embroidery might be more impressed with machine embroidery if they were to learn to operate specialized embroidery machines. It is standard procedure in the professional training of a Bonnaz operator to spend eight hours a day doing embroidery exercises on paper towels before being promoted to unbleached linen scraps. I spent a number of months at the Los Angeles Trade Technical College several years ago learning Bonnaz work in order to discover the variety of effects of which my Lintz and Eckhardt embroidery machine was capable. The same kind of rigorous and tedious training is given for operating monogramming machines, such as the Meistergram.

[8] Sales representatives of industrial monogramming machines are apt to say that all the machine will do is monograms; however, attention is called to the number of illustrations in this book where large shaded areas, such as doves, open books, lambs, etc., are shown for appliqué, and even for free, abstract stitchery. This is also true of domestic sewing machines; the persistence of the embroiderer can command the machine to a performance that the manufacturer never anticipated.

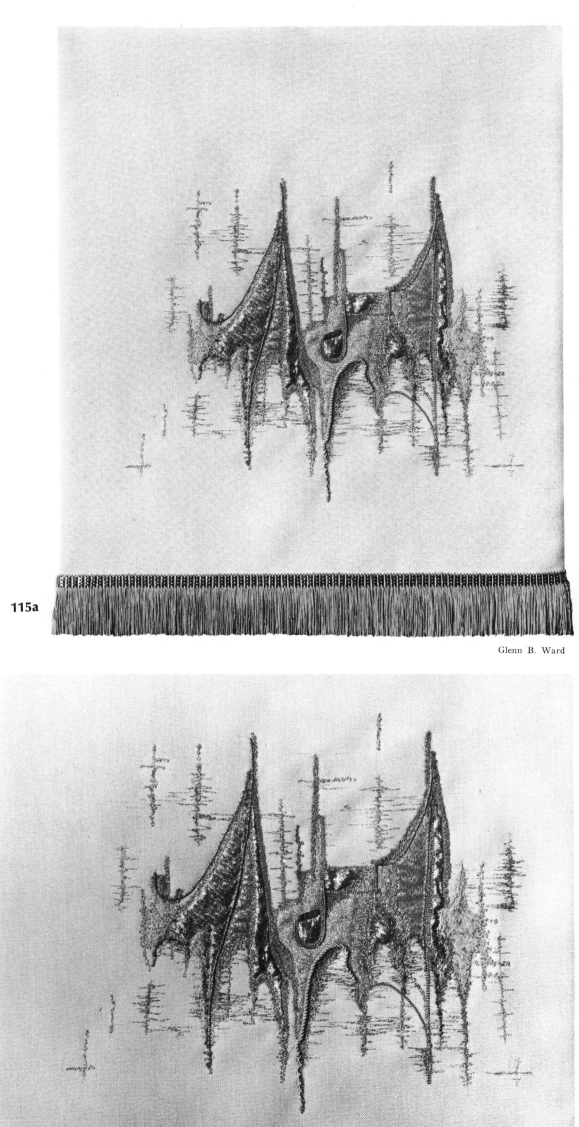

115a

Glenn B. Ward

115b

Glenn B. Ward

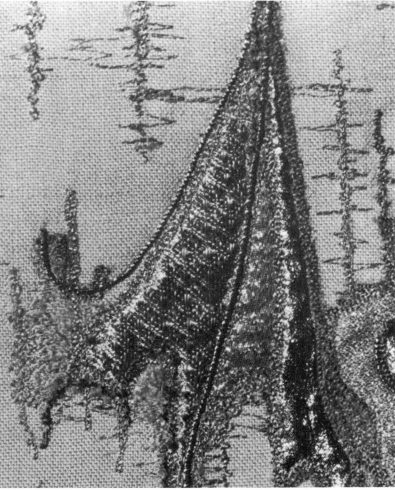

Glenn B. Ward   Glenn B. Ward

115 Pulpit antependium, Trinity United Presbyterian Church,
    Santa Ana, by Marion P. Ireland.
    Appliquéd gold fabrics, Bonnaz and Meistergram machine embroidery on coarse
    monk's weave fabric; handcouched cord:
    (a) full hanging, (b, c, d) details

116

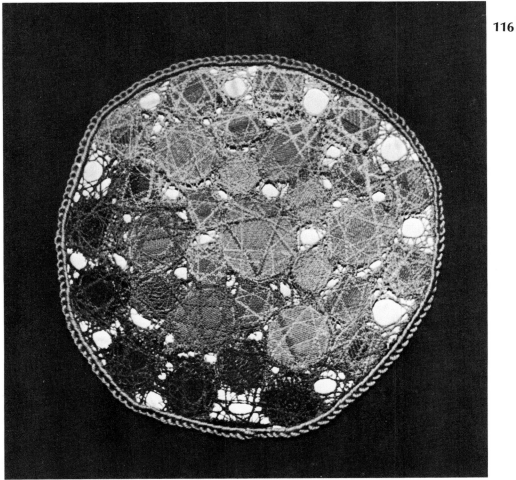

Courtesy of Bucky King

116 Machine embroidery by Everett K. Sturgeon;
    experimental burse: free machine embroidery and appliqué, orange, magenta,
    on dark red linen background

Libraria

the power tool is that it gives its own effects. I have tried to see how far and to what limits I could push the machine."

Appliqué

Appliqué is one of the most effective methods of embroidery, particularly for churches, where it must be seen from a distance. Great variety is possible, with or without additional surface embroidery, by machine or by hand. An exceedingly intricate example of extraordinary skill in both onlaid and inlaid (reverse) appliqué is shown in the wall hanging in Raus Church-house, Sweden, designed by Anna-Lisa Odelqvist-Kruse (Illustration 117). The wall hanging is done in linen appliqué, embroidered with linen thread, in rich, warm tones of reds—ranging from deep violet-reds to red-orange, with contrasting accents of emerald and lime greens and very pale green, with black. A circular geometric pattern interlocks like the mechanism of a clock, and a surface pattern of rectangles and squares contributes texture to this skillfully planned composition. Surface stitchery is used sparingly for linear detail.

A design may be completely successful when no decorative stitchery at all is used and the composition is made up of solid color areas, without

TEXTILE ART IN THE CHURCH

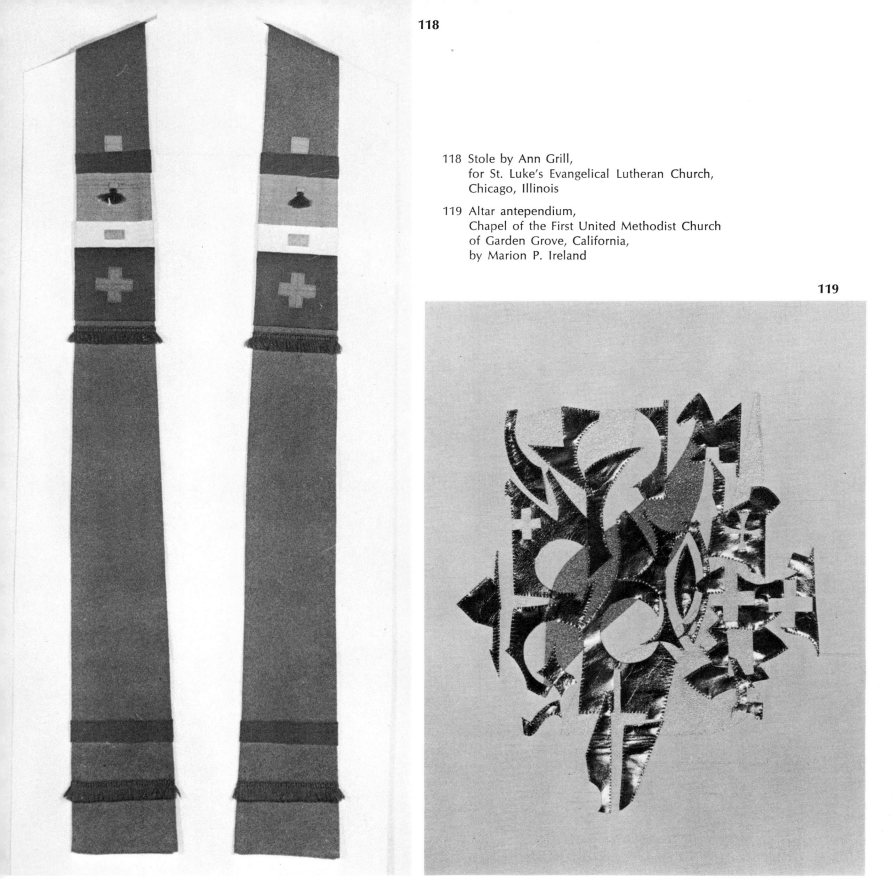

118 Stole by Ann Grill,
for St. Luke's Evangelical Lutheran Church,
Chicago, Illinois

119 Altar antependium,
Chapel of the First United Methodist Church
of Garden Grove, California,
by Marion P. Ireland

linear definition. The work of Ann Grill is notable in this respect (Illustration 118). Her designs have dignity, simplicity, and flawless technique. The color harmonies are subtle, and the fabrics are appropriate for the graceful folds of the eucharistic vestments. The appliquéd fabrics are laid by hand without visible stitches, so that no outline appears.

In applying leather, the stitches form an attractive indentation. This feature was used as part of the pattern on an altar cloth for the chapel of the First United Methodist Church of Garden Grove (Illustration 119; see Illustration

120 Red paraments, Geneva Presbyterian Church,
Laguna Hills, California, by Marion P. Ireland

Marion P. Ireland

104*). The relationship between the abstract design and the setting is shown in Illustration 92† to harmonize with abstract sculpture in the chapel. The design is worked in gold kidskin, over a free-form foundation of pale gold metallic fabric and silver-white metallic fabric, on a rough-textured white background. Shades of gold form a border at the bottom edge. The gold leather is soft and pliable, and reflects light in fascinating ways. In places the edge is not sewn down at all, as can be seen in detail (Illustration 119), relieving the monotony that would have resulted from completely outlined shapes. Some areas are padded, to create greater contrasts of light and shadow. Negative shapes are used, where I had cut out crosses and circles, creating a design in reverse. The natural graining of the leather adds texture and richness. The idea for the design originated with an assortment of shapes left from leather pieces which I had used for other embroideries. I visualized an abstract sculpture of gold leather, and the bronze work in this chapel provided the opportunity I was looking for to bring the idea into reality.

Leather was used along with a variety of fabrics in two sets of paraments for Geneva Presbyterian Church, Laguna Hills, California, William L. Pereira, architect (Illustrations 120, 121). The Old and New Testaments are represented

*P. 201.   †P. 176.

TEXTILE ART IN THE CHURCH

Marion P. Ireland

on the two red antependia for the Communion table, with a burning bush on
the left and the true vine on the right: both the bush and the vine are of
appliquéd leather. An effect of transparency and light is obtained with the use
of some nylon net, but principally through an interplay of different colors,
textures, and patterns of materials. The pulpit hanging for this red Pentecost
set is shown in Illustration 95*. The white set of paraments symbolizes the
Nativity and the Resurrection, with a golden star over the manger and a gold
Iota Chi to represent Christ victorious over death. In the Nativity, the manger
is of burlap supported by cross bars of suede leather—animal skin, suggestive
of the animals associated with the manger. Both Mary and Joseph are clothed
in dull, simple fabrics, but a radiant glow spills over on to them from the light
of the manger of Christ, the Light of the world.

The subject of the empty tomb has fascinated me for some time. I mentioned earlier, "What kind of tomb was it?" The *real* question is, "What
happened at the tomb?" I have shown only an entrance, radiant with light
bursting forth from it. The colors go darker toward the ground, where they
meet the shadow. The sacred monogram casts a shadow of a cross in the darkness which is suggestive of the stone that was rolled away. On a hill in the

*P. 183.

122 Banner, "Mother and Child," by Margaret Dickinson; Christmas banner for Grandview Presbyterian Church, Glendale, California

distance the three crosses stand, now empty. Incarnation and redemption are the themes symbolized here.

A lovely appliquéd "Mother and Child" Christmas banner was made for Grandview Presbyterian Church, Glendale, California, by Margaret Dickinson (Illustration 122). A handsome effect was achieved on a rough-textured back-

123 Banner, "Blue Madonna,"
by Norman Laliberté

ground material by drawing threads at intervals, allowing the light to come through. Several inches of threads were drawn from all four sides and knotted into fringe. The appearance is very similar to a handwoven fabric. A gentle dignity pervades the composition of simple applique laid with exposed edges, in keeping with the fringed borders. Accents of long, prominent jewels highlight the halos and sweeping lines of the garments. The hot pinks and pale lime greens harmonize well with the dull brick walls of the church.

Appliqué is sometimes applied by machine with joyous abandon. The banners by Norman Laliberté, designed to be seen from a distance, present a vigorous effect in design, color scheme, and rendering (Illustrations 42, 106,* and 123). When viewed along the walls of the nave in the Rockefeller Chapel at the University of Chicago, this is obviously *cloth*. The designs are made up of pieces of cloth, and the raveled or frayed edges reveal the basic stuff

*PP. 69, 203.

124 Lectern marker, First United Methodist Church of Garden Grove,
by Marion P. Ireland

125 Chancel area of the Lutheran Church of the Master,
   Lancaster, California; Power and Daniel, architects; paraments by Marion P. Ireland

—the threads from which the cloth is made. The collage banners utilize all sorts of materials, from tangles of thread to thick yarns, beads, and bells, so that the figures emerge from the cloth background in a third dimension. Laliberté's use of rich, glowing colors and subtle harmonies is discussed above.[9]

Fabrics of various patterns may be applied to contribute details of design in place of embroidery stitches. The red stole and lectern marker (Illustration 124) designed for Pentecost are appliquéd with a flame design made of novelty brocades and metallics. A wavy pattern of magenta and the same fabric in red-orange are laid in such a way that the wave pattern continues through the change in color, giving an effect of transparency and intertwining flames.[10] A multicolored metallic fabric and a dull red satin add variation to the flames, and an irregular swirl of couched gold cord is used for highlight. The wavy-patterned brocade is repeated on the upper part of the stole, to add interest to the portion that is seen when the minister stands behind the pulpit.

Effects of distance and foreground can be attained by the use of appliquéd shapes in the background and detailed stitchery in the foreground of the design. It should be mentioned that not only fabrics are used for appliqué; embroidery can be worked on another fabric and then laid on the main embroidery, either for a raised effect, an overlapping of figures or areas, or for large, solid embroideries that would pucker the fabric if worked directly on the background material.

[9] P. 203, Illustration 106; see also Norman Laliberté and Sterling McIlhany, *Banners and Hangings* (New York: Reinhold Publishing Corp., 1966).
[10] This same combination of flame fabrics is used as a background for a dove (Illustration 12, p. 35).

Marion P. Ireland

The purple paraments for the Lutheran Church of the Master, Lancaster, California (Illustrations 125, 126) were done according to this method and by embroidery directly on the material. For the pulpit the pastor wished an adaptation of the official emblem of the Lutheran Church in America (Illustration 50m*), and at the same time we wanted the Tree of Life to allude to the Crucifixion, hence the bowed arms on the cross arising from the roots of the tree. The circular background was a part of the official emblem, but was of little importance to the design. Therefore, it was of plain red-violet satin, unoutlined. The soil from which the tree emerges is suggested by a multicolored brocade of "stony" pattern, in predominantly blue-violet to red-violet hues. The tree and leaves are Bonnaz embroidery which has an interesting texture, and the fruit is satin stitch (worked on an industrial Meistergram machine, so that the fine threads could be built up into a solid, rounded shape). These symbols were kept in the foreground by their raised contours (the leaves worked separately and applied over a padding) and tex-

*P. 105.

126 Paraments for the Lutheran Church of the Master,
Lancaster, by Marion P. Ireland:
(a) purple pulpit fall with denominational insignia
of the Lutheran Church in America;
(b) Advent and Lent are symbolized
on the purple altar antependium;
(c) lectern marker, the Last Supper

126b

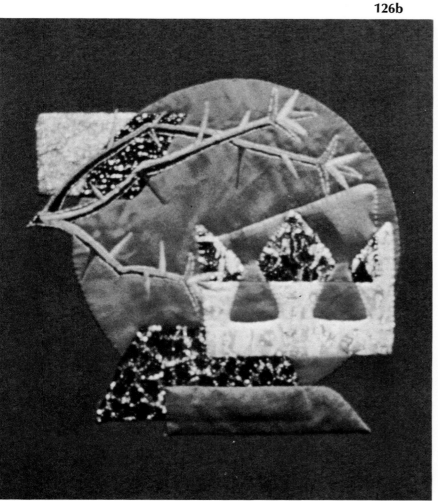

Marion P. Ireland

126c

Marion P. Ireland

tures and by being outlined with couching of a delicate bronze metallic twist. A burst of sunlight, at the upper right, is made of metallic fabrics and accented with gold Bonnaz streaks.

The matching altar cloth has a similar circle for background. A kingly crown for the Christ Child (Advent) is overshadowed by a crown of thorns (Lent), representing the two seasons when the purple paraments are used. The branch is worked in Bonnaz, and the thorns in satin stitch (Meistergram), couched by hand to match the pulpit design. A single marker is used on the lectern to balance the offset cloth on the altar and tall standing cross at the right of the altar. An appliquéd fish forms the background upon which the chalice and Host, grapes, and wheat are placed.

127 Altar antependia, St. Mark's Lutheran Church, Chula Vista,
by Marion P. Ireland:
(a) "Sermon on the Mount";
(b) the ship of the Church

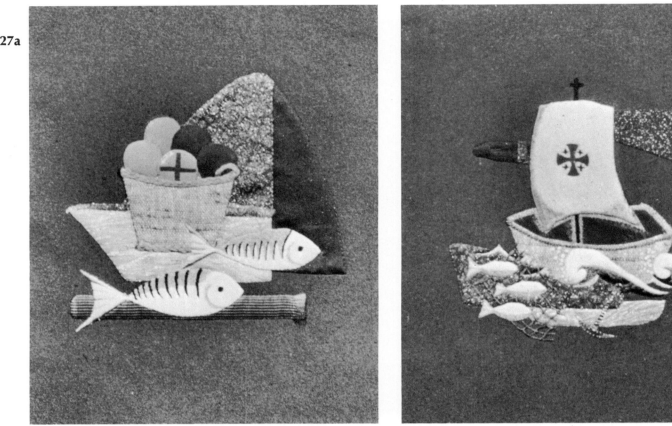

127a

127b

Marion P. Ireland

Marion P. Ireland

The Sermon on the Mount and the ship of the Church are the subjects of a pair of altar antependia for St. Mark's Lutheran Church of Chula Vista, California (Illustration 127). A rich green, coarse weave was selected for the material, and rude materials were used for the basket of loaves—burlap, hemp, and leather. The fish are machine embroidered and applied to the design, bringing them into the foreground, overlapping the flat background shapes (Illustration 127a). The ship's sail is also machine embroidered, and the hull is of burlap, leather, and hemp (Illustration 127b). A net of gold mesh suggests the fishermen disciples and the miracle of the filled nets. A gold leather anchor symbolizes hope.

The Eucharistic vestments made for the Church of the Resurrection, New York City, by Beryl Dean and Elisabeth Hopper, London, use the cross as a basic structure for an elegant composition of varied textures and materials (Illustration 33*). Here also the cross is treated with great ingenuity, and the surrounding symbols are linked with the cross into a composite design. The various raised and padded portions give the work a sculptural quality.

Lettering

A striking machine-embroidered cope bearing the inscription "Glory be to God on high, on earth Peace Good will toward men," was made by Pat Russell for the Church of the Holy Rood, Oxford, and illustrated in an article

*P. 58.

128a

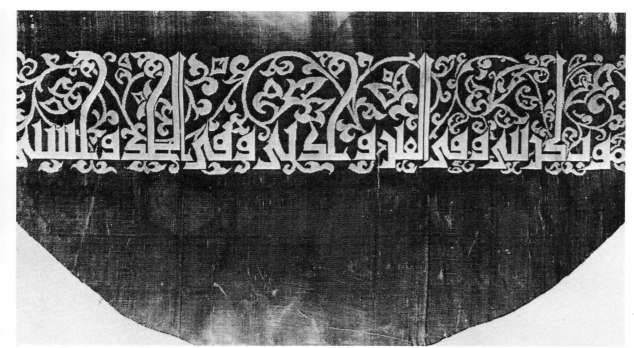

128 Kufic Inscriptions:
(a) plain compound twill,
fragment of tomb cover,
Persia, Buyid, eleventh century;
(b) plain compound twill,
fragment of tomb cover,
Persia, Buyid or Seljuk,
eleventh to twelfth century

128b

"Lettering and Embroidery." [11] Mrs. Russell maintains that we fail to look at the shapes of letters because we are so intent upon reading what they have to say. On the other hand, we can "look" at Greek or Chinese characters as patterns, without trying to understand them. Only by seeing the beauty of form in the lettering itself can the artist use it effectively in embroidery. If it were not for the inherent beauty of the letters themselves, Mrs. Russell says, the mere trick of erasing the readability would have no meaning in religious art.

Some of the most beautiful examples of lettering in embroidery and weaving are found in the Kufic inscriptions on Islamic textiles, such as the Persian tomb covers of the eleventh century (Illustration 128). It was the custom to weave quotations from the Koran into the borders of the textiles. We can gain inspiration from these intricate and graceful designs that may

[11] *Embroidery* (Diamond Jubilee Issue, 1966), p. 45.

129 Tapestry, "Magic Letters," by Marin Hemmingson,
designed as a tapestry for a children's library

open our eyes to ways in which we may use the lettering and words of our own Scriptures more effectively. A charming study in the beauty of letters, titled "Magic Letters," is woven in Gobelin technique by Marin Hemmingson (Illustration 129). The letters here are not meant to "say" something, but to stimulate the imagination. When lettering is designed to serve a liturgical function, legibility is as essential as ingenuity.

Lettering is combined with figures, as decorative detail, on a series of banners by Ann Hall for the Church of the Resurrection in Newington, Connecticut (Illustration 130). The banners are designed to be used as ambo pendants, and are made entirely of felt. Each piece is cut out and fitted into the design like pieces of a jigsaw puzzle, using iron-on interfacing as a foundation for the entire banner. The edges are then tacked down by hand. The artist's interpretation for the Advent/Christmas banner, "The Lord Lives With Us," is that God comes to us through each other. The Lenten banner shows figures turning their backs on one another, in isolation, rejecting one another. The Easter banner shows two figures who see the Risen Lord in the new light and proclaim him to all as Mary comes back from the tomb.

130 Banners for the pulpit, Church of the Resurrection, Newington, Connecticut, by Ann Hall. (a) Advent-Christmas banner; lettering provides the decorative detail on the garment of one of the four figures in this composition, achieving a three-dimensional appearance, the other figures seeming to be farther away. The decorative lettering also gives strength to the vertical lines and shapes.

130 (b) Lenten banner. The text, "My God, Why Have We Forsaken One Another?" is augmented by two figures with their backs to each other in isolation and rejection. The distribution of letters as texture for the two upright figures contrasts to the stark black figures below.

130 (c) Easter banner. The lettering "I have seen the Lord" is the decorative element in this composition, bringing the figures into the foreground, but taking precedence over them. Concentric circles are used effectively in balancing with the strong vertical forms of the two men.

131 Stoles by Ann Grill, for St. Luke's Evangelical Lutheran Church,
Chicago, Illinois:
(a) white;
(b) red

131b

131a

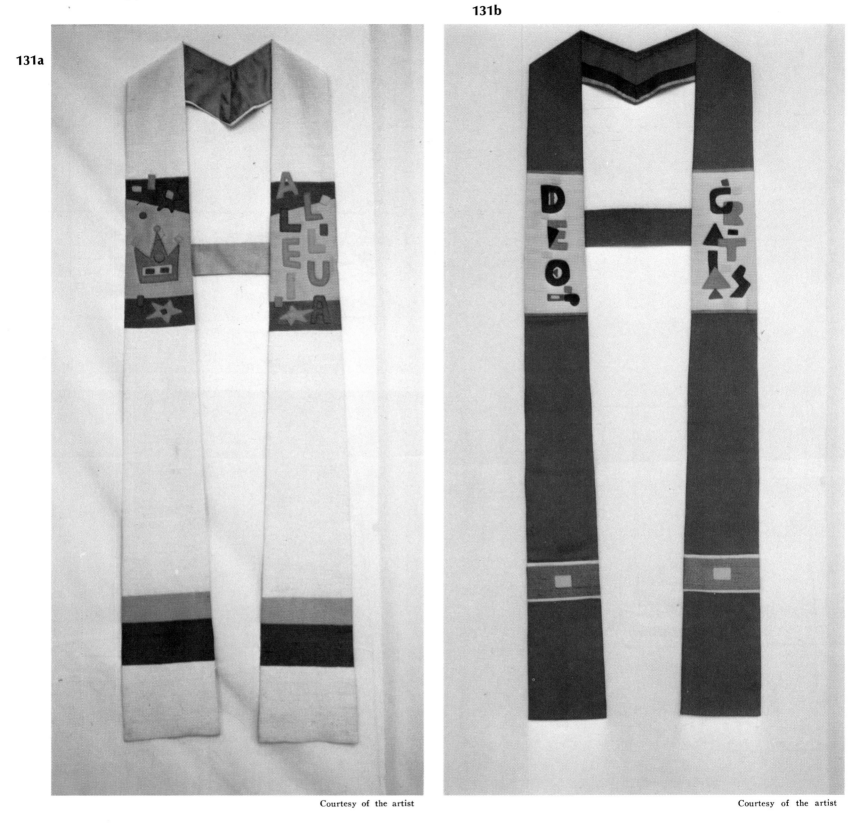

Courtesy of the artist

Courtesy of the artist

A decorative use of lettering which is seen both as design and message
is accomplished by Ann Grill (Illustration 131). Her understanding of letters
as elements of design is demonstrated by the fact that the design of each of
the stoles is composed of letters and symbols, and yet the two designs are
perfectly balanced. A highly decorative use of colors within the composition
prevents the design from becoming just an embroidered word. No decorative
stitchery is needed to adorn these well designed stoles.

TEXTILE ART IN THE CHURCH

132 Olivet Lutheran Church, Fargo, North Dakota
Sövik, Mathre and Madson, architects;
(a) white paraments;
(b) green paraments

132a

132b

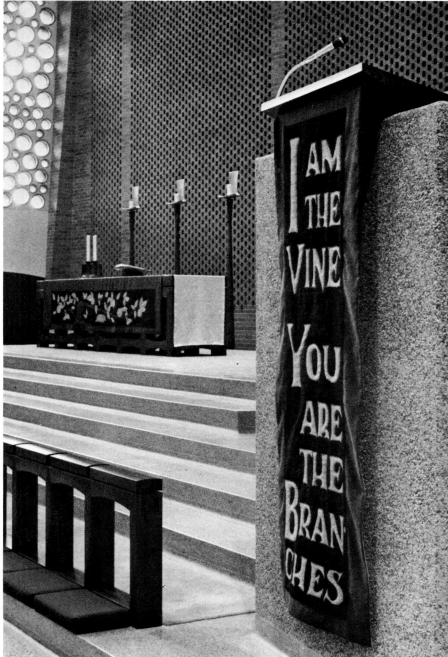

espie Studio

Gillespie Studio

The word "Hallelujah" forms the entire design on the white frontal for the Olivet Lutheran Church of Fargo, North Dakota (Illustration 132a). The variation of sizes of the letters interlocking and the combination of straight lines and simple curves creates a rhythmic pattern, in harmony with the evenly spaced communion rail and series of tall candleholders behind the altar. The textured wall treatments of brick and "bubble" pattern of glass are well complemented with this pleasing frontal. The green paraments for the same church (Illustration 132b) include a very long pulpit fall, with the words "I am the Vine, You are the Branches" appliquéd on wool. The frontal portrays the vine, with elongated branches spreading the full length. The green background is greatly enhanced with an area of blue behind the design.

133a

133 Purple paraments for Geneva Presbyterian Church,
Laguna Hills, California, by Marion P. Ireland:
(a) pulpit antependium, "Abide in me and I in you";
(b) lectern antependium, "Comfort ye my people"

133b

Courtesy of Louis Grossé

Verses of Scripture are part of the design on the purple antependia used during Advent and Lent at the Geneva Presbyterian Church, Laguna Hills, California (Illustration 133). The figure of Christ dominates both compositions, and the words supplement the portrayal.

Textile Paints and Dyes

Designs may be applied to cloth in ways other than embroidery, such as textile paints and dyes. Occasionally painting and embroidery are used together, the design being applied to the cloth by silk screening, stenciling, or free brush painting and accented with embroidery. The vestments made for Coventry Cathedral by Louis Grossé Ltd. include the combined use of stenciling, spraying with color, and appliqué—a method also used on the frontal for the Roman Catholic Church at Hayes, Middlesex (Illustration 134). This unusual frontal has a central *ichthus*, the fish, within a large anchor surrounded by twelve smaller fish representing the apostles. This frontal was commissioned to draw the eye to the altar, which was otherwise dwarfed by a magnificent Annigoni painting.

Silk screening on fiber glass was the technique employed for a very large reredos (35 by 50 feet) covering an entire wall in St. Paul's Cathedral, Peoria (Illustration 85*), made by Zelda Strecker. The wall is made up of fifty-two stretched fiberglass fabric panels with two symbols per panel. Behind these panels are fiberglass batts to provide acoustical absorption. The fiberglass

*P. 165.

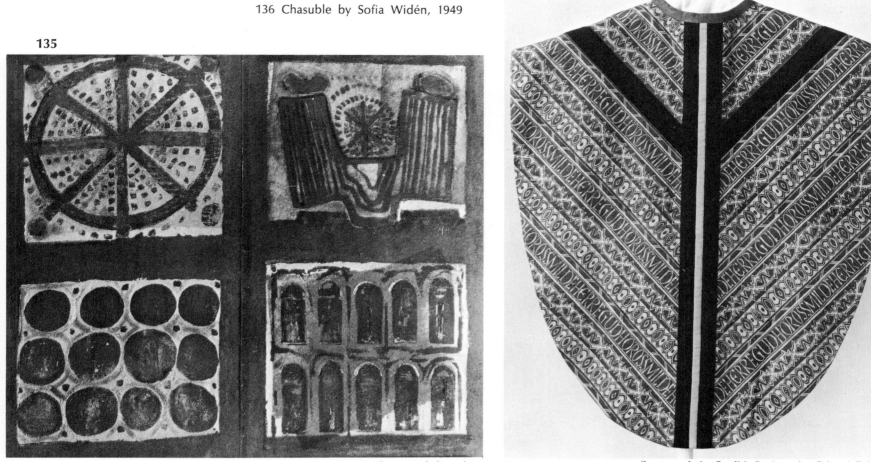

135 Reredos (section), St. Paul's Cathedral,
Peoria, Illinois, by Zelda Strecker

136 Chasuble by Sofia Widén, 1949

135

136

Courtesy of the artist

Courtesy of the Swedish Institute for Cultural Relatio

fabric is open meshed and allows the sound to pass through. The symbols were printed with a silk-screen process, with textile pigment, and silicon coated for protection. The artist says: "The colors have the same 'milky' quality as the interior brick and I feel that it becomes a *part of* the church rather than a furnishing."

The symbolic units contained in the squares of this reredos are repeated but in no set pattern. Illustration 135 shows a set of four squares in detail: (upper left) *Iota Chi,* monogram of Jesus Christ, in a circle; (upper right) the two natures of Christ, human and divine; (lower left) the twelve disciples; (lower right) the Ten Commandments. The symbols used are traditional, but stylized in a contemporary mode. The soft blue coloring which predominates blends into the blue of the ceiling, becoming—as the artist said—a part of the architecture.

Block printing on linen was the process used by one of the greatest designers of Sweden, Sofia Widén. A chasuble (Illustration 136) made by this artist was printed by the same method as the books before Gutenberg, by rolls of wood, carved with the design, dipped in color, and rolled over the linen. A complex design can be made in this manner, with the advantage that the blocks can be used over and over, in a variety of different color combinations, far more economically than by embroidery, once the blocks are made.

Batik is an ancient process, widely used in the Orient, India, and the Near East. It received its name from an ancient Malayan word *batik* meaning to trace, or paint. The process is termed "resist dyeing" because the design is

242

137

Marion P. Ireland

138

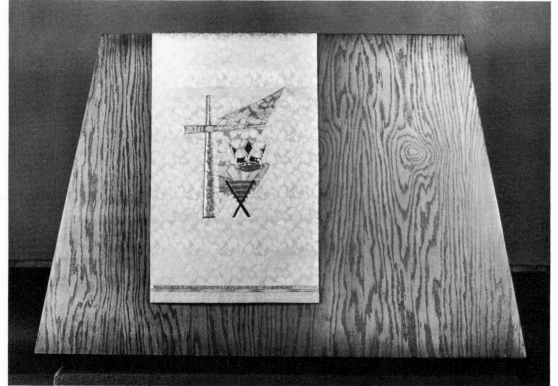

Marion P. Ireland

137 Banners, United Christian Church,
Los Angeles, California, by Mabel L. Martin.
Christmas banners worked in batik

138 Pulpit antependium, United Christian Church,
Los Angeles, by Marion P. Ireland

made with molten wax, which resists the dyes. After dyeing, the wax is removed, and other areas are waxed before dyeing in a second color. This
may be repeated as many times as desired, and a variety of interesting shades
and hues results from the overlapping of colors. Illustration 137 shows a pair
of Christmas banners by Mabel L. Martin, for the United Christian Church,
Los Angeles, California, each made with a single color, the design remaining
white. The thick and thin lines of the design create an effect of shading, even
though only a solid color and white are used. The banners are intended for
use only at a particular occasion rather than as part of the liturgical paraments, and therefore the spontaneity and simplicity of this method is appropriate and joyous in keeping with the spirit of the occasion. The Nativity
theme is also portrayed on the white pulpit fall, appliquéd and embroidered
with sparkling textures of fabric and gold leather, the angular lines designed
to relate to the "A" lines of the architecture (Illustration 138).

Weaving

The art of hand weaving has risen to new heights of popularity in recent years, and art exhibitions include an increasing number of handwoven textiles and works of art. No longer regarded as limited to flat surfaces, weaving now includes many novelties such as sculptural objects and open strands or screens. The practical value of this new exploration, as far as textile art for the church is concerned, lies in the variety of results that may be especially suited to garments, or to decorative and symbolic cloths which must be seen from a distance. A quality that is desirable for the first may not be appropriate for the latter.

The weaver must understand his art well enough to recognize this difference in function; otherwise, a chasuble may hang in stiff, ugly folds or a tapestry on a huge scale may lack the necessary firmness to support its weight. The body and texture are dependent upon the relationship between warp and weft threads, the type of weave, and the kinds of yarns. Techniques and fundamentals of modern weaving are demonstrated in a number of books, and some fine books are available illustrating modern tapestry design.[12]

Church textiles may be classified generally into two groups: (1) as fabrics, which may or may not be ornamented with some kind of design, and (2) as tapestry, which is woven ornamentation. In the former, the warp and weft threads are seen as fabric; in the latter, the warp threads are the support which is covered by the weft threads which make the design. Immediately, a question arises regarding this broad classification. We tend to assume that woven fabrics are used for vestments and tapestries are woven to hang on the wall. This, however, is not always the case. A beautiful cope was worked in tapestry by J. Plasse-le Caisne for the Chapel of St. Thérèse at Hem (Illustration 139), the same weavers who produced the Rouault "Holy Face" tapestry which is hung over the altar at Hem (Illustration 71*). Dossals are sometimes made of handwoven fabrics designed to hang behind the altar, and do not necessarily have a figured design. Although the word "tapestry" is defined as "a textile fabric decorated with ornamental designs or pictorial subjects, painted, embroidered, or woven in colours, used for wall hangings, etc.," tapestry, in the narrower sense, is a technique in weaving wherein design and background are woven together on a loom. The Bayeux Tapestry (Illustration 53†) is, strictly speaking, an embroidery.

Fabrics: Handwoven Vestments and Paraments

The trend away from what has come to be regarded as the traditional design for chasubles (a central orphrey on front and back, often with cross pieces of orphreys extending to the shoulders, and a central symbol) has encouraged the use of fabrics that are so designed as to be beautiful in their own right. The simple dignity of the vestments woven by Sister M. Augustina Flüeler of Switzerland (Illustration 140) is obtained from generously cut garments and fabrics designed to fall in graceful folds. A cross is only hinted at by means of the vertical stripes at the center and the narrow hori-

[12] See bibliography.
*P. 148.   †P. 117.

139

139 Cope, Chapel of St. Thérèse, Hem, France,
by J. Plasse-le Caisne

140 Chasuble by Sister M. Augustina Flüeler, Switzerland;
handwoven, with hood, stole, and burse

140

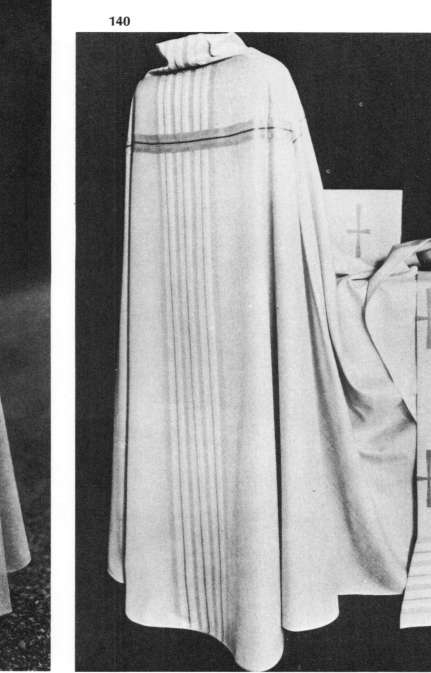

zontal stripe just below the shoulder line: the stripes suggest the erect figure of a wearer (and a chasuble is intended to be worn) as much as they do a symbol.

This is not to say that a chasuble is better if it is not ornamented; it is to stress the fact that the vestment must first be suitable. Only then can the decoration succeed. Handwoven vestments of outstanding design have been

141a

141b

141c

141d

141 Chasubles for Markus Church, Stockholm:
(a) designed by Marin Hemingson;
(b, c, d) designed by Barbro Nilsson

© Pål-Nils Nilsson /TIO

142 St. Markus Church, Stockholm, Sweden:
Two tapestries designed by Robert Nilsson
and woven by his wife, Barbro.
These are very rich in colors and made
on a wool warp with wool, some linen,
and silver and gold thread in the weft.
The golden relief of Christ between the
tapestries is designed by Robert Nilsson.
The three kneeling stools
are upholstered with lambskin.

woven at the Märta Måås-Fjetterström AB workshops at Båstad, Sweden, for
the St. Markus Church, Stockholm (Illustration 141). The vestments and altar
furnishings were woven in tapestry technique—the same technique that was
used for the beautiful pair of tapestries on the wall behind the altar (Illustrations
84*, 142, 143). A splendid harmony of beautiful fabrics is created: on the altar,
on the tapestries, and on the minister who officiates at the altar. A blend of
random threads throughout the background of the vestments unites design and
foundation. This is one of the unique characteristics of woven design. Other
excellent Swedish handwoven vestments are those made at Libraria (Illustrations 77a, 78a†), and at Licium (Illustrations 80-83‡).

*Pp. 162-63. †Pp. 155-56. ‡Pp. 158-61.

143 Details of tapestry in St. Markus Church, by Robert and Barbro Nilsson

143b

143c

144 Altar antependium, St. Martin's Church,
Hanover, Germany

From G. E. Kidder-Smith, *The New Churches of Europe*

Hand weaving makes possible the use of particular textures and blends of thread colors and tones, to complement the surroundings, for altar and pulpit cloths and dossals. The predominating feature in St. Martin's Church in Hanover, Germany (Illustration 144), is a brick mural relief, "The Twelve Gates of Jerusalem," by Claus Arnold. The mural fills the entire wall, and a simple slab altar stands in contrast to the brick and relief pattern behind and above it. A dark cloth is suspended from the front of the altar, creating impact by means of a solid area in contrast to the solid, unbroken lines of the light altar, and achieving a close relationship between altar and cloth. The surface of the cloth shows textures of thick and thin threads, which is harmonious with the relief pattern of the brick mural.

145 Tapestry pulpit antependium, Västerort Church,
Vällingby, Sweden, by Evy Parmsten.

The pulpit fall (Illustration 145) for the Västerort Church at Vällingby,
Sweden, Carl Nyrén, architect, was woven by Evy Parmsten. The theme is
based upon the "eye of the needle" or the "narrow gate" of the cross over
the altar, by Fritz Sjöström, which in turn was designed to conform to the
sense of space in the light from the ceiling window and in the slanting and
irregular surfaces. The eye of the needle is at the center of the cross, opening
to the light. The design for the pulpit fall grew from a series of studies of
the altar sculpture, and seeks to express opening and liberation, like a narrow
and closed room which receives light from an open door. This conception
is based on horizontal and vertical planes. The unity of the color of quite
heavy earth colors is broken by the white light of the door-opening and the
small dazzling "thorns" in cold blue. The pulpit fall was woven with flax
and wool yarn in Gobelin technique, translating the sculptor Sjöström's inten-
tions sensitively into textile form.

146 Tapestry, "Miraculous Draught of Fishes,"
by Märtta Taipäle, Finland

Tapestry: Wall Hangings

Tapestry weaving goes back to the earliest beginnings of thread interlacing
—a technique used to mark off areas of color and design. It is pictorial or
figurative in contrast to pattern weaving, and the various weft threads are used
only in certain areas rather than from selvage to selvage, as in plain weaving.
The process is very time consuming, but lasting. Examples from Peruvian and
Coptic weavers from the third century A.D., now preserved in museums, show
a high degree of excellence. These early weavers conceived their designs
within the weaver's idiom, whereas in later years tapestries were often designed
by painters, and the results were pictorial and decorative, although not necessarily uniquely belonging to the art of weaving.

A tapestry based upon the same theme as the one woven from the Raphael
cartoon, "The Miraculous Draught of Fishes,"* is woven by Märtta Taipäle,
of Finland (Illustration 146). Here, the primitive character of early tapestry
weaving is used—a character that seems particularly appropriate for the fish-

*Pp. 122-23.

147a

147 Tapestry weaving at the Gobelin factory and museum, Paris:
(a) a weaver works from the back of the warp threads;
(b) detail of the weaving from the back side of the tapestry, with tracing on the warp threads;
(c) right side of tapestry; mirror for the weaver to see the pattern and reflection of the cartoon behind her.

147b

Marion P. Ireland

Marion P. Irela⸱

ermen casting their nets into the sea almost two thousand years ago. There is refreshing strength and vigor here.

The great tapestries of Graham Sutherland (Illustration 65, the "Christ in Majesty" tapestry at Coventry*) and Jean Lurçat (Illustration 21, the "Apocalypse" tapestry at Assy†) were woven at Aubusson, as well as the works of other renowned artists of the twentieth century, such as Dufy, Coutaud, Rouault, Matisse, Leger, and Braque. Such weavers as the Gobelins and the Aubusson and Felletin factories, have maintained the high reputation that France has held since the Middle Ages.

Besides the experience of generations of expert weavers, Sutherland chose the firm of Pinton Frères at Felletin Aubusson partly for the fastness of the colors, which are specially dyed in small vats beside the River Creuse whose waters, being alkali free, are ideal for fixing dyes. Sutherland used thousands of different colors to transfer every subtle nuance from painting to tapestry. Lurçat, on the other hand, developed a standardized range of forty-four colors within which he did all his work. This range of colors forms a reference table in the Aubusson workshops, whereby the artist could "orchestrate" his drawings with numbers and the weavers could select the exact shade the artist intended.

*P. 139.   †P. 43.

147c

Marion P. Ireland

The revival of tapestry weaving in modern art owes much to the methods devised by Jean Lurçat. One of the greatest drawbacks in this art has been the tremendous expense of dyeing colors, due chiefly to the passion for multiplicity of shades desired by artists working in the late eighteenth and nineteenth centuries and into our own. At the beginning of the twentieth century, according to Lurçat, a medium-sized hanging took 889 colors.[18] This resulted in a tremendous inventory of odd lots after a work was completed. Lurçat's system of standardization, followed by both artist and weaver, resulted in a far greater degree of accuracy in reproduction from cartoon to tapestry. The translation from the artist's concept is hazardous at best, since neither weaver nor artist sees the whole woven design of a large work at one time until the work is finished and cut from the loom. Tapestries woven with the Gobelin technique are worked from the back; hence, the Raphael cartoon of the "Miraculous Draught of Fishes" at the Victoria and Albert Museum is in reverse of the woven tapestry made from the cartoon at the Vatican. Illustration 147 portrays tapestry weaving being done at the Gobelin factory in Paris. A full-sized cartoon is fastened to the wall behind the weaver, and mirrors are placed beyond the warp threads, so that the weaver can separate the warp and see the right side of the work as well as the cartoon behind her. Outlines are traced on the warp to show where the design is to be.

[18] Jean Lurçat, *Designing Tapestry* (London: Rockliff, 1950), p. 27.

148 Tapestry altarpiece, Chapel of the Swedish
     Covenant Theological Seminary at Lidingö, Sweden;
     artist-weaver, Sten Kauppi

Sune Sundahl

A strikingly original tapestry altarpiece was woven by Sten Kauppi in Gobelin technique for the chapel of the Swedish Covenant Theological Seminary at Lidingö, Sweden (Illustration 148). The design is a triptych, with the triumphal Christ at the center, the prodigal son on the left, and Golgotha on the right. The left panel, portraying the return of the prodigal son, shows a "sun-gold" form with outstretched arms, denoting the father. A black silhouette to the right of the father's head is the figure of the prodigal son, while the dark picture-form to the left depicts the envious son who had remained at home. The blue-black field in the center panel indicates the darkness of Golgotha. This darkness, as the spherical form of the earth, was broken through by Christ. The white triumphal central figure—Christ both crucified and risen—stands in close relationship to the tree-trunk cross. He belongs to the earth but reaches up with the pierced arms, which break through the cloud. A small gray form to the right can be interpreted as a skeptical or irresolute person, while the women to the left of the cross denote devotion to the faith. The motif on the right hand panel is of Christ bearing the cross, struggling with forces of evil which encompass him like a huge dragon, depicted in purple, red, and dark blues. Earth colors prevail throughout the three panels. A wonderful feature of this work is the blend of colors within areas. Technique and color blend go hand in hand here; the weave is very coarse, made up of clusters of yarns and strips of materials rather than single strands, and each group may contain more than one hue. This thickness of

149 Tapestry, "The Glorification of Christ,"
by Marijke Neyens-Wiegman,
St. Nicholas Church,
Limburg, Netherlands

weft allows the warp threads to show, creating a diagonal pattern to the weave. There are rich shadings within each color area, and splendid oranges and yellows for the prodigal son and his father. The forms of the women at the feet of the Lord are shaded in pinks, blues, and lavender. Only the central Christ figure is done in a close, single strand weft, to set it off from the rest. An architectonic unity is achieved in the calm, light interior of the chapel with the magnificent Gobelin tapestry, the long warp threads knotted in a self-fringe harmonizing with the vertical lines of wood paneling on the walls.

A tapestry was proposed by the architect G. J. van der Grinten for the wall behind the two altars in St. Nicholas Church, Limburg, Netherlands. The priest proposed the theme: the glorification of Christ. The design (Illustration 149) was the work of the artist-weaver, Marijke Neyens-Wiegman, who

150 Tapestry, Shepherd of the Hills Lutheran Church,
Edina, Minnesota, by artist-weaver, Jan Yoors.
Symbolism of the tapestry is related to the
shepherd theme in the congregation's name.

Robert Warn

expressed the subject with a large figure of Christ surrounded by his faithful,
shown as little figures of people. Under the crowd is one figure colored in
purple: the patron of the church, St. Nicholas. The tapestry is woven in
Gobelin technique, and measures 300 by 450 centimetres. The warmth of
fabric is particularly welcome here, relieving what would otherwise be rather
severely uniform wood paneling. The repeated rectangles of the tapestry
background create a pleasing relationship to the vertical lines of the wood
panels, the edges of the rectangles softened by a broken line, which is
characteristic of tapestry-weaving technique.

An unusual textile art project was done by the same artist for this church
at the suggestion of the architect. Fourteen little windows are placed in the
sidewalls, with panes of different sizes and placed on different heights. The
Way of the Cross is embroidered on transparent materials between the panes.
During the day, daylight falls through the transparents (negative) and at
night the lights in the church illuminate the objects (positive).

An impressive horizontal tapestry, designed and woven by the Belgian
artist Jan Yoors, of New York City (Illustration 150), spans the chancel wall
over the altar at Shepherd of the Hills Lutheran Church, Edina, Minnesota.
The theme—a flock of sheep, some with heads raised toward the cross,
others searching the ground—has special significance to this congregation.

151 Tapestry by Marion P. Ireland

The background is a bright, rich red, shifting to orange at the center behind the cross, which appears as part of the composition. The sheep are of a dull earthy color, with dark outline. The beveled facets of the brick wall cast pleasing vertical shadows as a counterpoint to the strong horizontal shape of the tapestry, which is the chief ornamentation of the church interior. An unusual arrangement was chosen for the altar cloths by the architects, Sövik, Mathre, and Madson: three parallel cloths suspended in front of the altar. The reason for the three-panel paraments was to avoid a large cloth area that would conflict in scale with the tapestry behind, and also to make a strong Trinity symbol. This arrangement of multipanels is used in other churches also by this same firm (Illustrations 9, 10*).

Many novel textures can be achieved in tapestry weaving by combining threads of different colors and textures and wrapping them around the warp threads in different ways. This is illustrated in a pulpit fall (Illustration 151)

*Pp. 33-34.

on which combinations of both color and texture were employed to achieve a glow of radiance behind the cross. The cross was given a dimensional effect by being raised in places with the Finnish *rya* technique of knotting bundles of yarn to form rows of loops. Some of the loops were cut to form a deep pile, and others were left, for variety. An analogous color harmony of greens was composed of twenty-one hues and variations from greenish-yellow to greenish-blue.

An attractive form of Scandinavian tapestry weaving is called *rölakan,* an example of which is shown (Illustration 76*) by Alice Lund. The Norwegian form is called *åklae,* and the Swedish, *rölakan.* It is a most exacting technique, worked in geometric patterns and worked out first on squared paper. In addition to carpets, the Norwegian technique is used for wall hangings, table covers, and other articles. The Swedish *flossa* technique is knotted and cut into pile, similar to the *rya,* which is believed to have originated in Finland but is now popular in Sweden as well. Many fine rugs and hangings in *rölakan, flossa,* and *rya* have been made by the Märta Måås-Fjetterström AB studios.

Carpets

Specially woven carpets have been included in the textile arts of St. Paul's Cathedral, Peoria (Illustration 85†), designed by William Donaldson and woven by hand in Puerto Rico. The large carpet in the narthex has a design of wavy lines suggesting the contours of the earth, the valleys and rivers of God's creation. A circular rug around the font has the signs of the zodiac and of the days of the week as a symbol of the sanctity of time. The carpet down the center of the nave pictures the fruits of the earth, and especially those of Illinois. The carpets surrounding the altar are abstractions.

The sanctuary carpet leading to the high altar at Guildford Cathedral is of striking design and color (Illustration 67b‡). Designed by the architect, Sir Edward Maufe, it was worked by nine ladies on a hand loom at the Royal Wilton Carpet Factory. Its weight is one thousand pounds. In both this cathedral and St. Paul's, Peoria, special carpets have been combined with the ambitious textile art project of needlepoint kneelers and wall coverings.

Conclusions

Many forms of textile art have been noted in this survey, reflecting a tradition that has existed as far back as human memory. Cloth has been associated with religious ceremonial as long as the Scriptures record, and the various ways in which it is used now have their precedent in the past. Within the spirit of the current reawakening in matters of liturgy and art, we must expect to see experimentation in all areas of the use of textiles in the church: vestments, paraments, banners, wall hangings, and others. Not all innovations will be appropriate, and fads may be introduced for the sake of novelty. The church is not the place for cuteness or mere cleverness. We have come to accept the phrase "new and improved" through the media of advertising as though the two were synonymous, whereas each new thing must seek to become an improvement. While the artist is challenged to create a kind of

*P. 154. †P. 165. ‡P. 142.

art that is alive and stimulating, the people of the church must also be challenged to be receptive to a lively idea that can stir them from a lethargy brought on by dull repetition of the expected, and make them eager for more and better religious art.

The purpose in assembling these examples has been to look beyond our immediate acquaintance with church art to recognize its shortcomings, and to find guidelines toward a true fulfillment of the use of beauty in the church today.

Appendix: Denominational Seals and Insignia

The insignia of various church organizations and denominations illustrated in Chapter V have, in some cases, been officially adopted; in other cases, they are used unofficially to represent aims, beliefs, or emphases of that particular religious body. The explanations and interpretations given here are derived from pamphlets, literature, and letters from the headquarters of each body.

The *oikumene* symbol of the World Council of Churches (Illustration 50a) was devised by a group of Christians in Germany during World War II. It is described in a pamphlet published by the Council, "What Is the World Council of Churches?" as follows:

> "The *oikumene* symbol of the Council is based on the ancient Christian image of the Church as a ship afloat on the sea of the world. The symbol carries the Greek word *oikumene* which is used in the New Testament to describe the whole inhabited earth. The circle surrounding the device represents the wholeness of the Church's mission to the entire world."

The official symbol of the National Council of Churches (Illustration 50b) has an official color combination of gold with green cross and lettering, when it appears in color. The symbolism is simple and straightforward, the map of the United States representing the nation.

The symbol used by the Executive Committee of the Southern Baptist Convention (Illustration 50c), and also by the Sunday School Board of the Southern Baptist Convention, is as near an official design as there is for this body. It contains the cross, the open Bible, and the world as the field. It sometimes bears the words "to lead men to God through Jesus Christ."

The official corporation seal of the International Convention of Christian Churches (Disciples of Christ) has the words "Building a brotherhood through voluntary cooperation," inscribed in a circle around the illustration shown (Illustration 50d). This simplified emblem is used on denominational stationery and literature.

The executive council of the United Church of Christ (Illustration 50e) has issued "An Authorized Interpretation of the Official Emblem of the United Church of Christ":

> "The emblem of the United Church of Christ is based on the ancient Christian symbol known as the Cross of Victory or the Cross Triumphant.

> "Traditionally, this symbol—the cross surmounted by the crown and all of it atop the orb—signifies the kingship of the Risen Christ over all the world. The orb, representing the world, is divided into three parts to signify the command of our Lord to his disciples: 'You shall be my witnesses in Jerusalem and in all Judea and Samaria and to the end of the earth.'

> "For the United Church of Christ this emblem, rich in the traditions of the past and alive with hope for the future, is particularly appropriate. For this reason, there appear on the perimeter of the emblem both the name of the Church and the text: 'That they may all be one.' "

The globe and open Bible also appear on the official insignia of the American Baptist Association (Illustration 50f). It is described as an open Bible bearing the denominational insignia spread over the world map.

"The intended interpretation is to convey our concept of the biblical commission to the churches of the New Testament that the gospel should be carried to all the world. It is likewise intended that wherever our name is seen, it should represent the fact that we are there to carry the full truth of an open Bible to that area of the world. . . .

"This insignia was first used in 1957 and has been used continually since that time. At first the insignia was round and later was changed to the oblong circle because we felt it better in design."

The scriptural basis for the official emblem for the Reorganized Church of Jesus Christ of Latter Day Saints (Illustration 50g) is found in Isaiah 11:1-9. In 1874 a resolution was passed by the General Conference of the church with reference to the emblem: "A lion and a lamb lying down at rest. Motto, 'Peace.'" In 1917 the resolution was adjusted to describe the emblem as containing "a child, a lion and a lamb. Motto, 'Peace.'" A letter from the First Presidency describes the symbolism:

"Although the seal has undergone some changes in details through the years, the basic motif has been maintained. The symbolism of the lion, the lamb, and the child together is expressed in the word 'Peace.' The lion (the symbol of power), the lamb (the symbol of meekness), and the child (the symbol of innocence) will dwell together in love and peace."

Two emblems are illustrated pertaining to the Episcopal Church in the United States of America. The first (Illustration 50h) is the insignia on the letterhead of the Executive Council. It includes the coat of arms of the Church and is supposed to symbolize God the Holy Trinity overshadowing the Episcopal Church and the world. The official seal of the Presiding Bishop of the Protestant Episcopal Church, U.S.A. (Illustration 50i) has the following official interpretation:

The Shield-Heraldic Blazoning

"Argent a cross throughout gules, on a canton azure nine cross crosslets in saltire of the field.

Popular Description

"On a white field a red cross the arms of the cross extending to the edges of field, on a blue union nine small white crosses arranged in the form of an X cross, the arms of the small crosses also being crossed.

Symbolism

"A red cross on a white field is the cross of Saint George and indicates our descent from the Church of England.

"The St. Andrew's cross in outline in the canton recalls our indebtedness to the Scottish Church in connection with the consecration of our first bishop. Bishop Seabury was consecrated at Aberdeen in 1784.

"The nine cross crosslets symbolize the nine original dioceses which met in Philadelphia and in 1789 adopted the constitution of the Protestant Episcopal Church in the United States of America.

"The colors red, white, and blue obviously represent our country and stand for the American branch of the Anglican Communion."

The official insignia of The United Methodist Church (Illustration 50j) consists of the traditional Christian symbol of the cross in combination with a two-prong flame. Thus it relates the church to God the Father by way of the second and third persons of the Holy Trinity—God the Son, symbolized by the cross, and God the Holy Spirit, symbolized by the flame. The dual tongues of flame also relate to the two denominations that merged to create the new United Methodist Church—The Methodist Church and the Evangelical United Brethren Church.

The official seal of the United Presbyterian Church in the U.S.A. (Illustration 50k) was adopted by the General Assembly in 1959, the year following the union of the Presbyterian Church in the U.S.A. and the United Presbyterian Church of North America. The design is a contemporary rendering of historical and biblical themes. The central figure is the Celtic cross, long associated with Celtic Christians whose origins are traced to the earliest Christian centuries. The circle is the most distinctive feature, probably stemming from a Constantinian device wherein the *Chi Rho* monogram was surrounded by a golden crown. In this sense, the circle is the emblem of Christ's victory over sin and death. The four symbols surrounding the Celtic cross are interpreted in a report made to the General Assembly, giving the regulation for the use of the seal, together with a description of it:

"The burning bush is found in the seal of the Church of Scotland and in the seals of several other Reformed Churches. It is based on Exodus 3:2: 'And lo, the bush was burning, yet it was not consumed.' . . .

"The dove is one of the earliest and most beautiful of the symbols which represent the Holy Spirit. In Matthew 3:16 we read: 'And when Jesus was baptized, he went up immediately from the water, and behold, the heavens were opened and he saw the Spirit of God descending like a dove, and lighting on him.' . . .

"The cross here used, with the wavy line at the head of the shaft, is sometimes called a chrism. It is the identification of Christ with the cross. The cross bears the Greek motto, IHCOYC XPICTOC NIKA, with the name of Jesus Christ contracted into IC and XC.

"The Orb (bottom circle) is divided into three parts with the base of the cross at the center representing Jerusalem. It calls to mind the words of Christ in Acts 1:8: 'You shall be my witnesses in Jerusalem and in all Judea and Samaria and to the end of the earth.'

"The Bible is presented opened with the Greek letter Theta (Θ) on the right-hand page and Lambda (Λ) on the left-hand page. These represent the words ΘEOY and $\Lambda O\Gamma OC$, meaning 'Word of God.' The arrow through the center of the Bible is formed by a line connecting the emblem Alpha and Omega. This is a reference to Christ based on Revelation 1:8: 'I am the Alpha and Omega.' The arrow is the symbol of martyrdom, reminding us that many have suffered death for love of Christ who is the Word of God Incarnate."

The official seal of the Presbyterian Church in the United States (Illustration 50l) was adopted by the General Assembly in 1956. The seal was originally designed by Dr. R. P. Kerr in 1887 for use of the Publication Committee. The elements of the seal and the historical background are as follows:

"The central element of the seal is the shield presenting the Church. It is divided vertically into two equal sections.

On the left side of the shield appears the burning bush representing indestructibility of the Church; on the right side a lamp standing for the witness-bearing nature of the Church. At the head of the shield is the star representing Christ, the Lord of the Church, and above the shield is the dove representing the work of the Holy Spirit. Around the shield is a laurel wreath symbolizing the Church triumphant. Across the bottom of the seal is a scroll bearing the motto 'Lux Lucet in Tenebris,' meaning 'the light shineth in darkness.'

"The symbolism used in the seal has specific roots in the Reformed tradition as well as their biblical derivation. The dove has its place in the symbolism of the United Church of Scotland, the Presbyterian Church of England, and the Presbyterian Church of Hungary. The star, the lighted lamp, and the motto are all derived from the Waldensian Church of Italy. The burning bush is taken directly from the seal of the Church of Scotland, but also finds its place on the seal of the Spanish Reformed Church and the Reformed Church of France. The laurel branches are reminiscent of the wreaths on the seals of the Swiss Reformed Church and of the Westminster Assembly of Divines of 1643."

The official seal of the Lutheran Church in America (Illustration 50m) is described by Edgar S. Brown, Jr., who had a part in establishing the design:

"The seal takes its design primarily from St. John 15:1-8: 'I am the true vine. . . . I am the vine, ye are the branches: He that abideth in me, and I in him, the same bringeth forth much fruit.' Here is our Lord, source of life and salvation, symbolized in the Tree of Life (Revelation 2:7, 22:2) and the Root of Jesse (Isaiah 11:10). Out of the tree grows the Cross, symbol of redemption (Galatians 3:13). The branches which flow forth from the tree are the faithful, the members of the Body of Christ, the Church, and the leaves and fruit symbolize the fruitful life in Christ.

"The design has added historical significance. Henry Melchior Muhlenberg, patriarch of American Lutheranism, had as his motto *Ecclesia Plantanda* ('The Church must be planted'). Thus the vitality of the symbol is a witness to the growth of the church from the days of our forebearers, but more importantly it is a reminder of the urgent task before the church.

"The style is contemporary. The light 'airness' of the circular treatment of the name of the church and the sharp, clean lines of the symbol provide a modern interpretation for the seal of a newly merged church."

The seal of the Lutheran Church—Missouri Synod (Illustration 50n) was designed by A. R. Kretzmann, who explains it as follows:

"Basically, the seal of the Missouri Synod centers around the shield of faith on which there is the cross and the first creed of Christendom, *Jesus Christus Dominus Est* (Philippians 2:11). Besides the cross of Christ there are three smaller crosses pateè for the three persons of the Holy Blessed Trinity, and three stars for the three ecumenical Creeds of the Christian church—the Apostolic, the Nicene and the Athanasian.

"The red bands which support the shield carry on them the three great emphases of the Lutheran Church—*Sola Scriptura*—*Sola Gratia*—*Sola Fide*. Between the red bands and the blue shield there are six stars (three on each side) symbolizing the six special confessional writings which set forth the doctrinal position of the Lutheran Church—the Small and Large Catechisms of Dr. Martin Luther, and the Augsburg Confession, the Apology of the Augsburg Confession, the Smalcald Articles, and the Formula of Concord. *The Book of Concord* in which all these creeds and confessions were gathered is shown as a supporting ornament of the shield of faith and on it are the words 'Concordia, A ✚ D MDLXXX.' In the center, at the base, subordinated to Christ and all the confessional symbols of the church, is the symbol, or seal, of Martin Luther. On either side of the base of the shield are found the symbols of the vine and the grapes as signs of the Old Testament church (Isaiah 5), and the New Testament church (St. John 15). The lettering around the outside of the shield is simply the official name of the church and the year of its founding—1847."

The insignia of the American Lutheran Church (Illustration 50o) shows the Holy Trinity and the open Bible in the two upper sections of the shield, and symbols of the sacraments —baptism and the Lord's Supper—in the lower sections. At the center of the cross which divides the shield is the Luther seal.

Glossary

Alb. From the Latin *albus,* white. A long garment with fitted sleeves, customarily made of linen, worn over the cassock and beneath the chasuble, and held in position at the waist by a cincture; derived from the everyday tunic of classical Greek and Roman dress.

Altar cloth. Covering for the Christian altar. Used from earliest times, at least during the Eucharist. Made of linen and silk, enveloped free-standing altars on all four sides during earliest centuries.

Ambo. From the Greek *ambon.* A raised platform in the early Christian basilicas from which the Scriptures were read and the Litanies conducted. Originally only one, and later, two, one for the Epistle and one for the Gospel; predecessor of the modern pulpit and lectern. After the fourteenth century, the ambo was replaced by a pulpit.

Amice. A rectangular piece of linen worn around the neck, over the cassock and under the alb and chasuble, with ties to fasten it to the body under the arms.

Antependium. From the Latin, *ante,* "before" and *pendere,* "to hang." An ornamental cloth to hang in front of the altar, pulpit, or lectern; varying in color according to the season. Also called parament, fall, or frontal.

Apparel. Ornamented band of cloth, interlined with stiffening, to be attached to amice as a collar; above hem of alb in middle of front and back, and outside of each cuff of alb. Derived from the *clavi* of classical times; revived as a border around hem of alb, in eleventh and twelfth centuries; reduced in present use to short pieces on hem and on each wrist.

Arabesque. From the French, meaning "Arabian" or "in the Arabian manner." Characterized by scrollwork contain-

ing intertwined foliage, tendrils, flowers, branches, etc. Inherited from the Graeco-Roman.

Aureole (or aureola). From the Latin *aurum;* a gold oval or elliptical radiance (or glory) around the entire body of a figure—Christ, the Virgin, an apostle, a saint, etc. Also called *mandorla* or *vesica pisces.* A radiance around the head is called *halo, glory,* or *nimbus,* with a halo generally used for saints; a glory (more elaborate than halo) for apostles; and a nimbus with figures of the persons of the Godhead. The tri-radiant nimbus (three arms of the cross radiating from the body or head), reserved for Christ only.

Baldachino. From the Italian *Baldacco* (Bagdad, for the place where the materials were obtained for its construction). A canopy over the altar (also called *ciborium magnum),* made of wood, stone, metal, with pillars for support, or a drapery of silk or velvet hung from the ceiling or wall. A Baldachino is sometimes used as a canopy over the bishop's throne.

Batik. From Malay, a resist process for decorating fabrics. Parts of the design not to be dyed are impregnated with wax, to resist the dyes. The fabric is dipped in color and then boiled to remove the wax. The process is repeated as many times as there are colors.

Bayeux stitch. Named after the eleventh-century Bayeux tapestry, which was embroidered in wool on coarse linen. A stitch with the threads laid side by side, not over and under as in satin stitch. The laid threads are then couched down, and the filled areas finished with outline stitch. Special effects are achieved by the direction of the stitches and the patterns of couching. Covers background quickly and economically.

Bestiary. Medieval book on zoology concerning real and imaginary animals interpreted as symbols of Christian truths; frequently illustrated; a source of motifs for church decoration, including sculpture, painting, manuscripts, etc.

Brocade. From the Latin *broccus,* stitching. Originally heavy silk woven in an elaborate pattern with gold and silver and colored threads. The face of the fabric is easily distinguished from the back by the various colors, carried across the back from one part of the pattern to where they reappear. The name now used for many fabrics resembling the historic brocades.

Burse. An envelope-like case, in which the Corporal is kept at the time of Holy Communion. Made of two squares of stiffened material, covered with linen, silk, or other rich material, usually in the color of the day or season.

Cassock. A long garment, usually black, form-fitting from neck to waist, flaring wider and fuller below the waist, and with narrow sleeves. Worn by the clergy, assistants, acolytes, and choristers as a basic garment. Originated in the Roman *vestis talaris,* an ankle-length garment retained by the clergy when, under barbarian influence in the sixth century, shorter garments, were adopted for secular use. In the Eastern Church, *rason.* In the Western Church, the cassock of the bishop is violet; the cardinal, red; and the pope, white.

Casula. From the Latin *casa,* house; *casula* means little house or tent. Originally, an outer protection against the weather; a garment of secular attire that enveloped the wearer. Predecessor of the chasuble and cope.

Chancel. From the Latin *cancellus,* lattice, railing, or screen (before the altar). Originally, the area immediately surrounding the altar, now called the sanctuary (a term generally misused to apply to the entire interior of the church, including both nave and chancel). The term chancel now refers to the entire area within the main body of the church east of (or beyond) the nave and transepts.

Chasuble. From the Latin *casula,* little house, tent. An outdoor cloak worn by both men and women, derived from the *paenula* and *planeta* in the Graeco-Roman world. Circular, shaped like a tent, with an opening for the head, and often hooded. In the West, its shape gradually altered by cutting away at the sides; in the East, the *phelonion* (counterpart of the chasuble) was gathered up or cut away in front; the corresponding vestment in the other Eastern rites is open all the way up the front and joined with a clasp, so that it somewhat resembles the Western cope.

Chroma. The intensity or saturation of color.

Ciborium. Latin, meaning cup; from the Greek *kiborion,* seed vessel of Egyptian lotus, resembling a cup, (a) A chalice-shaped vessel with a lid, used to contain the sacramental bread of the Eucharist; (b) the canopy (*ciborium magnum*) resting on four pillars over the altar in Christian basilicas and other churches. Also called the Baldachino.

Cincture. From the Latin *cinctura,* girdle. A band about 4 inches wide, worn around the waist over cassock or alb, tied or fastened, with ends hanging. May also be tasseled rope.

Clavi. From the Latin; plural of *clavus,* nail. Purple stripes from each shoulder to hem, front and back, on the ancient dalmatic; originally indicated rank of the wearer, but later worn by everyone. In the fourth century, shortened and the ends finished in a roundel or a decorative motif. Other developments or variations, elaboration and joining of clavi to borders at the hem

of the garment, decorative roundels and squares added at the shoulder and knees, as is the custom on dalmatics today.

Collage. From the French, a pasting, or something pasted. Primarily, pieces of paper and/or other materials assembled in a manner unrelated to conventional use. Sometimes an arrangement of fragments in conjunction with drawn forms, transforming the obvious through the juxtaposition of other images and materials.

Color. The quality of an object or substance with respect to the light reflected by the object; described by its hue (color name), its saturation (intensity or chroma), and its brightness (value, degree of lightness or darkness).

Colors, liturgical. A sequence of colors ascribed to vestments and paraments according to the various seasons and occasions of the Christian calendar. In the early centuries, special ones not prescribed; the best vestments being used for the most festive occasions, the old ones for the ordinary ones. The first known sequence of colors, the Augustinian Canons at Jerusalem in the early twelfth century, followed by that of Innocent III, for local usage in Rome before he became Pope in 1198. The latter eventually adopted, in general, as Western usage, although not excluding other systems. Eastern churches have no prescribed color systems corresponding to those of the West, the finest vestments being prescribed for the most festive occasions, somber colors for penitential seasons.

Complementary. A color opposite another on a schematic chart or scale (hue circle or color wheel), such as red opposite green, orange opposite blue, or yellow opposite violet. Produces the after-image of its complement if looked at for a period of time, immediately followed by focus on a blank white area. The relationship of pairs of colors, in which they complete or enhance one another.

Cope. A semicular cloak, fastened at the neck with a morse; worn at liturgical functions when a chasuble is not used. Originated with the Roman *paenula* or *pluviale.* Frescoes and mosaics of the sixth century show it as a vestment of the clergy; not generally regarded as a liturgical vestment until the ninth century. During the Middle Ages, worn by entire communities as a cloak for protection against the cold (*cappa nigra,* a cloak of thick, black material). A remnant of the original hood of the cloak retained as a flat shield-shaped or triangular ornament attached to the border at the back of the neck. Ornamentation usually most elaborate here, as well as on the borders or front panels, and the morse.

Corporal. From the Latin *corpus,* body, referring to the Eucharistic bread as the body of the Lord. A square piece of linen on which the bread and wine are placed to be consecrated in the Eucharist. A linen cloth used in this way in the fourth century; the distinction between the corporal and the linen altar cloth under a corporal, not apparent before the ninth century. Symbolic of the grave cloth for the body of our Lord.

Cotta. A shortened form of surplice reaching to the waist or fingertips; less fullness in the sleeves than a surplice, a square or rounded yoke, the body and sleeves usually gathered onto the yoke, but occasionally plain and cut to flare out at the bottom. Worn by acolytes and choirs in modern times in place of the more ample surplice.

Crewel. Embroidery with wool on a canvas ground. Also called "crule" or "cruell"; associated with the sixteenth and seventeenth centuries but still popular.

Dalmatic. From the Latin *dalmatica.* An outer garment introduced from Dalmatia about A.D. 190, and common in Rome by the third century. Shaped like a tunic, but wider with short, wide sleeves, decorated with clavi, and having an opening for putting on over the head. Purple clavi used to indicate rank of the wearer; wide for senators, narrow for equites and knights. Its rectangular shape was being altered by the fourth century, the body and sleeves being widened with diagonal seams; from the fifth century, the dalmatic was more elaborate, fitted, and shortened. From the time of the Crusades, it was a gentleman's long, loose-sleeved gown, which, by the eleventh century, was used as the Coronation dalmatic of the German Emperors. The dalmatic is worn by the deacon in the modern Roman Catholic Church or the Church of England.

Dossal. Also called "dorsal." A cloth, often embroidered, hanging flat or in folds back of an altar in place of a reredos. Originated probably as curtains hanging between the four columns of the ciborium in the Early Church.

Fall. A hanging, parament, or antependium of colored cloth, made to hang down in front of altar, pulpit, or lectern.

Fanon. See maniple.

Feast. Also festival, festal. (a) Every Sunday, a Feast Day commemorating the Resurrection; (b) Movable feast: Easter, Pentecost, or Whitsunday, governed by lunar reckoning; (c) Immovable feasts: anniversaries of the martyrs were probably the earliest; by the fourth century, festivals of fixed dates, especially Christmas and Epiphany, according to solar reckoning.

Fenestration. (a) Architectural term pertaining to the design and placement of windows and openings of a building. (b) Ornamental motifs with perforations or openings. *Fenestra,* a small opening.

Ferial. A day on which no feast is celebrated. In ancient Rome, *feria* was a religious holiday; today it has the opposite meaning. Ferial use, with regard to paraments and vestments, "ordinary" or "everyday." Before the development of liturgical color sequences for the entire Church Year, old Church orders frequently directed "old and shabby" for non-feast days, in contrast to the "best" for feasts. In Western usage today, green usually regarded as the ferial color between such seasons as Christmas-Epiphany and lent, and after Trinity Sunday until Advent. In Sarum usage, red the ferial color.

Flossa. Scandinavian rug-weaving technique. Swedish. Yarns knotted and cut into pile; similar to *rya;* used for rugs and wall hangings.

Fret. An ornament or ornamental border of Classic or Renaissance style, sometimes called a Key Pattern, consisting of straight lines turning at right angles in a repeat pattern, on garments and in architecture.

Frontal. A cloth hanging that covers the entire front of an altar. In the Middle Ages, sometimes made of precious metals. Many altars vested with both a full frontal and a frontlet—which extends the full length of the altar, but hangs only a short distance down from the top of the altar, or mensa. (The frontlet is sometimes called a superfrontal, although this term more correctly describes a decorative cloth hung above the altar in place of a reredos.)

Girdle. From the Latin *cingulum.* Also called cincture. Worn about the waist with an alb. In the Eastern Church, *zone,* worn only by bishops and priests, the *sticharion* worn by deacon being ungirdled.

Hanging. A colored cloth used as vesture for the altar, pulpit, or lectern. Also called parament, fall, or antependium. Usually in the liturgical color of the Church Year, with appropriate symbolism.

Houselling cloth. A long white linen cloth, to be spread in front of the communicants, or held by them, at the time of receiving the bread and wine of the Eucharist A medieval custom that has survived or been revived in some churches of Great Britain. *Housel,* medieval English name for the Eucharist.

Hue. The property of light by which the color of an object is named with reference to the spectrum, such as red, yellow, etc.

Immovable feasts. Festivals that occur on the same date every year, as contrasted with those whose date is dependent on the lunar cycle (Easter). Immovable Feasts include Christmas, Epiphany, saints' days, etc.

Kitsch. From the German *kitschen,* to throw together a work of art. Art produced to appeal to public taste, but of little or no artistic merit.

Lenten array. The shrouding of the crosses and images during Lent; not necessarily white, although Lenten white or unbleached linen are used. Other colors, such as blue or black, also used. As a Sarum use, it is still followed in some churches in England and in some Episcopalian churches in America.

Lenten veil. A great veil hung between the chancel and nave, from the beginning of Lent until Easter Even; used during the Middle Ages and survived until long afterward in many places.

Maniple. Also called *Fanon.* A silk band, 2 to 4 inches wide, shaped like a small stole, and worn over the left arm by the celebrant at Mass. Originally, handkerchief or napkin carried on the left hand; used in both pagan and Christian ceremony. First liturgical use, in Rome; used in Ravenna in sixth century, and all over Europe by the ninth century. Its use now gradually being discontinued.

Meander. A running pattern or border in the form of a fret or key design. An intricate fretwork; turnings or windings in a course of right angles.

Medallion. A large medal or tablet, usually round or oval, with a decorative design, object, or figure inside a border. An oval or circular panel; a portrait within an oval or circle; a decorative design often used in a carpet, a stained-glass window, or as a roundel at the ends of the clavi on a vestment, etc.

Mensa. From the Latin, meaning table. A single flat stone forming the top of the altar. Also called "altar slab" or "altar stone." Among early Christians referred to the large stone tablet set over or near a grave and used for the funeral banquet in memory of the deceased.

Morse. The clasp or fastening of a cope; often of precious metal, or jewels, or embroidered fabric.

Movable feast. Festival whose date is governed by the lunar cycle, such as the Christian Easter and Pentecost, that originated with the Jewish Passover and Feast of Weeks, which vary with the Paschal full moon. Various other feasts and fasts of Lent are movable with the date of Easter.

Munsell Color System. Developed by artist Albert Munsell (1858-1918). Now used as a basis for standardization of colors by the National Bureau of Standards and many commercial businesses. Based upon ten hues derived from 5 principal hues, in order to distinguish precise gradations within a decimal system. The Munsell color is described by its hue name, value (luminous reflectance), and chroma (colorimetric purity).

Needlepoint. Also called canvas embroidery. Wool yarn on canvas, with uniform stitches according to the spacing of threads in the canvas. Exceptionally durable for kneeling cushions, because of the closely applied, short stitches and the durability of wool. Needlepoint lace is worked directly on parchment paper, which is removed after the lace needlework is completed.

Omophorion. Greek. A bishop's stole used in Eastern Orthodox rites; hangs down front and back over his other vestments. A counterpart of the Western pallium; worn before the reading of the Epistle. The bishop wearing the omophorion symbolizes the image of Christ as the Good Shepherd carrying the lost sheep on his shoulders.

Opus anglicanum. A period of English ecclesiastical embroidery lasting from the eleventh century to the end of the fifteenth, reaching its peak between 1270 and 1330; universally esteemed for its excellence, beauty, and richness.

Orarium. See Stole.

Ornaments rubric. Ruling in the 1559 *Book of Common Prayer* that the ornaments of the Church and of the ministers should be those in use "by the authority of Parliament in the second year of the reign of King Edward VI."

Orientation. The construction of a church on its site so that its longer, or principal, axis runs east and west. The façades of basillica churches in Rome in the fourth century faced the east, with an apse for the altar at the west end, so that the celebrant faced east when standing behind the altar at the Eucharist. In Byzantine churches the high altar was placed in an eastern apse, a practice adopted later in England, Germany, and Spain. The practice of facing the sunrise to pray was derived from the pagans but given Christian significance by the symbolic reference to Christ as the Rising Sun.

Orphrey. An ornamental band or border of richly embroidered or woven material on an ecclesiastical vestment. Used chiefly on chasubles, copes, funeral palls, and altar frontals.

Ostwald Color System. Developed by physiochemist Wilhelm Ostwald (1853-1932). Color solid has twenty-four hues, derived from four major hues, with equal intensity at the equator but progressively whitened above and blackened below the equator. The twenty-four hues are placed so that psychological complementaries are opposite one another.

Paenula. A weatherproof garment made of leather or wool, bellshaped, with a hood; worn by everyone among the Etruscans in the fourth century B.C. By the end of the first century A.D., at the time of Tacitus (c. 55-c. 120), the paenula was being worn by lawyers and had replaced the toga for senatorial use. The forerunner of the casula, which in turn developed into the liturgical chasuble.

Pall. From "pallium," in the sense that it is a covering. (a) A small square of linen, stiffened with cardboard or other hard material, which is placed over the chalice at the Eucharist. (b) A large cloth, commonly black, purple, or white, which is spread over the coffin at funerals. Frequently, its design includes a cross, formed by two interesting orphreys running vertically and horizontally the length and width of the pall, with or without additional symbolic ornamentation at the intersection.

Pallium. Originally the outdoor garment of first the Greeks and later, the Romans. The Roman pallium, worn draped like a Greek "himation," was the characteristic garment of the scholar and philosopher, the conventional mantle of Christ. In the Roman Catholic Church, a circular band of white woolen material with a single band hanging down front and back; worn by the pope and granted by him to archbishops, and occasionally to bishops. *See Omophorion.*

Parament. (a) In secular use, a room decoration, such as a tapestry or wall hanging; (b) An ecclesiastical vestment, especially an adornment for the altar, pulpit, or lectern. Usually in the liturgical color of the Church year.

Pendant. A hanging ornament, such as a cloth marker suspended from the Bible or missal.

Phelonion. A liturgical vestment corresponding to the Western chasuble, worn by a priest in the Greek Orthodox Church.

Primary color. A color, such as red, yellow, or blue, which in mixture produces other colors.

Reredos. A decorative screen, wall painting, cloth, carving, or sculpture above and behind the altar. The earliest type, painting of scenes on the wall. During the Middle Ages, a variety of kinds used, including dossals of rich fabrics; jeweled metalwork; wood panels, either singly or in three panels, as a triptych; or carving in stone or alabaster. Sometimes covers only the width of the space occupied by the altar, or may cover the entire wall.

Rölakan. Also Röllakan. A Swedish and Norwegian weaving technique for repeat pattern for carpets, wall hangings, etc.

Roundel. Round or circular decorative panel, plate, etc. Popular for use at the ends of clavi on Roman tunics, for repeat pattern on carpets, brocades, and other textile ornamentation.

Rya. From the Finnish *Ryijy.* A knotted weave similar to "flossa" for rugs. Warp threads are covered with rows of plain weave between rows of knotted pile; the loops of yarn that have been knotted to the warp may be cut into pile or left as loops; hence, *rya* may have either cut or uncut pile, or a combination of both.

Sakkos. Also "saccos." A liturgical vestment in the Eastern Orthodox Church similar in form to the Western dalmatic. Probably dates from the eleventh century. Use formerly restricted to those of high rank, the archbishops and metropolitans; now worn by all bishops, in many countries, instead of a phelonion.

Sarum Use. Originally, a local medieval variation of the Roman rite in use at the cathedral church of Salisbury; attributed to St. Osmund (d. 1099), but actually developed over a long period of time. The earliest forms lacked many of the details added in later copies and revisions. Prescribed by the Consuetudinary, or cathedral statutes of direction for services, which was compiled by Richard le Poore (d. 1237). Further revised in the fourteenth century; followed in nearly all of England, Wales, and Ireland by the fifteenth century. Much of the material used by the Reformers for the first Book of Common Prayer (1549) was provided by books of the Sarum rite. Sarum Use has been revived in part by some Anglican churches, and by Episcopalian churches in the U.S.A.

Secondary color. A color, such as orange, green, or violet, which is obtained by mixing two primary colors.

Sticharion. Basic garment in the Eastern Orthodox Church.

Derived from the ancient tunic and worn by anyone who is vested, from the reader to the Patriarch.

Stola. A wide shirtlike undergarment, worn indoors by the Romans; outdoors, without a toga, by working people. A Roman woman's tunica. Originally without sleeves, usually made of white wool, and, later, of linen and cotton. Girded at the waist to the correct length according to sex and rank: long for women, knee-length for men, and shorter and deeply bloused for a centurion.

Stole. From Latin *stola.* Liturgical vestment about 8 feet long and 4 inches wide worn about the neck. Deacon's stole first mentioned in the East in the fourth century; in the West, known in Spain in the sixth century. In Western rites, worn by a deacon like a sash, over the left shoulder, the ends fastened under the right arm. Worn around the neck by a priest, with the ends crossed over the breast and held in place by the cincture when Eucharistic vestment are worn. At other times, the stole hangs straight down from the shoulders. In the Eastern Church, the priest's stole is called the "epitrachelion" and the deacon's the "orarion."

Surplice. From the Latin *superpelliceum,* over fur or hide. Originally worn over fur-lined garments. A loose vestment made of white linen, trimmed with lace or embroidery; variations in sleeves. Originally long, shortened somewhat in the thirteenth century, and very short by the seventeenth century. Waist or finger-tip length called a "cotta."

Tabernacle. From the Latin *tabernaculum,* tent. (a) A niche or arched canopy in a church. (b) An ornamental receptacle to contain the Blessed Sacrament in Roman Catholic churches. Since the sixteenth century, placed in the center of the High Altar.

Tapestry. (a) A weaving technique with colored threads woven by hand with bobbins upon a warp, whereby a design or pattern is produced completely covering the warp. (b) A wall hanging with woven design. (c) Any decorative fabric hanging, embroidered or otherwise.

Tertiary color. A color, such as gray or brown, produced by the mixture of two secondary colors.

Tippet (or *liripipe*). A broad black scarf worn over the surplice by Anglican clergy for services other than the Eucharist. It is uncertain which vesture the word indicated in the sixteenth and seventeenth centuries.

Tippet is presumed to have evolved from the long ends of the medieval hood, and hence was not originally confined to the clergy.

Triptych. A set of three panels, side by side, usually over an altar. Pictures, carvings, etc.

Tunic. Old Roman garment with short sleeves, worn girded up to knee length by men. Women wore the "tunica," with long sleeves and girded.

Tunicle. Also, dalmatica minor. Worn by subdeacons at Mass, and by bishops beneath the dalmatic and under the chasuble, but never under a cope. Like a dalmatic, but plainer with narrower sleeves.

Value. Degree of lightness or darkness of a color. Term assigned by the Optical Society of America to the designation of relative brightness. Used in the Munsell Color System to describe the lightness-to-darkness psychological attribute of color.

Velvet. From the Latin *vellere,* and Italian *svellere,* to pluck out; and the Latin *vellus,* fleece. A fabric of silk, rayon, nylon, etc., having a thick, soft pile. The loops forming the pile are cut for plain velvet, or combined with uncut loops for some figured patterns. Cut and uncut, became very sumptuous during the Renaissance. Process for making velvet known to have existed in Italy as far back as the late twelfth century.

Vestments. Garments worn by the clergy, assistants, and choristers during religious services; garments worn by the celebrant, deacon, and subdeacon, during the celebration of the Eucharist are termed "Eucharistic vestments."

Warp. The verticle or lengthwise threads in a woven pattern; those yarns that are mounted to the loom and placed lengthwise, being crossed by, and interlaced with, the weft threads.

Weaving. The interlacing of warp and weft threads to produce a fabric. Divided into four main groups: (a) single fabrics, with one warp and one filling (weft); (b) compound weave, with more than one warp or weft, or both; (c) pile or plush, with a pile or nap; (d) gauze or leno, warp thread twisted with threads of its own system, in addition to interlacing with filling (weft) threads. The term "woof" variously ascribed to the warp or the weft, as well as the texture of a fabric.

Weft. Filling. The threads interlaced horizontally with the warp threads in weaving.

Bibliography

I. CHURCH HISTORY: Ceremonial, Vesture, Color Sequences

Addleshaw, G. W. O. *The High Church Tradition.* London: Faber and Faber, 1941.

Andrieu, M. *Les Ordines Romani du haut moyen âge.* 5 Vols. Louvain, 1938.

Anson, Peter F. *Fashions in Church Furnishings, 1840-1940.* 2nd ed. London: Studio Vista, 1965.

Atchley, E. G. Cuthbert F., ed. *Ordo Romanus Primus.* The Library of Liturgiology and Ecclesiology for English Readers, Vol. 6. London: Alexander Moring, The De La More Press, 1905.

Barnes, Arthur Stapylton. *The English Liturgical Colours.* London: Church Printing Co., 1890.

Baumstark, Anton. *Comparative Liturgy.* Rev. by Bernard Botte, O. S. B. English edition rev. by F. L. Cross, 1958, from 3rd French edition of *Liturgie Comparée.* London: A. R. Mowbray and Co., 1958.

Beaton, Cecil. *The Glass of Fashion.* Garden City, N. Y.: Doubleday & Co., 1954.

Benoit, Jean-Daniel. *Initiation á la Liturgie.* Paris: Berger-Levrault, 1956.

Branting, Agnes. *Textil Skrud I Svenska Kyrkor från aeldre Tid til 1900.* Stockholm, 1920.

Braun, Joseph, S.J. *Die liturgischen Paramente in Gegenwart und Vergargenheit.* 2nd rev. ed. Freiburg im Breisgau: Herder and Co., 1924.

──────. *Die Liturgische Gewandung im Occident und Orient.* Freiburg im Breisgau, 1907.

Clarke, W. K. L., and Harris, C., eds. *Liturgy and Worship.* London: S.P.C.K., 1932.

Cox, J. Charles. *English Church Fittings, Furniture and Accessories.* London: B. T. Batsford, 1923.

Davies, Horton. *Worship and Theology in England.* 4 Vols. Princeton: Princeton University Press, 1961-62.

Dearmer, Percy. *The Ornaments of the Ministers.* The Arts of the Church Series. London: A. R. Mowbray and Co., 1908.

──────. *The Parson's Handbook.* 1st ed., London: Grant Richards, 1899. 13th ed. rev. by Cyril E. Pocknee, London: Oxford University Press, 1965.

Didache. Ed. and trans. by J. A. Kleist, Paramus, N. J.: Paulist/Newman Press, 1948.

Dix, Dom Gregory. *The Shape of the Liturgy.* 2nd ed. rep. Naperville: Allenson, 1954.

Duchesne, L. *Christian Worship, Its Origin and Evolution.* trans. by M. L. McClure. 5th ed. London: S.P.C.K., 1949.

Eeles, Francis C. *Notes on Episcopal Ornaments and Ceremonial.* Alcuin Tract XXV. London: A. R. Mowbray and Co., 1948.

Frere, W. H. *The Principles of Religious Ceremonial.* London: A. R. Mowbray and Co., 1928.

──────. *A Collection of His Papers on Liturgical and Historical Subjects.* Ed. by J. H. Arnold and E. G. P. Wyatt. London: Humphrey Milford, Oxford University Press, 1940.

Garside, Charles, Jr. *Zwingli and the Arts.* New Haven: Yale University Press, 1966.

Hargreaves-Mawdsley, W. N. *A History of Academical Dress in Europe until the end of the Eighteenth Century.* Oxford: The Clarendon Press, 1963.

Haulotte, Edgar. *Symbolique du vêtement selon la bible.* "Théologie" 65. Paris: Aubier, 1966.

Hope, William St. John, and Atchley, E. G. Cuthbert F. *English Liturgical Colours*. London: S.P.C.K., 1918.

_____. *An Introduction to English Liturgical Colours*. New York: The Macmillan Co., 1920.

James, E. O. *Seasonal Feasts and Festivals*. London: Thames and Hudson, 1961.

_____. *Sacrifice and Sacrament*. London: Thames and Hudson, 1962.

Jungmann, Josef A., S.J. *The Early Liturgy*. Notre Dame, Ind.: University of Notre Dame Press, 1959.

_____. *The Mass of the Roman Rite: Its Origins and Development*. Trans. by Francis A. Brunner, C.SS.R. 2 Vols. New York: Benziger Brothers, 1950.

King, Archdale A. *Liturgies of the Past*. London: Longmans, Green and Co., 1959.

_____. *Liturgies of the Primatial Sees*. London: Longmans, Green and Co., 1957.

_____. *Liturgies of the Religious Orders*. London: Longmans, Green and Co., 1955.

_____. *Liturgy of the Roman Church*. Milwaukee: Bruce Publishing Co., 1957.

_____. *The Rites of Eastern Christendom*. 2 Vols. Rome: Tipografia Poliglotta, 1947.

Legg, J. Wickham. "An Early Liturgical Colour Sequence, hitherto but little known, following the Use of the Crusaders' Patriarchal Church in Jerusalem in the Twelfth Century" and "Survival of the Use in Sicily of the Lenten Veil hung between Quire and Presbytery in the first decade of the Twentieth Century," *Essays Liturgical and Historical. Studies in Church History*. London: S.P.C.K., 1918.

_____. "Notes on the History of the Liturgical Colours," *Transactions of the St. Paul's Ecclesiological Society*, I, London, 1882.

MacAlister, *Ecclesiastical Vestments*. London, 1896.

Malais, L'Abbê. *Des Couleurs Liturgiques*. Paris: Paul Leprêtre et Cie, 1878.

Maxwell, William D. *An Outline of Christian Worship: Its Development and Forms*. London: Oxford University Press, 1936.

McArthur, A. Allan. *The Evolution of the Christian Year*. New York: Seabury Press, 1953.

_____. *The Christian Year and Lectionary Reform*. London: SCM Press, 1958.

McCloud, Henry H. *Clerical Dress and Insignia of the Roman Catholic Church*. Milwaukee: Bruce Publishing Co., 1948.

Morse, H. E. *English Liturgical Colours. Observations on "Notes on the History of the Liturgical Colours" by J. Wickham Legg*. London: Masters and Co., 1882.

Murray, Robert, ed. *The Church of Sweden, Past and Present*. Trans. by Nils G. Sahlin. Sponsored by the Swedish Bishop's Conference. Malmö: Allhem, 1960.

Norris, Herbert. *Church Vestments, Their Origin and Development*. New York: E. P. Dutton and Co., 1950.

Oakley, F. *Historical Notes on the Tractarian Movement*. London, 1865.

Ollard, Sidney L. *Short History of the Oxford Movement*. 2nd ed., rev. London: A. R. Mowbray and Co., 1933.

Ouspensky, Leonid, and Lossky, Vladimir. *The Meaning of Icons*. Boston: Boston Book and Art Shop, 1952.

Piepkorn, Arthur Carl. *The Survival of the Historic Vestments in the Lutheran Church after 1555*. 2nd ed. Graduate Study Number I, Saint Louis: Concordia Seminary, 1958.

Pocknee, Cyril E. *Cross and Crucifix*. London: A. R. Mowbray and Co., 1962.

_____. *Liturgical Vesture: Its Origin and Development*. London: A. R. Mowbray and Co., 1960.

_____. *The Christian Altar in History and Today*. London: A. R. Mowbray and Co., 1963.

Primus, J. H. *Vestments Controversy: Historical Study of the Earliest Tensions Within the Church of England and The Reigns of Edward the 6th and Elizabeth*. Amsterdam: Vrije Universiteit, 1960.

Pugin, A. Welby. *Glossary of Ecclesiastical Ornament and Costume, Compiled from Ancient Authorities and Examples*. Rev. by Bernard Smith. 3rd ed. London: Bernard Quaritch, 1868.

Rock, Daniel. *The Church of Our Fathers as Seen in St. Osmund's Rite for the Cathedral of Salisbury*. 4 Vols. Ed. G. W. Hart and W. H. Frere. 1st ed. 1849. London: John Murray, 1905.

Roulin, Dom E. A. *Vestments and Vesture. A Manual of Liturgical Art*. Trans. by Dom Justin McCann. Paramus, N. J.: Paulist/Newman Press, 1950.

Rousseau, Olivier, O.S.B. *Histoire du mouvement liturgique*, also an English trans. Paris: Éditions du Cerf, 1945.

Srawley, J. H. *The Liturgical Movement: Its Origin and Growth*. Alcuin Club Tracts XXVII. London: A. R. Mowbray and Co., 1954.

Staley, Vernon. *Ceremonial of the English Church*. 4th ed., rev. London: A. R. Mowbray and Co., 1927.

_____, ed. *Essays on Ceremonial*. The Library of Liturgiology and Ecclesiology for English Readers. London: Alexander Moring, The De La More Press, 1904.

_____, ed. *Hierurgia Anglicana*. Part 1. London: Alexander Moring, The De La More Press, 1902.

_____. *The Seasons, Fasts, and Festivals of the Christian Year*. London and Oxford: Mowbray and Co., 1910.

Stolt, Bengt. *Kyrklig skrud enlig svensk tradition*. Stockholm: Diakonistyrelselses Bokförlag, 1964.

Vasiliev, A. A. *History of the Byzantine Empire, 324-1453*. 2 vols. Madison: University of Wisconsin Press, 1961.

Walker, Charles. *The Ritual Reason Why*. 1st ed., 1866; rev. by T. I. Ball, 1901. London: A. R. Mowbray and Co., 1936.

Ware, Timothy. *The Orthodox Church*. Baltimore: Penguin Books, 1963.

The Warham Guild Handbook. 2nd ed. London: A. R. Mowbray and Co., 1963.

White, James F. *The Cambridge Movement*. Cambridge: Harvard University Press, 1962.

Zernov, Nicolas. *Eastern Christendom. A Study of the Origin and Development of the Eastern Orthodox Church*. New York: G. P. Putnam's Sons, 1961.

II. ART HISTORY AND CRITICISM

Banateanu, Tancred, et al. *Folk Costumes, Woven Textiles, and Embroideries of Rumania*. Bucharest: State Publishing House for Literature and the Arts, 1958.

Coulton, G. G. *Medieval Faith and Symbolism*. New York: Harper & Row, 1958.

Jobé, Joseph, ed. *Great Tapestries: The Web of History from The Twelfth to Twentieth Century*. Time/Life Books, 1965.

Johnstone, Pauline. *The Byzantine Tradition in Church Embroidery*. Chicago: Argonaut, Inc., 1967.

Kitzinger, Ernst. *Early Mediaeval Art*. Bloomington: Indiana University Press, 1964.

Kuh, Katharine. *Modern Art Explained*. London: Cory, Adams, and Mackay, 1965.

Lowrie, Walter. *Art in the Early Church*. New York: Pantheon Books, 1947.

Mâle, Emile. *Religious Art: From the Twelfth to the Eighteenth Century*. New York: Pantheon Books, 1949.

McClinton, Katharine Morrison. *Christian Art Through the Ages*. New York: The Macmillan Co., 1962.

Panofsky, Erwin, trans. *Abbot Suger on the Abbey Church of St.-Denis and Its Art Treasures*. Parallel texts in Latin and in English. Princeton: Princeton University Press, 1946.

Rice, David Talbot. *The Art of Byzantium*. New York: Harry N. Abrams, n.d.

————. *The Beginnings of Christian Art*. Nashville: Abingdon Press, 1957.

Santangelo, Antonio. *A Treasury of Great Italian Textiles*. Trans. by Peggy Craig. New York: Harry N. Abrams, 1964.

Schuette, Marie, and Müller-Christensen, Sigrid. *A Pictorial History of Embroidery*. New York: Frederick A. Praeger, 1963.

Stenton, Sir Frank, et al., editors. *The Bayeux Tapestry: A Comprehensive Survey*. Greenwich, Conn.: Phaidon Publishers, 1957. 2nd ed., rev., 1965.

van der Meer, F., and Mohrmann, Christine. *Atlas of the Early Christian World*. London: Thomas Nelson and Sons, 1958.

Weibel, Adèle Coulin. *Two Thousand Years of Textiles*. Pub. for The Detroit Institute of Arts. New York: Pantheon Books, 1952.

Weigert, Roger-Armand. *French Tapestry*. Trans. by Donald and Monique King. London: Faber and Faber, 1962.

III. LITURGY AND WORSHIP

Abba, Raymond. *Principles of Christian Worship*. New York: Oxford University Press, 1957.

Abbott, Walter M., S.J., ed. *The Documents of Vatican II. The Message and Meaning of the Ecumenical Council With Notes and Comments by Catholic, Protestant, and Greek Authorities*. Trans. by Joseph Gallagher. New York: Guild Press, American Press, Association Press, 1966.

Benoit, Jean-Daniel. *Liturgical Renewal: Studies in Catholic and Protestant Developments on the Continent*. London: SCM Press, 1958.

Brenner, S. F. *The Art of Worship*. New York: The Macmillan Co., 1961.

Coffin, Henry Sloane. *The Public Worship of God: A Source Book for Leaders of Services*. Philadelphia: The Westminster Press, 1956.

Edwall, P., Hayman, E., and Maxwell, W. D., eds. *Ways of Worship*. New York: Harper & Row, 1951.

Hebert, A. G. *Liturgy and Society: The Function of the Church in the Modern World*. 1st ed., 1935. 9th ed. London: Faber and Faber, 1956.

Hedley, George. *Christian Worship*. New York: The Macmillan Co., 1953.

Jasper, Ronald C. D., ed. *The Renewal of Worship*. London: Oxford University Press, 1965.

Koenker, Ernest Benjamin. *The Liturgical Renaissance in the Roman Catholic Church*. Chicago: University of Chicago Press, 1954. St. Louis: Concordia Publishing House, 1966.

————. *Worship in Word and Sacrament*. St. Louis: Concordia Publishing House, 1959.

Ladd, W. P. *Liturgical Interleaves*. New York: Oxford University Press, 1942. Republished by Seabury Press, 1961.

MacGregor, Geddes. *The Coming Reformation*. Philadelphia: The Westminster Press, 1960.

Macleod, Donald. *Presbyterian Worship: Its Meaning and Method*. Richmond: John Knox Press, 1965.

Nathan, Walter L. *Art and the Message of the Church*. Philadelphia: The Westminster Press, 1961.

O'Shea, William J. *The Worship of the Church: A Companion to Liturgical Studies*. London: Darton, Longman & Todd, 1960.

Paquier, Richard. *Traité de Liturgia. Essai sur la fondement et la structure du cults*. Neuchâtel and Paris: Delachaux and Niestlé, 1954.

Phifer, Kenneth G. *A Protestant Case for Liturgical Renewal*. Philadelphia: The Westminster Press, 1965.

Reed, Luther. *The Lutheran Liturgy*. Philadelphia: Muhlenberg Press, 1947.

————. *Worship*. Philadelphia: Muhlenberg Press, 1959.

Ritual Notes. A Comprehensive Guide to the Rites and Ceremonies of the Book of Common Prayer of the English Church. 10th ed. London: W. Knott and Son, 1956.

Shepherd, Massey H., Jr., ed. *The Liturgical Renewal of the Church*. New York: Oxford University Press, 1960.

————. *The Oxford American Prayer Book Commentary*. 2nd ed. London: Oxford University Press, 1951.

————. *The Reform of Liturgical Worship: Perspectives and Prospects*. The Bohlen Lectures, 1959. New York: Oxford University Press, 1961.

Strodach, Paul Zeller. *A Manual on Worship*. Philadelphia: Muhlenberg Press, 1946.

Taylor, Michael J., S.J. *The Protestant Liturgical Renewal. A Catholic Viewpoint*. Paramus, N. J.: Paulist/Newman Press, 1965.

Underhill, Evelyn. *Worship*. New York: Harper & Row, 1936. Torchbook ed., 1957.

White, James F. *The Worldliness of Worship*. New York: Oxford University Press, 1967.

IV. CHURCH ART AND ARCHITECTURE

Bouyer, Louis. *Liturgy and Architecture*. Notre Dame, Ind.: University of Notre Dame Press, 1967.

Chagall, Marc. *The Jerusalem Windows*. Text and notes by Jean Laymarie; trans. by Elaine Desautels. Rev. ed. New York: George Braziller, 1967.

Damaz, Paul F. *Art in Latin American Architecture*. Preface by Oscar Niemeyer. New York: Reinhold Publishing Corp., 1963.

Dahinden, Justus. *New Trends in Church Architecture*. Trans. by Cajetan J. B. Baumann. New York: Universe Books, 1967.

Dillenberger, June, *Secular Art with Sacred Themes*. Nashville: Abingdon Press, 1969.

Eversole, Finley, ed. *Christian Faith and the Contemporary Arts*. Nashville: Abingdon Press, 1962.

Fletcher, Banister. *A History of Architecture on the Comparative Method*. 1st ed. 1896. 17th ed. rev. by R. A. Cordingley. New York: Charles Scribner's Sons, 1961.

Freehof, Lillian S., and King, Bucky. *Embroideries and Fabrics for Synagogue and Home. Five Thousand Years of Ornamental Needlework*. New York: Union of American Hebrew Congregations and Hearthside Press, 1966.

Getlein, Frank and Dorothy. *Christianity in Modern Art*. Milwaukee: Bruce Publishing Co., 1961.

Hammond, Peter. *Liturgy and Architecture*. London: Barrie and Rockliff, 1960.

————, ed. *Towards a Church Architecture*. London: The Architectural Press, 1962.

Hazelton, Roger. *A Theological Approach to Art*. Nashville: Abingdon Press, 1967.

Henze, Anton, and Filhaut, Theodor. *Contemporary Church Art*. New York: Sheed and Ward, 1956.

Kampf, Avram. *Contemporary Synagogue Art. Developments in the United States, 1945-1965*. New York: Union of American Hebrew Congregations, 1966.

Matisse, Henri. *Les Chapelles du Rosaire à Vence par Matisse, et de Notre-Dame-du-Haut à Ronchamp par le Corbusier* [pseud. Jeanneret-Gris, Charles Edouard]. Paris: Éditions du Cerf, 1955.

McClinton, Katharine Morrison. *The Changing Church: Its Architecture, Art, and Decoration*. New York: Morehouse-Gorham, 1957.

Mills, Edward D. *The Modern Church*. New York: Frederick A. Praeger, 1956.

Nathan, Walter L. *Art and the Message of the Church*. Westminster Studies in Christian Communication, ed. Kendig B. Cully. Philadelphia: The Westminster Press, 1961.

Pichard, Josef. *Modern Church Architecture*. Trans. by Ellen Callman. New York: Orion Press, 1960.

Régamey, Pie-Raymond, O.P. *Religious Art in the Twentieth Century*. New York: Herder and Herder, 1963.

Reinhold, H. A. *Liturgy and Art*. XVI, Religious Perspectives, ed. Ruth Nando Anshen. New York: Harper & Row, 1966.

Rubin, William S. *Modern Sacred Art and the Church of Assy*. New York: Columbia University Press, 1961.

Shear, John Knox, ed. *Religious Buildings for Today*. An Architectural Record Book. New York: F. W. Dodge Corp., 1957.

Smith, G. E. Kidder, *The New Churches of Europe*. London: The Architectural Press, 1963.

Spence, Basil. *Phoenix at Coventry: the Building of a Cathedral*. New York: Harper & Row, 1962.

Vogt, Von Ogden. *Art and Religion*. 1st ed., Yale University Press, 1921. Rev. ed., Boston: Beacon Press, 1960.

White, James F. *Protestant Worship and Church Architecture: Theological and Historical Considerations*. New York: Oxford University Press, 1964.

V. SYMBOLISM AND AESTHETICS

Bevan, Edwyn. *Symbolism and Belief*. Boston: Beacon Press, 1957.

Bouyer, Louis. *Rite and Man*. Liturgical Studies VII. Notre Dame, Ind.: University of Notre Dame Press, 1967.

Cope, Gilbert. *Symbolism in the Bible and the Church*. London: SCM Press, 1959.

Daniélou, Jean, S.J. *Primitive Christian Symbols*. Trans. by Donald Attwater. Baltimore: Helicon Press, 1963.

Dillistone, F. W. *Christianity and Symbolism*. Philadelphia: The Westminster Press, 1955.

Eliade, Mircea. *Images and Symbols: Studies in Religious Symbolism*. Trans. by Philip Mairet. New York: Sheed and Ward, 1961.

Ferguson, George. *Signs and Symbols in Christian Art*. New York: Oxford University Press, 1954. 2nd ed., 1955.

Goldman, Bernard. *The Sacred Portal: A Primary Symbol in Ancient Judaic Art*. Detroit: Wayne State University Press, 1966.

Goodenough, Erwin R. *Jewish Symbols in the Greco-Roman Period*. 13 Vols., Bollingen Series XXXVII. New York: Pantheon Books, 1953-1965.

Johnson, P. Ernest, ed. *Religious Symbolism*. Institute for Religious and Social Studies. New York: Harper & Row, 1955.

Langer, Susanne K. *Feeling and Form*. New York: Charles Scribner's Sons, 1956.

————. *Philosophy in a New Key*. 1st ed., 1942. 3rd ed., Cambridge: Harvard University Press, 1967.

————. *Problems of Art*. New York: Charles Scribner's Sons, 1957.

MacGregor, Geddes. *Aesthetic Experience in Religion*. London: Macmillan & Co., 1947.

May, Rollo, ed. *Symbolism in Religion and Literature*. New York: George Braziller, 1960.

Minchen, Basil. *Outward and Visible*. London: Darton, Longman and Todd, 1961.

Parker, DeWitt H. "The Problem of Aesthetic Form," *Problems in Aesthetics*, ed., Morris Weitz. New York: The Macmillan Co., 1959.

Webber, F. R. *Church Symbolism. An Explanation of the More Important Symbols of the Old and New Testament, the Primitive, the Medieval and the Modern Church*. Cleveland: J. H. Jansen, 1938.

VI. COLOR

Billmeyer, Fred W., Jr., and Saltzman, Max. *Principles of Color Technology*. New York: John Wiley and Sons, 1966.

Birren, Faber. *A Survey in Words and Pictures, from Ancient Mysticism to Modern Science*. New Hyde Park, N. Y.: University Books, 1963.

Bond, Fred. *Color, How to See and Use It*. San Francisco: Camera Craft Publishing Co., 1954.

Chevreul, M. E. *The Principles of Harmony and Contrast of Colors and Their Applications to the Arts*. Based on the first English edition of 1854, as translated from the first French edition of 1839, *De la Loi du Contraste simultané des Couleurs*, with a special introduction and explanatory notes by Faber Birren. New York: Reinhold Publishing Corp.; 1967.

Evans, R. M. *An Introduction to Color*. New York: John Wiley and Sons, 1948.

Jacobson, Egbert. *Basic Color, an Interpretation of the Ostwald System*. Chicago: Paul Theobald, 1948.

Munsell, A. H. *A Color Notation, an Illustrated System Defining All Colors and Their Relations Measured by Scales of Hue, Value and Chroma*. First ed., 1905. 10th ed., rev. Baltimore: Munsell Color Co., 1947.

VII. TECHNIQUES: Embroidery, Weaving, and Textile Ornamentation

Albers, Anni. *On Weaving*. Middletown, Conn.: Wesleyan University Press, 1965.

Anders, Nedda C. *Appliqué, Old and New*. New York: Hearthside Press, 1967.

Beitler, Ethel Jane. *Create with Yarn: Hooking, Stitchery*. Scanton, Pa.: International Textbook Co., 1964.

Beutlich, Tadek. *The Technique of Woven Tapestry*. London: B. T. Batsford, 1967.

Birrell, Verla. *The Textile Arts, a Handbook of Fabric Structure and Design Processes: Ancient and Modern Weaving, Braiding, Printing, and other Textile Techniques*. New York: Harper & Row, 1959.

Black, Mary E. *New Key to Weaving*. Milwaukee: Bruce Publishing Co., 1957.

Blumenau, Lili. *Creative Design in Wall Hangings, Weaving*

Patterns, Based on Primitive and Medieval Art. New York: Crown Publishers, 1967.

Davis, Mildred J. *The Art of Crewel Embroidery.* New York: Crown Publishers, 1962.

Dean, Beryl. *Church Needlework.* London: B. T. Batsford, 1961.

————. *Ecclesiastical Embroidery.* London: B. T. Batsford, 1958.

———— *Ideas for Church Embroidery.* London: B. T. Batsford, 1968.

Enthoven, Jacqueline. *The Stitches of Creative Embroidery.* New York: Reinhold Publishing Corp., 1964.

Forman, W. and B., and Wassef, Ramses Wissa. *Tapestries from Egypt, Woven by the Children of Harrania.* Trans. by Jean Layton. London: Spring House, 1961.

Howard, Constance. *Inspiration for Embroidery.* 2nd ed. London: B. T. Batsford, 1968.

Kafka, Francis J. *The Hand Decoration of Fabrics.* Bloomington, Ill.: McKnight and McKnight Pub. Co., 1959.

Karasz, Mariska. *Adventures in Stitches: A New Art of Embroidery.* New York: Funk and Wagnalls, 1959.

King, Bucky. *Creative Canvas Embroidery.* New York: Hearthside Press, 1963.

Krevitsky, Nik. *Stitchery, Art and Craft.* New York: Reinhold Publishing Corp., 1966.

Kybalová, Ludmila. *Contemporary Tapestries from Czechoslovakia.* Trans. by Olga Kuthanová. London: Allan Wingate, 1963.

Laliberté, Norman, and McIlhany, Sterling. *Banners and Hangings.* New York: Reinhold Publishing Corp., 1966.

Laury, Jean. *Appliqué Stitchery.* New York: Reinhold Publishing Corp., 1966.

Lurçat, Jean. *Designing Tapestry.* Trans. by Barbara Crocker. London: Rockliff, 1950.

Moseley, Spencer; Johnson, Pauline, and Koenig, Hazel. *Crafts Design, an Illustrated Guide.* Belmont, Calif.: Wadsworth Publishing Co., 1962.

Overman, Ruth, and Smith, Lula E. *Contemporary Handweaving.* Ames: Iowa State College Press, 1955.

Van Dommelen, David B. *Decorative Wall Hangings.* New York: Funk and Wagnalls, 1962.

Wilson, Erica. *Crewel Embroidery.* New York: Charles Scribner's Sons, 1962.

VIII. ARTICLES AND PERIODICALS

Articles for recommended reading

Charlot, Jean. "Catholic Art in America: Debits and Credits," *Liturgical Arts,* XXVII (Nov., 1958).

Kenny, J. P., S.J. "Towards an Esthetic of Sacred Art: Four Canons," *Liturgical Arts,* XXXV (Aug., 1967).

Hofmeister, Philipp, O.S.B. "Gibt es in den Ostkirchen einen liturgischen Farbenkanon?" *Ostkirchliche Studien,* XIV (1965).

Marx, Dom Michael, O.S.B. "The Altar of the Lord's Supper," *Liturgical Arts,* XXXIII (Nov., 1964).

Mathews, Thomas, S.J. "The Future of Religious Art," *Liturgical Arts,* XXXV (Feb., 1967).

d'Ormusson, Wladimir. "The Contemporaneity of Sacred Art," *Liturgical Arts,* XXV (June, 1956).

Pryor, Jerome, S.J. "The Art of the Past, the Art of the Present, and the Art of the Church," *Liturgical Arts,* XXXIV (Nov., 1965).

Periodicals with mailing addresses

Art d'Église, Abbaye de Saint-André, Bruges 3, Belgium.

Arts and Architecture, 3305 Wilshire Blvd., Los Angeles, Calif. 90005.

Christian Art, Christian Arts Associates, 1801 West Greenleaf Ave., Chicago, Ill. 60626.

Craft Horizons, American Craftsmen's Council, 44 West 53rd St., New York, N. Y. 10019.

Embroidery, The Embroiderers' Guild, 73 Wimpole St., London, England.

Faith and Form, Guild for Religious Architecture, 1346 Connecticut Ave. N.W., Washington, D.C. 20036.

Handweaver and Craftsman, 220 Fifth Ave., New York, N. Y. 10001.

L'Art Sacré, Les Éditions du Cerf, 29, Bd. de Latour-Maubourg, Paris, France.

Liturgical Arts, Liturgical Arts Society, Inc., 521 Fifth Ave., New York, N. Y. 10017.

Studia Liturgica, Postbus 2, Nieuwendam, Holland.

Una Sancta, 195 Maujer St., Brooklyn, N. Y. 11206.

Worship, The Order of Saint Benedict, Inc., Collegeville, Minn. 56321.

Dalmatic: 51, 55-58. *See also* Vestments

Daniélou, Jean: *Primitive Christian Symbols,* 91*n*, 92*n*, 95

Dead Sea Manual of Discipline: 88

Dean, Beryl: 30, 31, 133, 136, 232

Dearmer, Percy: 74*n*, 82, 127. *See also* Alcuin Club; Warham Guild

Dickinson, Margaret: 226. *See also* Grandview Presbyterian Church, Glendale, California; banner

Didache: 91

Djellaba: 46, 56. *See also* tunicle

Dominican: 28, 42, 128, 130, 144. *See also* Couturier; Régamey; Chapel of the Rosary, Vence, France; Chapel of St. Thérèse, Hem, France; Sacred Art Movement

Donaldson, William: 218, 258. *See also* St. Paul's Cathedral, Peoria, Illinois; Carpet

Dossal: 23, 113, 152, 176-77, 244. *See also* Dean; Queen Anne Lutheran Church, Seattle, Washington

Dunfermline Abbey, Scotland: 67, 116. *See also* Pulpit

Dunn, Frederick Wallace (architect): 165. *See also* St. Paul's Cathedral, Peoria, Illinois

Durandus: 126

Durham, Anderson and Freed (architects): 176. *See also* Queen Anne Lutheran Church, Seattle, Washington; Dossal

Easter: Resurrection symbols, 164, 167, 171, 225; colors, 76, 78, 80, 84. *See also* Church Year; Christian Year; Colors, liturgical

Ecclesiological Society: 82. *See also* Church of England; Cambridge Camden Society

Embroiderers' Guild, London (Journal, *Embroidery*): Diamond Jubilee, 132, 133

Embroidery: *Opus Anglicanum,* 118-20; Order of Golden Fleece, 121; Embroiderers' Guild, 132

   techniques: appliqué, 30, 35, 41, 146, 156, 172, 176, 200, 222-32; stitchery, 135, 138, 206, 222; collage, 30, 135, 172, 206, 229; crewel, 210; Bayeux stitch, 210-11; canvas work, 212, 214; needlepoint, 212, 214, 216; petit point, 213; Gobelin stitch, 213, 218

   machine: 30, 167, 219-22, 232; Bonnaz, 219, 230, 231; Meistergram, 219, 230, 231. *See also* Appliqué; Collage

Emil Frei Studios (stained glass): St. Paul's Cathedral, Peoria, Illinois, 165

Emmanuel College, Cambridge, England: frontal by Dean, 29. *See also* Dean

Episcopal Church, U.S.A.: stole for sacramental use, 50; maniple still used, 53; liturgical renewal, 82. *See also* St. Paul's Cathedral, Peoria, Illinois; St. Mark's Church, New Canaan, Connecticut; Anglican; Church of England; Vestments; Colors, liturgical

Epitrachilion: 48, 53. *See also* Church, Greek Orthodox

Evangelists: Piper tapestry, Chichester, 29, 93; Sutherland Tapestry, Coventry, 93, 140; Kuemmerlein banners, 171; iconography, 171

Faith Lutheran Church, Prairie Village, Kansas: chancel hanging, Kuemmerlein, 171

First United Methodist Church, Escondido, California: 37, 38, 185. *See also* Whittemore (architect)

First United Methodist Church, Garden Grove, California: 171-76, 184, 185, 201, 202, 223. *See also* Whittemore (architect); Thompson (sculptor); Maes (stained glass)

First United Methodist Church, Santa Monica, California: 188

Fitz-Gerald, Clark (sculptor-designer): reredos, St. Mark's Episcopal Church, New Canaan, Connecticut, 166

Fitz-Gerald, Leah (designer): paraments, frontals, St. Mark's Episcopal Church, New Canaan, Connecticut, 167, 207

Flüeler, Sister Augustina: woven vestments, 244-45

Frei, Emil. *See* Emil Frei Studios

Frontal: 24, 32, 63, 64, 143; Emmanuel College, Cambridge, by Beryl Dean, 29; Chelmsford Cathedral, by Beryl Dean and Patricia Scrase, 30; St. Margaret's Church, King's Lynn, by Beryl Dean, 30; St. Thomas Church, Stockholm-Vällingby, 32; Epiphany Chapel, Winchester, by Margaret Kaye, 135; St. Mark's Episcopal Church, New Canaan, Connecticut, by Leah Fitz-Gerald, 207; Roman Catholic Church, Hayes, Middlesex, by Grossé, 24

Frontlet (superfrontal): 32, 64; Guildford Cathedral, 143; Markus Church, Stockholm, 163

Galbraith, John (architect). *See* United Christian Church, Los Angeles, California

Gallican Rites: 75, 77. *See also* Colors, liturgical

Geneva Presbyterian Church, Laguna Hills, California: 224, 225, 241. *See also* Pereira (architect)

Gobelin: tapestry works, 194, 252, 253; stitch, 213, 218; weaving technique, 213, 253; tapestry by Marin Hemmingson, 234; pulpit fall by Evy Parmsten, 250; tapestry by Sten Kauppi, 254, 255; tapestry by Marijke Neyens-Wiegman, 255-56. *See also* Tapestry

Golden Fleece, Order of: 56, 107, 121. *See also* Dalmatic; Cope; Vestments; Embroidery

Goldman, Bernard: *The Sacred Portal:* 87

Goodenough, Erwin R., *Jewish Symbols in the Greco-Roman Period:* 87, 88*n*

Gothic: 21, 28, 30, 31, 116; chasuble, 56; revival, 56, 64, 67, 126; Suger, father of Gothic architecture, 107; sculpture, Pisano pulpit, 66

Grandview Presbyterian Church, Glendale, California: banner, by Margaret Dickinson, 226; antependia, by Marion P. Ireland, 202

Gregory V, Pope: Color Canon, 76

Grill, Ann: Stoles, 223, 238

Grossé, Louis, Ltd.: Development of the Chasuble (diagrams), 55; vestments for St. Paul's Cathedral, Peoria, Illinois, 58, 166; copes, 59; vestments for Coventry Cathedral, 241; frontal, Roman Catholic Church, Hayes, Middlesex, 241

Guéranger, Dom Prosper: French liturgical movement, 82, 126

Guildford Cathedral, Surrey, England: embroideries designed and supervised by Sir Edward Maufe (architect) and Lady Prudence Maufe, 142-44; lectern fall designed by Alix Stone, 143; carpet, 206, 258; kneelers, 214, 215. *See also* Laudian; Frontal; Kneelers; Carpet

Hall, Ann: Banners, 234

Härlanda Church, Göteborg, Sweden: carpet, antependium, and kneelers, 154. *See also* Lund; Heybroek

Harmon, Robert: stained-glass designer, 165. *See also* St. Paul's Cathedral, Peoria, Illinois

Hazelton, Roger: 25, 42

Hem, France. *See* St. Thérèse Chapel

Hemmingson, Marin: tapestry, 234

Herrick Memorial Chapel, Occidental College, Los Angeles: paraments, 38-41, 183. *See also* Ladd and Kelsey (architects)

Heybroek, Folke: altar antependium, Härlanda Church, Göteborg, 154

Hippolytus: 92

Tertullian: 87, 90

Textile paints and dyes: 206, 241-44; frontal, Coventry vestments, by Grossé, 241; reredos, Peoria, 241; batik, 242-43; block printing, 242. *See also* Batik; Printing; Stenciling

Thompson, J. E. (sculptor): First United Methodist, Garden Grove

Tippet, 50. *See also* Vestments; Episcopal

Torah Curtain, Temple Israel: 178-80

Tractarian movement: 82, 128. *See also* Oxford Movement

Trinity, symbol of: Piper tapestry, 29; Trinity Lutheran, Lisbon, 32, 33, 185; paraments, Shepherd of the Hills, Edina, 34, 257; colors, Sarum sequence, 78; colors, 84; banner, Kuemmerlein, 167, 171; frontal, St. Mark's, New Canaan, 207

Trinity Lutheran Church, Lisbon, North Dakota: 32, 33, 185. *See also* Sövik, Mathre and Madson (architects)

Trinity United Presbyterian Church, Santa Ana, California: pulpit fall, 186-87, 220-21. *See also* Whittemore (architect); Embroidery, machine

Tunicle: 46, 51, 56. *See also* Vestments

Underhill, Evelyn: 88n

United Christian Church, Los Angeles, California: banner, pulpit fall, 243. *See also* Galbraith (architect)

United Church of Christ: 36, 104. *See also* Congregational

United Methodist Church. *See* Methodist Church, United

van der Grinten, G. J. (architect): 255. *See also* St. Nicholas Church, Limburg

van der Meer and Mohrmann: 90

Våsterort Church, Vällingby, Sweden: pulpit fall, Parmsten, 250. *See also* Nyrén (architect); Sjoström (sculptor)

Vatican: 129

Vatican Council II: 61, 82, 133. *See also* Roman Catholic Church

Veil: 25, 46, 146

Vence, Chapel of the Rosary. *See* Chapel of the Rosary, Vence

Vestments: 23-25, 44, 45, 47, 48, 71, 81, 109, 181, 207; Eucharistic, 47, 166, 232; Western and Eastern counterparts, 47-49; black gown, 47, 59, 60, 164; choir, 60, 61. *See also* Alb; *Burnūs;* Burse; Cassock; Chasuble; Cope; Cotta; Dalmatic; *Djellaba; Mandias;* Maniple; *Paenula; Pallium; Phelonion;* Surplice; *Sticharion; Sakkos (saccos);* Stole; Tippet; Tunicle; *Zone*

Vitruvius: 73

Warham Guild: 67, 127

Westminster Abbey: 26

White, James F.: 21, 24

Whittemore, Hal C. (architect): 37, 171, 185. *See also* First United Methodist, Escondido; First United Methodist, Garden Grove; Trinity United Presbyterian, Santa Ana

Widén, Sofia: 152-54, 242. *See also* Printing; Chasuble; Kung Karl's

Willet Stained Glass Studios: American Lutheran, Oslo, 164; St. Mark's, New Canaan, 167

Wilson, Erica: kneelers, St. Mark's, New Canaan, 216

Winchester Cathedral, England: frontal, Kaye, 135

World Council of Churches: 104

Worship cover designs: Kacmarcik, 185

Wren, Christopher: 125

Yoors, Jan: tapestry, Shepherd of the Hills, Edina, 188, 256, 257

Zernov, Nicolas: 115n

Zone or girdle, Eastern, 53

Zwingli, Ulrich: 60

Designer: Harry Lynn Towns
Typesetter: Parthenon Press
Printing: Parthenon Press/4 Color Offset
Textpapers: Northwest Paper Company/80# Mountie Matte
Endsheets: Northwest Paper Company/100# Mountie Matte
Printed 2 colors
Binding: Columbia Bolton Buckram
Bound by: Parthenon Press

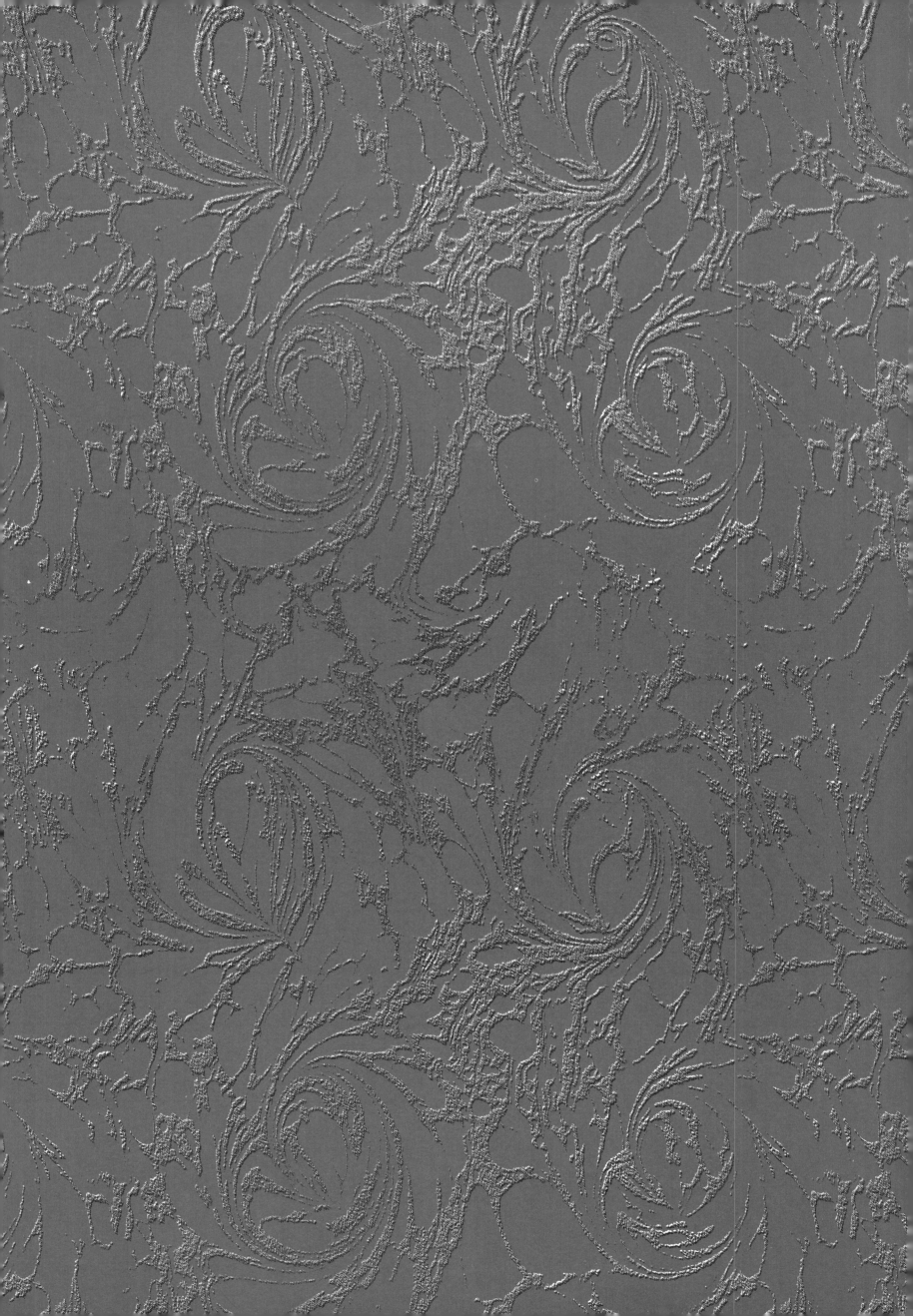